Participatory Video

Participatory Video

Images that Transform and Empower

Edited by
Shirley A. White

SAGE Publications
New Delhi ❖ Thousand Oaks ❖ London

First published in 2003 by

Sage Publications India Pvt Ltd
B-42, Panchsheel Enclave
New Delhi 110 017

Sage Publications Inc
2455 Teller Road
Thousand Oaks, California 91320

Sage Publications Ltd
6 Bonhill Street
London EC2A 4PU

Published by Tejeshwar Singh for Sage Publications India Pvt Ltd, photo-typeset in 10/12 pt Charter BT by Line Arts, Pondicherry and printed at Chaman Enterprises, New Delhi.

Second Printing 2004

Library of Congress Cataloging-in-Publication Data

Participatory video: images that transform and empower/edited by Shirley A. White
  p. cm.
  Includes index.
  1. Community development—Developing countries. 2. Economic development—Developing countries—Citizen participation. 3. Video recording—Social aspects—Developing countries. 4. Video tape recorders and recording—Social aspects—Developing countries. 5. Communication in community development—Developing countries. 6. Communication in economic development—Developing countries. I. White, Shirley A., 1931–
HN981.C6P376   306.4'85—dc21   2003   2003003670

ISBN: 0–7619–9762–8 (US-Hb)   81–7829–247–5 (India-Hb)
        0–7619–9763–6 (US-Pb)   81–7829–248–3 (India-Pb)

Sage Production Team: Sunaina Dalaya, Sushanta Gayen and
Santosh Rawat

Contents

List of Figures and Tables

FIGURES

TABLES

Foreword

The word 'participation' is kaleidoscopic; it changes its color and shape at the will of the hands in which it is held. And, just like the momentary image in the kaleidoscope, it can be very fragile and elusive, changing from one moment to another.

Shirley White (1994)

In a time when everyone is talking about the potential of new information and communication technologies, a book which reminds us of how participatory video is being a powerful catalyst for development is a welcome change. Communication practitioners are constantly faced with the challenge of adapting to the needs of a global information society, drawing upon the lessons learned in the past 30 years about applying participatory communication processes to local environments. This book will make an important contribution in meeting this challenge.

We are living in an era that presents new opportunities for development communication practitioners. Processes of democratization and decentralization are renewing old development trends, creating a new scenario. Communication technologies are becoming more appropriate for developing countries. Pluralism and media liberalization have encouraged the decentralization of information production, shifting control away from central governments. Horizontal "people to people" processes are replacing the "authority driven" top-down communication tradition. Participatory approaches have paved the way for community-based ownership of various communication media such as newspapers, radio, and video.

The notion that the ultimate purpose of development is human and social, and not only economic is now more widely accepted. It is recognized that there can be no sustainable development unless people become the agents of their own development—not just beneficiaries—participating fully at every stage of the development process. There is more recognition of the role played by the knowledge and experience of rural and indigenous people. And, there is increasing recognition that participatory communication approaches are powerful tools to foster positive change and to empower people to forge their own destiny.

Many participatory communication experiences have taken place over the last 30 years, with some being more successful than others. Much has been written by academics on the theory of participation and participatory communication, with attempts to define and elaborate both concepts. In her introductory chapter, Shirley White describes some of them. However, there is now a general consensus that there is no unique recipe or model for a participatory process or a participatory communication approach. Approaches will vary according to different geographic conditions, societies, cultures, and environmental conditions. In the words of the Spanish poet Antonio Machado: "Traveler there are no paths; paths are made by walking."

Yet, even more than scholarly theories and definitions, what is seriously lacking is information on practical, innovative participatory communication programs at the grass root level. The sharing of these experiences can provide guidelines and lessons learned for communication practitioners in the future, as well as contribute to the creation of conceptual frameworks. *Participatory Video: Images that Transform and Empower* does exactly this, by addressing this problem, raising questions and, providing some answers.

For Shirley White, this book emanates from a lifetime of work done with video for participatory development and social change, and from her collaborative effort with many students and communication professionals. It shares the experiences of numerous individuals and organizations from all corners of the globe. These accounts show how powerful video images have been used to promote changes in attitudes and social behavior, helping communities identify development solutions that are within their reach. Video has been used to reach the policymakers, to empower women behind the camera, to share stories and experiences, to rescue the culture and heritage of poor peasants and indigenous people. As a mediation tool, the power of video was used to help resolve conflicts, achieve consensus and find common ground for collective action. Video has been used for role modeling, as a medium to expose social injustice, to lend a voice to the voiceless, to challenge public stereotypes and for many other development processes involving illiterate communities. The various accounts presented in this book demonstrate how powerful images can be in documenting realities, sharing those realities, and using the realities to bring about significant changes.

This book describes one of the first instances of the use of video for social change, the Fogo Island Process, which was developed in the late 1960s and 1970s. This innovative experiment used video as a tool for social dialog, as a problem-solving mechanism leading to collective action, for empowerment and decision-making. It was one of the first experiments in community feedback and image control in the filmmaking process. It created a network and opened channels of communication among the island communities as also between the island and the government. It defined a series of guiding principles and conceptual framework that has influenced many participatory communication programs throughout the world. As illustrated by the experiences in this book, the principles and criteria developed by Don Snowdon and his colleagues for the successful use of participatory video are valid even today, not only for the use of video as a tool, but also as process. The fundamental importance of the process is stressed in all the stories recounted here: participatory communication is a social process, and technology and media are the tools that facilitate this process. Thus, video programs should be produced with and by the people, about their social problems, themselves, and not just produced by outsiders; when produced by outsiders the professional quality of the communication programs becomes secondary to the content and process involved in the production of a message or a program.

The importance of a well-trained facilitator to act as a mediator and support for the video process is an essential prerequisite for success. This is pointed out by Shirley White and confirmed by many of the 14 contributing authors. Participatory communication approaches require a number of skills, including fluency in local dialects, knowledge of local conditions, beliefs, culture and customs, ability to translate technical jargon into locally understandable concepts, as well as group dynamics and group facilitation skills. There is a need to train a new set of communication specialists and field agents who can be mediators and act as brokers between communities and the local authorities and institutions. Participatory communication approaches require new participatory and interactive learning processes, preferably field-based. Students can best learn through field experience and through practice rather than only through classroom training. Curricula should not be limited to technology and media production, but also include the economic, social, political, and cultural processes related to development communication.

Listening to people is one of the first steps and an essential prerequisite for participatory communication. Listening goes beyond learning about their perceived needs. It involves listening to what people already know, what they aspire to become, what they perceive as possible and desirable, and what they feel they can sustain. It involves taking into account their knowledge and culture. Establishing trust is another essential prerequisite for successful participatory communication efforts and video activities. This takes time, usually more time than traditional donor-driven projects foresee. But this is a problem common to all participatory approaches in development projects and programs.

Participatory communication, especially when dealing with social and political injustices, can only take place if there is political space and a political will on the part of governments and local authorities. However, there also has to be commitment and political will on the part of the people. They have to realize that they are subject to risks. Participation in activities for social change can raise conflicts within the community. Methods must be found to engage people meaningfully, while providing adequate protection and conflict management measures.

The sustainability of participatory video initiatives, the need for new institutional frameworks involving all stakeholders, and the need for participatory evaluation of media are other essential issues addressed in this book. Possibly, one of the greatest challenges facing participatory communication specialists today is over the question of marrying the potential of new information and communication technologies (ICTs) to the benefits of small and local participatory media.

ICTs are in the limelight, and there is a great rush on the part of development agencies to make use of ICTs at all costs. Experiments with ICTs are demonstrating that the benefits of the information revolution can have positive repercussions for economic and social development. But infrastructure, access, and use are still limited in the rural areas of developing countries. Computers, connection fees, and online charges are too expensive. Computers are hard to use, especially for those who cannot read or write. Most of the information on the Internet is produced in English, and has little local relevance. Thus, traditional media still plays an important role. A combination of both traditional and new media will probably yield the best results. The next few years will witness a number of experiments that will mix new information technologies with more traditional media, optimizing the worth of both. It is already happening with community radio, with rural communication centers, and will certainly take place with linkages between video and the Internet. Communication practitioners must adapt to the realities of the new information age and learn to select the most appropriate communication channels and technologies. What is important is to apply the same principles, criteria, and lessons learned from use of other technologies and participatory approaches in the past, to the selection and use of new information and communication technologies. This is a complex challenge.

This book demonstrates how video is becoming an increasingly powerful tool that can transform and empower disadvantaged individuals and communities. This power results from many years of experience with video and its utilization in the field and in the classroom. *Participatory Video–Images that Transform and Empower* will be a valuable resource for communication scholars, practitioners, students, and development agency staff. It brings together practical information on innovative experiences with the use of participatory video and contains a thoughtful analysis of some essential issues to be taken into account in planning and implementing a participatory video process. It is hoped that it will provide inspiration and guidance to a new generation of communication development specialists. In the words of Shirley White: "It is hoped that the book will inspire further exploration of the uses of video and the interface of video with other technologies that can enhance the power of images ... and participatory processes."

Silvia Balit
Rome, Italy June 2002

Acknowledgements

This book is the result of a long and laborious process, of writing a publication on Video Communication, which has been long overdue. After more than 30 years experience in media production and training, teaching and doing research, I have accumulated a wealth of information and understanding. Along the way, ordinary people, college students and adult learners have enriched that experience. I have always realized that sharing my experiences and resources might be useful to others, but time constraints continually prohibited that sharing. Writing has always slipped down on the list of priorities.

My entire career has focused on video in its various incarnations, beginning with early broadcast television in the 1950s (I was but a child). I owe my enduring commitments to video communication to my first boss, George Round, who was the director of public relations for the University of Nebraska and extension editor for the Agricultural Extension Service. We went on the air with one of the first educational television programs in the USA, *Backyard Farmer*, which during six fall and winter months was transformed into *House and Home*. This program is still being produced for the University of Nebraska Statewide Television and continues to follow essentially the same format it used from the beginning. I was George's assistant, doing the needful, including organizing content and scripting. He was the emcee and the producer. One day, after I had worked on only two programs and was headed into the third in about four hours, George telephoned and said "Sorry, something has come up and I can't make the show tonight. You will have to take over." I was speechless and panic-stricken. But, I did it and from that time onward became the emcee on *House and Home* and a backup for *Backyard Farmer*. This was George's favorite trick—to thrust his young proteges into new challenges of performance. It worked.

Another person at the university who "mentored" my on–the–job learning in television broadcasting was Jack McBride. He was the super producer for University of Nebraska Television in its formative years and the mastermind behind the State of Nebraska's exemplary and extensive Educational Television Network. Those were exciting, and highly creative years in educational broadcasting, with very few rules and wide open frontiers for experimentation. There were also others who nurtured my creativity, motivation and curiosity—Rolly Graham, Virginia Trotter, Dee Clouse, and Ron Hull. Interestingly, as I have plunged deeper into participatory video over the past two decades, I have constantly returned to those early experiences for operational and theoretic clues.

For the first 10 years after completing graduate studies, I worked in administration. There I was able to reinforce the explorations of others who were pioneering in video communication—my staff at Kansas State University (KSU) and Ken Thomas, my mentor at KSU. After this I assumed the role of professor at Cornell. In the early 1970s I established a Video Communication Laboratory that instituted an ambitious program of off-campus training and classroom instruction supported by an access facility. Fortunately, my first two graduate students who became assistants in the lab, Mary Richards and David Way, had been active participants in establishing Public Access Cable Television in Reading, PA. Their experience was invaluable in setting up a viable program for faculty and off-campus extension agents. Mary's graduate research explored the relationship of rural residents to technology and developed a model for a Community Communication Center. These ideas were later refined by Jill Parker when she conceptualized the Data Donor Network, another aspect of the center, and explored the Knowledge Gap hypothesis as an input to the Development Communication Research Project at the University of Pune in India. That research project, which was negotiated in 1984, focused heavily on the use of video at the village level. There more of my graduate students made vital contributions to that project and to my thinking about video—Jyoti Khare, Randy Arnst, and Pradeep

Patel. Meanwhile, other students were also working with me to build the video lab program of teaching and research—Geri Gay, Nancy Smith, Mike Tolomeo, Ken Abbott, Nash Bly, and several others including our "manager," Sandra Goodine. During those years, a voluminous amount of creative training material and instructional techniques was developed. Every student added a new dimension to the programs of the lab and to my sense of the power of video.

As a result of my close association with the Development Communication Research Project in India which began in 1982, my focus for video communication shifted to development and participatory communication. Working with K. Sadanandan Nair and his staff at the University of Pune was a whole new learning experience. Their research and experimental work in the villages of Maharashtra was another pioneering experience with video. When the video lab program ended we transformed the video courses, strengthening their focus on development and participatory approaches. It was encouraging to see both graduate and undergraduate students become excited about "process" video, which for them was a total conceptual turnaround from their notion of television. Again, graduate students played an important role in shaping those learning experiences—Shonini Ghosh, Ron Hess, Robert Rieger, Barb Seidl, Priya Suri, Ricardo Gómez, Rezwan Razani, Simone St. Anne, and Eric Nielsen.

The content in this book has roots in my total experience with video communication, as I have lived it over my career. It not only shares my experiences and knowledge of video as it is now being explored on the development scene, but also draws on the expertise of 14 other people—some my former students. Their explorations span a wide spectrum of video and its power as a visual communication media.

The idea of a book evokes enthusiasm, particularly when it focuses on information and issues that are meaningful and important. However, the execution of a book is "more than a process." Supportive people are critical to that process. Mary Jo Dudley who has shared my enthusiasm has been a sounding board throughout. Tejeshwar Singh of Sage Publications who endorsed this book with enthusiasm and provided ready counsel and feedback on its progress was always positive about the project and extremely patient. I appreciate the technical support provided by the Department of

Communication at Cornell, and the assistance from Michele Finklestein and Joan Sweeney.

And, once again I thank my husband, Al White, who has suffered the evolution of another manuscript. As always, he has been totally supportive, encouraging me to spend time with my computer in lieu of the kitchen.

My sincere thanks to all...

Shirley A. White
June 1, 2002

1

Introduction: Video Power

————————— ❋ —————————

Shirley A. White

*No matter where on the globe one might be, you could not possibly
address the topic of Video Power without immediately recalling
the powerful images of '9/11'–September 11, 2001. The instantaneous transmission of images of the New York trade towers
exploding and crumbling to the ground are emblazoned on one's
memory. There has been a continuous stream of images that record the daily significance of war, liberation, and terror since.
These powerful visual messages have come both from the cameras of professionals and from ordinary people. The home videos
salvaged from the ruins of the 'War on Terror' tell stories from an
intimate and shocking historical perspective. The 'image data'
embodied in these tapes is startling in its content and staggering
in its implications. More startling are the images of the terrorist's
murder of an American journalist—so indicative of the magni-
tude of terrorism issues currently being addressed.*

This book was conceived from numerous examples of people's participation and video's power in the "development process" over the

past three decades. *Images that Transform and Empower*—little did we know that we would now find a world context in which the link between video images as a means to transform and empower would be so clearly understood. The power of the images we have seen so much of in the media over the past months is linked to life situations that severely impact on the well-being of individuals. Unfortunately, these images have been representative of the negative aspects of human relationships.

The chapters in this book focus on life situations that have found video to be empowering and transforming, but in a positive sense. Critical development needs clearly include countries that are the current and future sites of the War on Terror. These countries are poverty-stricken, politically turbulent and unstable, and in a continuing state of turmoil that can be attributed to their conflict-ridden human relationships and cultural practices. Video, without a doubt, can take on an even more significant role as these frontiers are challenged.

The images of twisted ruins, smoking ashes, clouds of dust, and tireless workers at "Ground O" are strikingly similar to the often seen images of ravaged people and countries struck by war, drought or natural disasters. Victims of such natural and man-made tragedies suddenly thrust into cycles of despair. The way out of those cycles almost always becomes a matter of access to resources—emotional support of family and friends, financial support for rebuilding the basics of living, options, choices and courses of action which remove human vulnerability. But when resources are not available, the cycles dissipate into conditions of helplessness, hopelessness, powerlessness, and erosion of human dignity and life space. There is little escape from this stark reality.

This is the condition of the nearly three billion people around the globe who are regarded as "living in poverty." In reality, they are barely "existing" in poverty-stricken conditions. Their homes are meager, whether a cardboard, tin roofed cubicle in the slums of Mumbai, or a thatched roof house outside Nairobi. Men, if at all present, may be jobless or sporadically employed. Their discouraging quest for regular, much less meaningful work may often find them capable of disruptive behaviors, which harm their wives and children. Women too seek employment and are quick to accept menial or demeaning tasks when doing so means their children and husbands will enjoy the benefit of food and clothing. Their long days begin at dawn, preparing food for the family, collecting dung or firewood for warmth and cooking, going to the well for water. Rural women are found doing backbreaking labor in the fields, caring for animals (if they are fortunate enough to have some) and many times rock picking for road building and construction. Urban women are found doing this as well. It is not unusual to find women of the city become scavengers, along with their children, to provide for the basic needs of their family. Their children roam the streets, snatching food from vendors, who many times, turn their heads and look the other way.

One of my most haunting images of India is of Indian women laborers. During my first visit to India, the driver drove me cautiously, horn blaring, through the streets of Calcutta to my hotel at midnight. Men, women, children, dogs, water buffalo, and cows scampered from the street where they were sleeping. In the dark I could only "feel" what was happening. I woke from a sleepless night, shuffled to the shuttered window, opened it and looked below. In the early light of dawn, from six floors above, I could identify a curving line of movement toward a huge open pit. As the images came more clearly into focus, I realized that that movement was of Sari-clad women carrying large, obviously heavy, baskets on their heads. They were walking, almost in cadence, a few feet behind one another. When they reached the huge pit, they dumped their loads into a large container. Awestricken, I watched for some time until the vibrant colors of their Saris reflected the morning light. I later learned that the women were a part of the 'crew' building the new subway in Calcutta. This was in 1982, and this was only the first in an unending stream of powerful images that attest to the conditions of poverty and vulnerability of women in India.

Women of poverty are the key actors in many of the chapters of this book. However, the most vulnerable victims of poverty, undoubtedly, are the children. Men, the world over are viewed as protectors of the family, but poverty wipes out any protective shields, irrespective of who wields them. Every individual is faced with a fight for survival. Globally, the conditions of poverty are unfortunately not improving. While video, as a tool to communicate these conditions cannot eradicate the problems, the problems can certainly be shared, stated, and exposed through images.

This powerful tool however, must continue to be used by people living in poverty and become their "voice." Its use does not depend on traditional literacy, i.e., people being able to read or write. Present day technology has become increasingly "user-friendly" and with some basic assistance, can be mastered by anyone at a functional level. At the same time, professional videographers can also play an important role of communicating the life situations of the poor through powerful images. While the main focus of this book is on participatory video, it takes into account the wide range of approaches to using video's powerful images to transform people, relationships, perceptions, and understandings.

Part 1: The Power of the Process

If one were to state the major objective of participatory development and communication it would be "to empower people to shape their own destiny." Ideally, the participation process enables people achieve an identity, chart their life course, experience freedom in their life space and reach for their human potential with dignity and respect. Participatory communication has the capacity to connect human beings as they experience social change. It is a democratic process, characterized by dialog, creative and consensual thinking, and collective action.

In Chapter 2, Shirley White endeavors to provide a frame of reference for understanding and practicing participatory approaches to development, and situates participatory video within those approaches. She presents the linkages between development participation and participatory communication, and identifies some of the issues to be addressed in the participation debate. Outlining of the dimensions of involvement and the importance of culture as a dominant force are important aspects of Chapter 2. She points out that: "Heritage provides a secure foundation for development endeavors that individuals and communities deem useful to their progress. The greater the cultural diversity in a community, the greater the effort to evolve mutually agreeable directions will be."

Chapter 3 focuses on the participatory video process. It carefully identifies and discusses the social–psychological aspects of transformation and renewal in relation to transactional communication perspectives. White notes:

While video is a tool, it becomes *more* than a tool when used within developmental conceptual frameworks such as self-concept, reflective listening, dialog, conflict management, or consensus building. It then becomes a vital force for change and transformation of individuals and communities. It has unlimited potential.

Chapter 3 elucidates the transactionalist communication perspectives, identifies transformative process skills and the pathways to self-realization. Trust and relationship building, and the fostering of a creative communication climate are also discussed. White concludes her discourse by sharing a personal experience that proved to be a defining moment in experiencing the power of video.

In Chapter 4, Renuka Bery places video in the relationship of participation and empowerment noting that the participatory video context is one where it is safe to "tell risky stories." These stories can be powerful enough to inspire change.

Participation motivates individuals to work collectively to take action. Empowerment involves personal growth and taking risks. And video is a medium in which to share stories. The convergence of these philosophies with a practical tool sets the stage for participatory video that empowers.

Bery probes further into the power of the participatory video process and presents a useful framework to categorize various forms of participation placing them on a continuum. She discusses the video process as one that equalizes power. She also looks at the aspects of defining the self, building self-confidence, exercising one's voice and effecting change, but from the point of view of power equalization and empowerment.

Stephen Crocker's Chapter 5 is significant as it helps us appreciate the historical aspects of participatory communication and the role of video/film media in promoting and facilitating social change. He traces the genesis of the famed "Fogo Process" and the evolution of participatory communication and participatory video from those roots. The early experiments with the "Fogo Process" made another important contribution to development thinking. It helped in conceptualizing and operationalizing the role of *social animator* that has evolved or matured into the concepts of *catalyst communicator* or *facilitator*. Crocker states: "The Fogo Process provides real evidence of how people who have been marginalized by the economic and political structure of the world system can renew and empower their local communities and transform the conditions of uneven development."

Together these four chapters set the stage for moving through the other three sections of this book. At times development practioners take on points of view about participatory approaches or become involved in participatory approaches without much understanding of the participatory process. These chapters can serve as a springboard for further exploration and study for those who wish to dig deeper and enhance their own capabilities.

Part 2: Video that Transforms

That video has the power to transform is a well documented phenomenon and fact. The four chapters presented in Part 2 of this book offer different perspectives about the power to transform from the viewpoints of a video producer-director, researcher, field project director, and a development consultant. Mary Jo Dudley's overview sets the stage for reflecting on the power of video in these diverse contexts and perspectives. In Chapter 6, Dudley looks at the inherent impact of the video process and its transformation and empowerment qualities. She elaborates on several aspects of the process—how video can be used to document, produce, and change one's reality, how the tool empowers those who control it, and how construction of one's own public image provides ways to analyze the structures of power within which the image is embedded. She uses specific grass root situations to illustrate the points she makes.

In Chapter 7, Barbara Seidl displays a remarkable responsibility toward her role as a professional videographer documenting exemplary development projects. She is the kind of person who is sensitive about the documentation task, fully realizing that the very presence of a "camera crew" is an intervention in the life of a community. Her commitment to the "Participatory Message Development Model" is impressive, particularly since she has been able to hang on to her convictions that this approach is one that best serves the "subjects" of her documer.tation. She notes that, "this model dictates that the videographer has nothing to do with defining truth," and that the videographer simply becomes a vehicle for "telling someone else's story." When documenting that someone else's story, that someone "knows what is and is not important." The theme of deference to the people and the community appears throughout her presentation.

In this chapter Seidl shares insights vis-à-vis the three phases of the video documentation process—preproduction planning, on site production, and postproduction and broadcast/screening of the finished video. The intent of her message is to provide persons who would engage in video documentation with an understanding of the potential benefits and risks of the process in order to use the tool to optimum advantage. For each phase, she considers the positive and negative influences—both intentional and unintentional—of the video documentation process on the development project. She shares her firsthand experiences about working with development agencies. Her "stories from the road"—from Nepal, Bolivia, Zambia—put a human face on the impact of development and vividly illustrate the transformations that result from video storytelling.

Chapter 8 presents a contrast of the traditional documentary and participatory documentary approaches. Sadanandan Nair and Shirley White share one story from their experimental research with video in the villages of Maharashtra, India. The contrast in the perspective of professional videographers "looking at" and 'interpreting' the daily life of village women and the perspective of village women looking at their daily life is stark. The two perceptions of reality are truly counterpoint.

Their account of women taking over "storytelling" explains how the participatory process emerged from their research and experimentation. This work provided firsthand observation that became a part of the foundation for constructing the Nair/White "Participatory Message Development Model" which Seidl has dubbed "unorthodox," but highly influential. Putting cameras in the hands of the women, takes participation to a deeper, even more involving level, in contrast to the professional videographer—enabling people to tell their own story. Taking over "the decision-making vs just participating" in the decision-making, truly delivers control to the people with the story.

The brief experience the women had with the researchers was transforming. They had formed alliances and gained confidence that their points of view were valuable. They were proud of the videotape they produced and felt valued because they had been given full rein to tell their own story in their own way. They painted a picture of "well-being" rather than "ill-being" for their families and their village.

In Chapter 9, Ricardo Gómez' account of how video has transformed the lives of Colombian children is truly amazing and heartwarming. He traces a decade of involvement of children with video and the impact the experience has had on their sense of belonging to their collective roots and perceptions of themselves. In Chapter 9, he details how the viewfinder of a camcorder transformed the children's worldview, their sense of teamwork and cooperation, and their sense of self in relation to others. Over the decade of involvement, the children transformed into budding adults, taking on responsibilities for the growth and development of younger children. In a sense, Gómez recounts a process of "growing up with video."

It is not common to find a development project that provides sustained leadership to a community for a decade or more. The kind of reflections shared in Chapter 9 illustrate the deep satisfaction of sustaining a process of development that continues to facilitate opportunities for people to alter not only their life situation, but also their lives in a broader sense. The opportunities have included the increased access to communication technologies, which have opened up greater potential not only for the individuals of this story, but for their respective communities as well.

These four chapters in Part II of this book give us graphic evidence of the power images wield in transforming lives. They raise the question of why more concrete work has not been done to further develop the conceptual foundations for participatory video. Not only are there few definitive concepts, but there is remarkable absence of any well-formulated theories to undergird the participatory video practices. While projects have been routinely evaluated, the lessons learned and understandings that have resulted have not led to significant theoretic work on the part of academics or other development professionals.

Part 3: Video that Empowers

The chapters in Part 3 of this book focus on video as a tool for empowerment. The four chapters present diverse perspectives—video for role-modeling, video to give individuals a public voice, video to empower the woman behind the camera, and video as a medium to expose social injustices. All four accounts however demonstrate how video serves to empower women to address their personal situations and take control of their lives.

Carol Underwood has been central to a large research project, *Arab Women Speak Out*, which involved over 60,000 women in Egypt, Jordan, Palestine, Tunisia, and Yemen. The project used video to profile women who could provide realistic role models for women of the region. From over 100 nominations, 30 women were selected to be profiled in the videos. Case studies of the women became a part of the documentation process. Training manuals were developed to run parallel with the videos and training in the use of the material was provided to development workers. Technical assistance was provided for each organization that participated. These trainers, in turn conducted small group sessions for women in their respective countries.

Chapter 10 presents the background of the development of this project. The results from an extensive impact evaluation are shared. The project that began in 1999 is still underway. Underwood says that the *Arab Women Speak Out* project gives women a platform where they can, and have consistently chosen to reclaim their voices. Viewing the videos and participating in group discussions about the issues raised has allowed women to make "dramatic changes in their lives."

Chapter 11 unfolds a story of commitment and facilitative "savvy" of a single individual who has made a huge contribution to the empowerment of women in a community through establishing a technology access center. Padma Guidi, shares a powerful account of a center in Guatemala which focuses on the empowerment of non-literate indigenous women. Its primary mission is to bring the "rural and private voices of women" into a global forum through auto-reflexive methodologies for using multimedia, Internet, and video. Their agenda is to use "technical empowerment" to enable women approach issues "which are personal and of deep concern to the community" as technical competencies overcome the handicap of not being able to read or write, enabling communication via oral and visual means.

The women who have been trained in the center are producing videos with significant social messages using participatory methods. In learning to use communication technologies these women have inevitably changed their lifestyles and widened their contacts. The Internet is enabling them to connect with other women like themselves, becoming active in making linkages worldwide. This program is now well established, and women of the community have assumed the necessary leadership roles to sustain the life of the Center.

Chapter 12 extends the theme of women's empowerment via technical competencies. Sabeena Gadihoke shares her insights about empowerment-oriented visual media and the issues of access and control for women. She points out that many preconceived notions about gender roles are often reinforced when teaching technology. She discusses strategies for the democratization of video practice from the point of view of a camerawoman and trainer concerned with the access of this technology to others. It presents an experiential account of Sabeena's concerns about the meanings created by the camera, focusing on the representation of underprivileged women in the "Third World."

In Chapter 13, Mary Jo Dudley illustrates how Colombian domestic workers have used video to explore their personal stories, and subsequently challenge public stereotypes. The chapter discusses how these domestic workers organized themselves and expressed their interest in learning how to produce videos with the hope that it would give greater visibility to their situation. Since many of them could not read or write, they felt they could express themselves through their own words and images to tell their stories. The first phase of their learning was sharing their own personal experiences with their work through videotaping. Each woman shared her history of relationships and work experience. This exercise was truly empowering for those women who had not talked about or shared their feelings and thoughts about their roles as a domestic workers.

The chapter recounts the way the women articulated their roles, challenging the stereotypical presentation of the domestic worker through mass media, and how they were ultimately able to advocate better working conditions and respect. Most importantly the chapter discusses now they were able to give public visibility to the prevalent illegal and unfair employment practices. This is one project that from the beginning had a goal of empowering women to take control of their situations and their lives.

Part 4: Video Action, Access and Impact

The final four chapters are intended to showcase a number of examples of how video power is being utilized for development purposes. They also take a look at participatory video models and the diverse approaches that are being utilized to meet specific development project needs. The information presented should be considered within the conceptual frames of reference that have been covered in previous chapters—ones that provide understanding of empowerment, transformation and renewal as it is impacted through video.

Chapter 14 recounts the experience of an international agency in producing a 30 minute video to address the HIV/AIDS issue. The *Springs of Life* videotape captured the devastating effect of the disease—powerful images of people living with the disease and families contending with its impact on their lives. The video explored issues such as the debate on whether AIDS is a curse, the struggle of children orphaned by AIDS, and the challenge of modeling healthy family relationships.

Ndunge Kiiti and Wilfred Amalemba share their insights; what they learned about the process of "doing video" and the effectiveness of this visual medium. They examine the production aspects as well as the distribution and broadcast/screening aspects of using video for education on social issues. They conclude:

Springs of Life proved to be a key that opened opportunities for us to reach unreachable audiences. Through the video we have 'gone where MAP Staff could not venture,' we have changed people we have yet to come into physical contact with, we have taught and spoken to multitudes at a cost incomparable to what physical travel would have afforded.

David Booker shares findings from his research in India about development agencies that are endeavoring to facilitate participatory video in Chapter 15. In this chapter he highlights some of the obstacles, successes and insights arising from some Indian communication initiatives in using video based on data he gathered from 62 development organizations. He discusses his inquiry into their successes and failures in using participatory approaches and reports the suggestions and tactics used by the field level practitioners.

Chapter 15 provides substantial background regarding use of participatory video. Here, Booker cautions how that one needs to be very clear from the beginning whether production for mass media is an objective or whether local inputs, facilitation and process is a major goal. Based on his observations, he discusses important aspects of the uses of participatory media by development agencies, and some historical aspects of its evolution.

Discussion of the power of video would not be complete without consideration of the interface of broadcast television and participatory approaches. In Chapter 16, Korula Varghese addresses this issue and discusses a participatory community broadcast model. He examines the status of community controlled media. He notes: "The increasing accessibility and decentralization of mass media in developing countries offers a great opportunity for communities to extend their challenge for unmediated self-expression into media spaces offered by existing broadcasting structures and emerging cable systems."

The Participatory Community Broadcasting Model (PCB) he discusses is relevant for those communities that aspire to have a voice in presenting their stories. The participatory production process is designed to enable nonprofessionals from the community to control the development of programs, from ideas to the final videotape ready for transmission. The model welds the talent of professional videographers to the indigenous perspectives of nonprofessional community spokespersons who have a grasp of the realities within the story to be told. Professionals are challenged to "technically reproduce nonprofessionals" ideas into a finished television program that is faithful to the realities of the nonprofessional.

Chapter 17 is the grand finale for this book. It takes a kaleidoscopic view of video—a *World's Eye View of Video Power in Context*. Here, Shirley White profiles some 20 development projects that represent the broad scope of functions and roles video is playing in facilitating change. This chapter offers a small sampling of what is happening with video throughout the development world.

Two more significant contributions of this chapter are the identification of Internet Websites that are important sources of information about uses of video and broader communication for development agendas, and the presentation of a Community Communication Center Model (CCC). The Web is undoubtedly a vital source of information but not accessible in many more remote corners of the world. Internet access is necessary, as is access to other communication technologies. In the future the interface of video and Internet will facilitate access to images as well as words.

The CCC Model not only lays out a mechanism for accessing the tools of communication technology but also conceptualizes a facility that can become a *communication environment* to serve as a port of entry into the community's participatory development. The center is depicted as a dynamic place where dialog and interaction is ongoing and where people can expect to find a link to community organizations and services. White challenges those who advocate the use of communication technologies in developing remote communities to take a holistic view of the cultural context within which these technologies become accessible, and to consider the economic and human realities. But most important, it is vital that we not make the assumption that when tools and access are provided, effective use of these tools will follow.

A Final Point

Throughout these chapters, the authors have endeavored to share their personal experiences, points of view, and lessons learned in regard to video's power as a development tool. They are sharing their personal experiences with you. Most would agree that participatory video is destined to become an even more powerful and useful tool in articulating the needs and visions of the poor in the future. The power of video to transform behaviors is not yet fully explored. Additionally, it is not adequately theorized nor are informed links made between theory and practice. In fact, participatory communication as a practice is clearly lacking in meaningful conceptualizations and useful theory.

We know that technology will continue to change. For example, one can envision or perhaps experience the interface of Internet and "streaming video." This means that it will be possible to capture powerful images with locally accessed video cameras and help them find their way via Websites into global transmission. It is not assumed that either video or the Internet are currently available or affordable to remote, isolated, poverty-stricken communities. But, these two complementary technologies hold promise for revolutionary changes that can play a crucial role in uplifting poverty conditions. Pioneers in the use of participatory video would agree that the potential is now established.

The recent report from the World Bank, "Voices of the Poor Crying out for Change," is an illuminating picture of poverty's realities.[1] As I read it, I thought: "If only these heartbreaking quotes also carried the image of the person." Coupled with the worldwide distribution on the Internet, I'm positive the responses would be more dramatic. Another significant aspect of this report, in addition to its vivid depiction of the plight of the poor, is that it incorporated the participatory research process.

The contributors in this book were encouraged to put down their ideas and accounts of their experiences in useful and concrete form. Each chapter can lead you into areas of thought and inquiry that can further enlighten your understandings about the power of video. Our goal is to encourage free and reflective experimentation with video to accomplish specific personal growth or communication objectives. Information about each contributor is available at the end of this book. Feel free to contact them to share your ideas or experiences, to comment, to inquire or dialog about their presentations as well as other issues of mutual concern. My goal as the editor of this volume is to lead you into further inquiry and understanding of participatory video and its use and potential for development.

Note

1. The complete set of reports is accessible via http://www.worldbank.org

Part 1

The Power of the Process

2

Involving People in a Participatory Process

——————— ✴ ———————

Shirley A. White

The participatory process is a person's active involvement in interaction, dialog, sharing, consensual decision-making and action-taking. Participatory communication is the foundation of this process. Empowering people around the globe to express themselves, develop their human potential, and begin to seize opportunities to lift themselves out of poverty and become a person valuable to the self and the community, has been the ultimate outcome of the participation process.

Involving people in a participatory process has become a normal expectation in the development context. This is a phenomenon, however, that has evolved over the past three decades. In the beginning, giving grass roots people a say in determining their course of development posed a threat to the hierarchical power structure of the development community. Gradually, a partnership in development has evolved, and at present there is a reasonable degree of comfort in the shared responsibility for uplifting and liberating depressed peoples and communities.

Communication technologies have played an important role in this liberation from isolation and despair. Video and radio, in particular, have given "voice" to this liberation. Both are tools that can be used by people who do not know how to read or write. Images give power to voice, conveying thoughts and emotions in unimaginable ways. The participatory model has transformed people from "objects" of communication, learning, and research, into active "subjects" who are shaping their life space, through knowledge and action.

Participation as Process

Participation issues surfaced in the 1970s and have dominated the development scene since. International organizations, regional and local agencies, and volunteer organizations have gradually recognized that a participatory approach requires not only a totally different mindset, but also a whole new set of attitudes and behaviors in order to achieve genuine participation. In this discussion of participation as a process, we will focus on the aspects of *participatory communication*. However, this concept must be understood within the broader connotation of *participation in development first*.

Understanding Participatory Development

Two international organizations have come to the fore with a commitment to make the development process participatory: The United Nations Food and Agriculture Organization (FAO) and the World Bank. FAO has a longer history of active interest and program focus on participation while the World Bank has made significant commitments over the past decade. Both have extensive Websites that articulate their interests and also offer a vast array of information and training resources to policymakers and development planners and practitioners.[1]

FAO sees participation

as an equitable and active involvement of all stakeholders in the formulation of development policies and strategies and in the analysis, planning, implementation, monitoring and evaluation of development activities. To allow for a more equitable development process, disadvantaged stakeholders need to be empowered to increase their level of knowledge, influence and (have) control over their own livelihoods, including development initiatives affecting them.

They point out that participation is, "seen as an organized effort within institutions and organizations to increase stakeholder access and control over resources and related decision-making that contributes to sustainable livelihoods."[2]

The World Bank's definition runs parallel to that of FAO: "*Participation* is a process through which stakeholders influence and share control over development initiatives and the decisions and resources which affect them." The World Bank has developed a useful Sourcebook that supports their definition of participation. They note that: "The Sourcebook is not a policy document on participation. It is primarily intended for readers who have already decided to use participatory approaches in their professional work." Terminology like *Community-driven Development* is used to highlight the fact that community groups are given control and authority over the decisions and resources, which affect their lives. "At the local level, *Social Capital* is the networks, shared values and associated norms which enable communities to effectively organize themselves and assume the responsibilities of participating in decision-making and resource allocation."[3]

Access to and a measure of control over resources is a major reason for a participatory approach to development. The process requires constant readjustment between the provider of resources and the community, allowing locals optimal, if not maximum, influence in decision-making and control over the development initiatives that impact their lives. It is important to recognize that citizen participation is the key to the sustainability of those initiatives and ownership of outcomes. If this is so, then it follows that the *participatory communication process* is also key to and inherent in participatory development and sustainability, if projects are to be relevant and appropriately institutionalized.

Understanding Participatory Communication

Participatory communication as a utopian "ideal" concept has become "real" practice in Third World development over the past 20 years. Somehow the belief that it could be so, doesn't seem as bold to us today as it did when scholars and development practitioners were offering their definitions of the concept some two decades ago. At that time, we did believe that participatory communication was a timely conceptualization and would in time become common development practice. The surprise is that it has happened so quickly. Now, attention to facilitative communication practices, at least in most development circles, is a mandate.

The concept of participatory communication perhaps deserves some definition for clarity. Nair and White (1987) have projected a definition of communication for development that reflects the need for participation:

> *Participatory development communication* is a two-way, dynamic interaction, between "grass roots" receivers and the "information" source, mediated by development communicators, which facilitates participation of the "target group" in the process of development (p. 37).

There are now many definitions of participatory communication. Some are media-centered, reflecting the ways communication channels and techniques are used to encourage people's participation in development and to provide information. Others are centered on the human aspects of development, encouraging participation and dialog. The goal of communication becomes that of conscientization, leading to an anchoring of cultural identities that liberates people from powerless positions and places them in a position to construct their own future.

An insight into the nature of *participatory communication*, its ideological, practical, and functional dimensions is useful for everyone whose mission it is to bring about "development." This is a complex idea and difficult to facilitate in the real world of development. An understanding of the concept comes from first hand experience,by working directly with the people at the grass roots, from facilitating and implementing projects, from conducting participatory research and planning, and from observing community action over time.

According to Nair (1994), those who conceive of development as a process of social transformation view participatory communication as a necessary instrument and condition for change. Highly contextual, participatory communication functions as a catalyst for action and as a facilitator of knowledge acquisition and knowledge sharing among people. He notes:

> ... the viewpoints on participatory communication, what it is and what it entails, differ widely. On some points there tends to be a common understanding: that it is a dynamic process, that it is dialectical and dialogic, that it brings about a transformation in communication competencies and social behaviours among those who engage in the process. Participatory communication for development begins with the premise that all people have a right to voice their views and become active partners in the development processes which impact upon their lives. As a human interaction, it is both a process and a product; it is both a means and an end; it is both a right and a need. As a dialogue between power holders and the powerless, it is both empowering and disempowering (p. 2).

Participatory communication is not simply a matter of studying about and dialoging with so-called "stakeholders" to make it possible for message designers to put forth more palatable information for a hungry audience. It also must be conceived as process methodology that involves people in an interactive way, making communication resources accessible to them directly, in turn, helping the grass roots people acquire the knowledge and skill that enables a partnership in generating messages.

Through that process, a person experiences self-awareness and becomes conscious of social issues that affect their lives. The transformative dynamic of communication exchanges acts as *a catalyst* for identifying one's own problems, recognizes possible routes to empowerment and self-reliance, and builds a sense of *independ*ence through *inter*dependence. Participatory community communication revolves around constructing opportunities for dialog in a context of commitment and concern about development. It has the potential to generate self-confidence, self-esteem, self-respect and self-definition in relation to the community.

The outcome of participatory communication for the people is consciousness-raising. By reflecting about their own condition, they are better able to think about and articulate social action that they believe would improve their well-being. Additionally, people develop communication skills, acquire new knowledge and contribute indigenous knowledge to development decision-making. Ultimately, the participation process can lead to resource acquisition that enables people to reach common goals within the community, making it possible for people to live and work harmoniously. Above all, those who control the resources for development will seek the input of local people in the development process—an input that is valued and sought through interaction, involvement, patient trust, and confidence building. At the same time, grass roots people, i.e., stakeholders, have to believe that their own individual efforts can make a difference when they are truly co-equal partners in development. In the end, they will feel a strong sense of ownership of projects undertaken.

Necessary Conditions for Participatory Development

Before the focus shifted to people's participation, earlier development models were based on the assumption that expert knowledge and practice was correct and that indigenous peoples were either uninformed or following incorrect practices. In this situation instituting participatory development represented a drastic change in direction. In addition, top-down models became obsolete overnight. This new approach required totally different assumptions. A new point of view in order to develop an appropriate perspective became critical. With this in mind, I would regard the following as necessary conditions for participatory development:

- ♦ Commitment by development planners and donors to human resource development.
- ♦ Understanding of the cultural aspects of the community.
- ♦ A critical mass of interested people in the community.

♦ Competent facilitators willing to and capable of enabling others.
♦ Training programs for building competencies, participatory planning, and action.
♦ Full interactive participation in defining, prioritizing and implementing development programs.
♦ Instutionalizing mechanisms to ensure sustainability: coalition building; setting up education and training facilities; establishing a resource base for continued development; creating linkages to advisors, resource providers, governmental bodies, and neighboring communities.
♦ Withdrawal of outside facilitators, when projects are completed.
♦ Provision of ongoing guidance and consultation to communities as needed.

Participatory development is people-centric. Localized indigenous knowledge is now combined with expert knowledge and outside experts become partners with the local citizenry. As partners they engage in ongoing dialog. Participatory communication, which undergirds all action, is process oriented, stressing critical thinking and reflection. The most important outcomes of participatory communication are the presence of local people in decision-making, project design and implementation as well as evaluation. The people must come through the process with newly acquired skills and a sense of being in control.

The Participation Debate

There has been considerable debate in development circles over the concept of participation and participatory processes during the past decade. Yielding the position of the "expert" as the ultimate authority in searching out "what is" and "what isn't" real, and "what is" and "what isn't" legitimate or necessary, has been painful. The shift from a "top-down" mode of information and knowledge dissemination to a "participatory" mode of information and knowledge generation has been a transformational force. Traditional communication theory and research models patterned after the

prediction models of the hard sciences for which there were dis-
crete measures, have given way to qualitative and interpretive models. Today anthropological perspectives are regarded as more valid,
reliable, authentic and explanatory, and thus, useful. However,
this juxtaposition will continue to be debated until these issues are
sorted out. Interestingly, at the "grass-roots," external interventions in the name of development are now not tolerated without
considerable struggle. Though top-down strategies have dominated development for a long time within villages and rural areas
the world over, people still value their indigenous knowledge and
know they must be a part of the development dialog. Their voice is
increasingly heard in decision-making circles and the poor have
become an active force in formulating policy.

No matter how paternalistic or dominating the external forces in
the development environment may have been in the past, grass
roots people *have* adopted new ideas and their knowledge base has
widened. For example, in India, village women who are concerned
about the well-being of their children no longer cling to health
practices relating exclusively to indigenous knowledge. They now
visit and use modern allopathic practitioners and modern medicine
rather than use primitive systems of medicine. Even though indigenous systems of medicine still exist and many of its practices useful,
the health care system has changed drastically, offering modern
medical approaches instituted through decades of development.
More importantly however, health care needs and services have
become more relevant because people are playing a role in determining what they will be. This is only one example.

The Current Concept Dilemma

The current direction of development, which increasingly emphasizes "people's participation," has made earlier development communication models obsolete, thus requiring scholars to rethink
their theoretic positions and theories. It has become necessary for
practitioners to reinvent their personal style and up-date their
approaches to the local (micro-level) communication environment.
Communication models, systems and technologies, also develop
much differently when issues of partnerships, stakeholding, coop-

eration, win–win conflict resolution, and collaborative community action are to be incorporated.

Popular education, participatory research, and localized alternative communication systems that integrate modern and traditional communication systems and technologies could conceptually benefit through the utilization of useful new models of participatory communication. Development educators, researchers, development communicators, and community citizens all must therefore become more facilitative, as they work toward common goals. The participatory development paradigm recognizes diversity and pluralism and the fact that there are many pathways to development. Consequently, message functions reflect the felt needs of local people, facilitating self-help, self-reliance and independence. Local strategies of communication are showing more promise for behavioral change than has been realized with regional, national or centralized strategies.

Relevant media content has become a contentious problem and its effects perplexing, thereby making a case for strengthening micro-level systems that can be more socially relevant and locally controlled as well. As the voice of the local people and bureaucratic power structures cannot be ignored, the communication dilemma has to be confronted. Communication systems and approaches to message-making must reflect a collaborative, interactive, dialogic, transactional relationship among stakeholders. No development stakeholder can cling to privileged knowledge, privileged information, and "power–over" models, but must embrace practices of sharing knowledge, information and power. Embracing the ideas of interaction, dialog, and information exchange that are components of a transactional or dialogic model of communication assures that a transformation will take place throughout the participatory process. The ultimate goal of empowering local people to take control of their life space is more realistically reached.

Alfonso Gumucio–Dagron[4] would concur with my observations, I believe. He makes a case for a new kind of communicator who can facilitate the participatory perspectives. He notes that: "If participation is not encouraged, communities are passive about development projects that are supposed to improve their living conditions. Communities do not have the sense of ownership of projects that were decided and implemented with a top-down approach." He sees participation as an absolute necessity, but maintains that development practitioners face extreme difficulty in translating and implementing what is written in their project documents into a process at the community level. Participation may be a part of policy,

> ... but there is no mechanism to guarantee it will happen. Few agencies have at the field level people that have certain knowledge and experience in community participation. Most of them just improvise by adding the participation and communication tasks to the job description of any professional, regardless of his or her academic background and experience. Often, the responsibility is given to experts who spend most of their time flying from one continent to another, attending important program meetings, reading and drafting sharp documents with recommendations, but have little or no experience of working at the community level. They miss the whole cultural dimension of development (p. 2).

We can only hope and believe that this lacunae is steadily being remedied as stakeholders come to understand and internalize the expectations and behaviors of the participation process and how to communicate effectively as partners in development.

Issues to be Addressed

There are many issues, which arise as we debate the pros and cons of people's participation. If we are to become increasingly more effective in promoting participation then they must be addressed. Four important issues have been identified:

♦ *Lack of appropriately trained development communicators.* Participation in development and participatory media development are at present understood conceptually, but remain operationally inadequate. For this situation to improve there is a need for more educated development communicators who are proficient in participatory approaches. The fact that the development communicator roles are often assumed by people educated in other disciplines results in less than competent handling of the participation facilitator role. This problem is often present in the use of participatory video where the leadership of these projects is often in the hands of technicians and individuals who operate from the "product" rather than "process" perspective. Professionals who assume these leadership roles must have appropriate academic preparation.

♦ *Insufficient individual and community networking.* The participatory process implies that local people be brought together in groups to pursue mutual interests and projects. This is impossible unless linkages between individuals of a group are made—linkages that result in interpersonal trust and commitment. Some linkages may come about naturally, but more often group situations must be constructed to encourage linkages. The same is true among communities. It is only when community networking occurs that more expansive development projects take root and become sustainable. The key to establishing networks is creating a context of ongoing dialog, consensual thinking, and shared commitment to action among leaders of neighboring communities.

♦ *Inadequate attention to social norms and cultural differences.* There exists a high degree of complexity in rural communities. In many countries the extent of cultural diversity is mind-boggling. Very often, because of the complexities and the personal nature of social and cultural perspectives, such differences are ignored by development facilitators. There will be no sustainable outcome for projects unless the issues of diversity are addressed, sensitively and openly. So, it is imperative that communication facilitators confront differences head on and bring participants to a position where they can relate to each other beyond their differences and establish some common ground.

♦ *Lack of commitment to sustainability.* All the parties involved in development endeavors must be able to see beyond the life of the project. It is unlikely that a vision of the future will be present at the onset of any participatory project. However, one of the built-in process goals needs to focus on "where from here, and how are we going to get there." Development facilitators need to continually look for ways to alert participants to the connections between their current efforts, and future well-being. If they are able to do so, they will look forward to becoming self-sufficient and becoming increasingly less dependent on the facilitator. The day the facilitator can walk away from a project confident that it will continue on its own should be anticipated from the beginning and celebrated at the finale.

Conflicts of Interest

This may be the only spot in this book where I can air one of my pet peeves: development exploitation. As an academic, I have suffered continuous disbelief and frustration over the extent of exploitation of the "know nots" by the "know it alls." For many years, I believed that the motivation for involvement in development efforts was one of helping the oppressed, the downtrodden and the poor. It was a rude awakening to find that for many people, motivation was the opportunity for making money especially through consultancy. I was shocked when one of my colleagues explained the reason behind his interest in becoming a part of the projects: "Have suitcase, will travel." Travel was a personal goal, and there was always time to tack several personal days on to a schedule, sometimes paid ones. This is a huge conflict of interest, whether inside or outside of academia.

Organizations can also be opportunistic. Their motivation to "help" may center around building the organization, more than on building the community. The picture of organizations competing for the time and involvement of the same people is a common one. A spirit of competition, rather than cooperation prevails at the expense of the community. In some cases organizations are advocating courses of action or use of products that will result in direct financial gain, e.g., medical or agricultural products.

The conflict of interest problem is present with media organizations as well. Enabling communities to become proficient in media production and establishing their own indigenous media organizations can be a threat to externally controlled media. Participation, which inevitably leads to capacity building and independent thought and action, is a threat to the status quo and to the power holders, both in the community and in development organizations.

Myths of Sustainability

It is expected that participatory approaches will result in more active citizens, responsible for their own futures, and capable of achieving goals and maintaining courses of action and direction that have resulted from a systematic process of addressing development issues. Unfortunately, this has not been so for many development projects. Perhaps "myths" may not be the word most appropriate for these comments, 'misconceptions' perhaps may be a better one, or may be even "false assumptions."

- *Development facilitators are capable of promoting meaningful participation among local people.* Capabilities are in question here. Enabling others to become involved in community action is not an easy task. Many times the individuals who have potential to become leaders and initiators are the most reluctant to become active. While it is ideal to engage a wide range of citizenry, it is also a fact that not everyone has the capability, or willingness to develop the necessary capabilities to play crucial roles in the community. Appropriate persons therefore need to be identified in an equalitarian fashion. Facilitators need endless patience, and must themselves be willing to step out of their "expert" role and become co-learners in projects. Relinquishing control carries its own risks, the greatest of which is that projects will not precede "my way" or may take a turn not anticipated by the facilitator and sponsoring agency.
- *Local people will automatically wish to become involved.* Participation carries with it personal sacrifices. Low resource people often pay dearly for becoming involved. They give up their time, they may have to spend money to participate, i.e., buy new clothes, pay for transportation, buy food, or arrange for childcare, for example. They may also face criticism from their families, their friends, or from people in the community. This is a variable directly affected by family norms, cultural practices, and political forces. The poor are totally involved in the day-to-day task of just keeping their families fed and functioning. This preoccupation can paralyze any thinking that their life may change if they involve themselves in external activities.

- *Capacity building is positive.* There is no question that capacity building is a must. However, it sometimes happens that local people, who acquire new communication skills, increase their economic position, or who become politically active, may have just gained the necessary tools to manipulate others for their own interests. Many examples come to mind: the bright and self-serving tenant farmer who manipulated his neighbors and acquired their land to become a new land baron; the village woman who used her new found video skills to bar other women from learning so as to seek payment for her services; the local politician who found clever ways to "skim" money from projects for which he was successful in finding funding. New capacities often need to be accompanied with guidance and frameworks for responsibility.

- *Participatory approaches will cure all development ills.* There is a possibility that participation brings with it red flags that signal the need for caution and care in the many aspects of its catalytic action. There is a need for constant feedback, dialog among stakeholders, and ongoing interaction and reflection over changes that are taking place with individuals and within communities. Many "ills" can be cured, but learning appropriate treatments that will not have adverse long-range effects is the ultimate challenge.

Essentials of Involvement in the Participatory Process

If a person is to take action, change and control his/her environment, becoming more self-reliant and self-determined, then genuine participation is necessary. People must be able to educate themselves, becoming more reflective through the development of thinking, acting and problem-solving abilities. Authentic or genuine participation can result in a sense of power, which in turn increases one's control over their environment and enables them to shape their own destiny.

Dimensions of Involvement

People's capacity to benefit from meaningful involvement is important when development participation is people-centered rather than focused solely on economic goals. Given a people-centered approach, let me outline what I think the dimensions of involvement are. Interestingly, these appear to be nearly parallel to the dimensions of personal change.

- *Awareness.* Rural people lead basic lives. Their daily patterns give priority to meeting the immediate needs of their families—food, physical well-being and maintenance of their living environment. The "work" that provides resources for meeting these needs, takes precedence over external activity. Recognizing the possibilities to reach out from their immediate "life space" to be a part of development projects may be unfathomable. Personal contacts, media messages, or direct requests from organizations will create awareness of the opportunity.

- *Active Interest.* Interest follows opportunity awareness. If individuals can understand the opportunity in highly personalized terms, they are more likely to become involved. If they can see benefits for themselves and their families, or ways to improve their economic status through improved "make a living" practices they will seek, and be open to receiving more information. It is only when the most personal needs of people are accommodated is it likely that they will become interested in the wider issues of the community.

- *Motivation to participate.* The promise of things or money or other "hand-outs" has characterized participation in some cases. But when the promises have not been fulfilled, apathy and distrust have been the result. When the only promise is to enable people to think for themselves, do for themselves and collectively chart a path of progress for their community, there may be even more skepticism. Initially, people may become involved out of curiosity, but when given the opportunity to be recognized and have a "voice", the enthusiasm builds. Video has proven to be a powerful tool for motivating participation, when used in the initial stages of involvement. Being a part of a discussion, voicing points of view, then viewing these discussions has a somewhat 'magical' effect on individuals. It arouses a confirming force within the individual, prompting further participation.

♦ *Testing and trust building.* Facilitators may find the road to building trust fairly long. In communities where disappointments have been a routine experience, there will be a trial period for the people to see that becoming involved in collective activity can produce desirable outcomes. In the past, whenever development has been imposed upon people, they have had only one choice, "take it or leave it." This imposition has erased the value of indigenous knowledge. Once people discover that indigenous knowledge is valued, the door to building trust and bringing about social transformation is opened.

♦ *Assuming a role and responsibility.* Interpersonal or social trust is the key. Once established it becomes rather straightforward to lead people to define the goals they wish to pursue and sort out the role they might play. A facilitator leads people through their own ideas and expectations for defining roles. Assignment of responsibilities is also up to the group. The facilitator gives participants the tools for building relationships, organizing projects, assessing alternatives and solving the problems to be encountered. In this process task trust develops, i.e., someone will do what he/she commits to do.

♦ *Project action and partnership.* Development projects are a partnership between external sponsors and internal participants. As projects unfold, it is expected that the community, with consultation and guidance from the external sponsors and their facilitators, will carry out the implementation. With the expectation that project decisions are reached through consensus, community leaders will actually share the facilitation roles. Ongoing evaluation is important in order to give community leaders the information they need to successfully carry out the project and make the necessary changes in the direction required. Above all, the community will be involved in such a way that will enable them to take ownership of the process and the outcomes.

♦ *Reflection.* Participatory processes require ongoing reflection. Facilitators will have to structure the opportunities for group reflection and give participants the tools they need to engage their own reflective thought processes. Reflection is a "reporting" activity, not a "blame game." That is, data and observations should simply state the realities of what is happening and formulate options for correcting any flaws that are identified. It is not a process of self- or other-condemnation.

♦ *Confidence, self-development, satisfaction, feeling of usefulness.* These are positive outcomes of involvement. As individuals experience success in expressing views, learning new things, using indigenous knowledge and skills, they will develop the confidence to continue to be involved. They will recognize their own self-development and the fact that they are becoming different people. Feelings of satisfaction and usefulness result from being able to play a part in community effort and be recognized and valued for that part. This is not to say that all outcomes of involvement will be positive. In some respects, we might expect positive outcomes to be directly correlated with the effectiveness of the facilitator. But when outcomes are negative, a facilitator must help people understand the "whys" and avoid the "blame game."

♦ *Commitment to continued activity.* Given that an individual does experience positive outcomes of their involvement and understand the negatives, they will be more willing to continue activity. Hopefully, there will be adequate resources for continued development projects that are locally identified. Frequently the experience that individuals have leads them into further education, paid employment, or assumption of direct leadership roles in the community. Personal growth, increased capacity, new challenges, or uplifted economics are immediate outcomes that provide a base of future involvement.

♦ *Leadership niche in community.* Beyond becoming capable and motivated to assume active roles in community leadership, the foundation is laid for a permanent leadership niche in the community. Individuals now become active community facilitators enabling others to become involved and experience the personal growth they themselves have

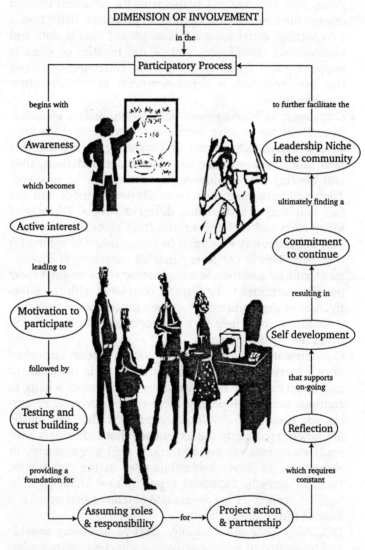

Figure 2.1
Dimensions of Involvement in the Participatory Process

benefited from. In time, no one will be left behind because individuals of the community will be assuming a personal responsibility for injecting their friends and neighbors into active community involvement.

The Facilitator as a Communication Catalyst

White and Nair (1999) have presented the concept of a "catalyst communicator," which is pertinent to thinking about the role to be played by a facilitator in involving people in the participatory process. They view the facilitator as a communication catalyst. They describe this person as "putting people together in order to make things happen, to catalyze thinking, motivation, interaction, action, reaction, and reflection." Through partnership and participation, grass roots people learn to more effectively communicate with others on their own behalf. "A generalized knowledge and understanding regarding needs, aspirations, goals, and anticipated outcomes is assumed to be present before these human linkages are made, " they say.

> *The transformation goal of the CC (Catalyst Communicator) is to unlock the human potentials of individuals, increasing their capacity to think, to relate, to act, and to reflect from a foundation of communication competencies.* The courage to launch out on an expanded vision of their own quality of life and what it takes to achieve it, will be an important outcome when this transformational goal is reached. The interesting thing about this transformational process is that it also brings about parallel changes within the catalyst communicator (p. 40).

Their explanation of the concept goes on to present a matrix of catalyst communicator competencies outlining in detail the interactions within an analysis of belief, knowledge, and skill along with identifying specific activities and characteristics. From their perspective, it is ideal that a facilitator has strong academic and/or an experiential background in communication theory and practice.[5]

Shared Ideas, Knowledge, Goals, and Responsibility

Meaningful involvement requires sharing. Inherent in the participation process is ongoing sharing. The initial bringing together of individuals from a community can establish a norm of sharing very quickly. I had the opportunity to observe the techniques of Kathy Colverson (1996), who conducted a participatory research project on women's access to agricultural information in Honduras, as she encouraged sharing behaviors among her interviewees. She was probing into the issue of women's marginalization in agriculture—an issue which when confronted gave rise to defensiveness in all corners. She was intent upon uncovering the innermost thoughts of women about the issue.

Before she began the research, her first step was sharing some of her experiences with groups of women. On one occasion, I observed her with a group of women who were operating a nursery school for children of field workers. They served a lunch of gruel (cooked cornmeal in water) each day. Although cabbage was produced in the area, all the good produce went to market and the culls and scraps were fed to the pigs or just thrown away. (Kathy said in some cases the pigs were better fed than the people.) The people knew they could eat the cabbage, but they did not know how to prepare it. In a very interactive way Kathy did a small workshop on how to make cabbage rolls, utilizing the corn with a small amount of rice and beans as stuffing. Each woman made a roll and placed it in the cooking pot. Their greatest satisfaction was the delight of the children with their new food. Kathy's satisfaction was that the women had acquired useful knowledge about nutrition and skill in preparing a nutritious meal.

Through this type of mutual sharing Kathy gained the confidence of the women who in turn were more than willing to talk freely in personal interviews about their status as women farmers. More importantly, this process involved an ongoing sharing of ideas and knowledge that resulted in the setting of goals and discussion of responsibilities for bringing about change. This small example highlights the very personalized aspects of the sharing process.

In the process of sharing, people can arrive at more clear understandings of their own life circumstances. By sharing, people can realize that they are not alone with their problems. Through a sharing experience, people can exchange and acquire useful knowledge and understanding. Courage to confront comes through consensual thinking. Dialog is instrumental in setting goals that are relevant to all members of a group or to a community. Shared responsibility produces mutual commitment. These are but a few.

Capacity Building and Institutionalization

Capacity building goes beyond but does not exclude individual growth. Hopelessness and lack of opportunities for self-expression or assumption of responsibilities outside their family context, makes people often lose confidence in, or perhaps not even recognize their own abilities. Involvement through participation initiates a process that results in acknowledging and awakening abilities.

Over time the capacities for uplifting life are increased through development of self-esteem, acquisition of new knowledge and skill, confidence in assuming an active role in the community. Learning to use the tools of the media is instrumental to capacity building. Use of participatory communication tools creates opportunities for people to involve themselves in activities that are empowering. New organizations, systems and patterns of communication can evolve and become an integral part of the community structure, thus institutionalized to serve the formerly unempowered.

Empowerment

Though empowerment is usually conceptualized as moving out of a condition or sense of deprivation or oppression, it can also be looked at as a positive, holistic outcome of self-discovery, successful human interaction, and the ability to dialogue with people different from one's self (Crabtree, 1998, p. 189).

It is essential for people to understand that empowerment can result from participatory involvement in development endeavors. For those who have been forever powerless, this promise will no doubt seem an impossible one to keep. However, most will find that their aspirations for a better life provide a compatible framework for participation that holds the promise of empowerment.

Narayan, et al., (2000b) characterize the powerless as "trapped in a many-stranded web." This web is one which is linked with deprivations—a struggle against "ill-being," a struggle for livelihood, social deprivation, and lack of access to information or education. Personal incapabilities are a barrier to providing adequate resources for families or to belong to society. This web strangles feelings of self-worth and fosters low self-confidence and self-esteem. Only through empowerment and by reducing vulnerability can some escape.

Empowerment implies a change in power relations. The first step is ensuring the voices of the poor are heard. This requires strong facilitation and mentoring on the part of development agencies. The poor need to be heard in decision forums of the community and play an active role in policy-making. This suggests that the power holders be willing to listen to these voices and that services be made available for addressing problems that poor people identify. The "Agenda for Change" (Narayan, et al., 2000a) suggests that progress across several themes is necessary for empowerment. People must move:

♦ From material poverty to adequate assets and livelihoods.
♦ From isolation and poor infrastructure to access and services.
♦ From illness and incapability to health, information, and education.
♦ From unequal and troubled gender relations to equity and harmony.
♦ From fear and lack of protection to peace and security.
♦ From exclusion and impotence to inclusion, organization and empowerment.
♦ From corruption and abuse to honesty and fair treatment (p. 266).

Critical Reflection

Critical reflection is a Freireian concept and a key one, pertinent to the participatory process. It is the process of "action–reflection–

action" that makes *conscientisation* possible. In participatory involvement, this suggests that at each step participants share an experience, think about it, then talk about it, draw conclusions and map out the next step. *Critical reflection* would include self-reporting of one's own actions, examining self–other relationships, sorting through options, recognizing outcomes, establishing causality, and outlining future alternatives.

People can diagnose their own situations and realities. They readily recognize their feelings of shame, hopelessness, depression, dependency, and fear, all of which have a bearing on their ability to move out of their current conditions. The process of critical reflection is helpful but *the process must be a part of their learning through participatory involvement.* An important element in learning to reflect is that self-blame, self-condemnation, or devaluing yourself or others, are all against the "rules."

Culture and Continuity

The cultural context and heritage of a community are strong factors in how people within communities relate to one another. Culture provides a meaningful framework for order and harmony in relationships. There are key factors that have strong bearing on the behavior of people who live in the same geographic area. These factors become determinants of community building and continuity of social practices. Some of these are ethnicity, race, religion, caste and social status. These account for significant differences in attitudes, beliefs, personal ethics and standards, values, and norms of behavior. Vast differences in perspectives are rooted in these cultural factors. So any involvement in the participatory process will be accompanied by sensitivity, respect for diversity, and tolerance of differences.

The Cultural Context for Participation

It has taken a substantial amount of time for developers to recognize the crucial role of culture in socio-economic development. The ideas for "knowledge sharing" and "participatory communication" surfaced and have steadily gained credence, providing a more people-based, thus culture-based perspective on Third World development. One of the strongest cultural forces in development is religious values that impact heavily on attitudes toward modernization and economic action. Another important force is the psychological factor of need for achievement, which is rooted in the value orientation of a community or ethnic group. Factors such as kinship and joint family structures, ritual obligations and caste solidarity contribute to the cultural context for participation. The interplay of these cultural factors can strengthen or weaken the development process. The interplay also accounts for competition, irreconcilable differences, and even violent actions.

Many anthropologists agree that education, i.e., knowledge acquisition, has the potential of altering cultural patterns and making people more receptive to modernization and the process of economic development. Alexander and Kumaran (1992) made a comprehensive study of the role of culture in development. They argued that culture, being a component of the socio-economic system, tends to be in coherence with other components of the system. Thus, cultural changes would be necessary in order to meet the requirements of development. The cultural context would thereby be altered by development.

The Pattern of culture in a developed area is likely to be different from its pattern in an underdeveloped area. While the cultural pattern in the underdeveloped area is likely to be characterized by a low level of knowledge about various aspects of day-to-day life, and less economically rational values, those in developed areas are likely to be characterized by higher levels of knowledge and more rational values (p. 26).

Their research showed a strong interrelation between knowledge and values, indicating, "knowledge is a powerful cause of change in value orientation." They found significant variation in the patterns of culture that they attribute to levels of education and exposure to mass media. This suggests that expansion of knowledge is brought about through education. We might safely conclude that it is probable that economic development increases the opportunity for education that in turn brings with it changes in the cultural context and framework of the community.

Cultural Renewal: A Transformation Model

True social transformation calls for both cultural and structural change. Popular participation in communication for development provides hope for cultural and eco-sensitive change. Development can only be successful when framed within the cultural expectations of indigenous people. Nair and White (1994) have framed a perspective for change they call *cultural renewal*, defined as "a dynamic process of goal-oriented cultural and structural change facilitated by pro-active indigenous communication transactions amongst local people...." It is a process whereby their cultural heritage and practices are shared, evaluated and modified in order to recognize ethnic diversity and live in harmony with differences. This perspective seeks to activate a horizontal communication process that can question the forces responsible for their deprived lives, research and reflect upon the issues, and enable people to act upon cultural and structural conditions of dependency that have been formerly legitimized.

The *cultural renewal* perspective attaches high value to participatory forms of communication. Participatory action for development is expected to bring about structural change and redistribution of power and resources, which if accomplished would result in cultural renewal and delegitimization of cultural exploitation. The Cultural Renewal Model interfaces two processes—development and cultural renewal. It is based on the assumption that the development process must continually build within it mechanisms that recognize and harmonize cultural diversity. People of diverse ethnicity, cultural practices, religious orientations, and value orientations must live peaceably with each other in the same communities, sharing the same pool of community resources.[6]

Cultural Conflict Resolution

One is reminded daily that cultural conflict has created great chasms in human relationships in many parts of the world. Conflict is an inescapable aspect of human behavior, usually based on incompatible points of view, ideologies and beliefs. Rival factions, organizations, and communities have built up animosities, over centuries or otherwise extended periods of time. It is almost always a struggle for power and control over one another. Unfortunately, seriously conflicted cultural contexts are often the ones that are potential sites for necessary development action.

Conflict can be either constructive, or destructive. It must be kept in mind that no change is possible without conflict—the greater the change, the greater the conflict. This is the challenge to participatory communication. The development facilitator, as a catalyst communicator, can enter a conflicted community and readily recognize conflicts. Bringing the people together and giving them tools to address their differences is the first order of the day. Creating an opportunity for them to talk about and share their differences will quickly lead to the identification of common interests and aspirations. Participatory Video (PV) has played a vital role in this process throughout communities on all continents. Chapter 17 highlights projects that have used PV to facilitate involvement in participatory communication and development processes. There should be no illusions however, that this can be a laboriously long and risky process.

Media Issues

There is no doubt that western media has been an intrusive cultural force. As television has become available in developing countries, so has western software. By the time local broadcasting capabilities are developed, they are often modeled after western programming. Social change in these countries is heavily influenced by socio-cultural patterns depicted in imported media. Western movies and music have impacted youth culture, in particular. In development, training models and the media used within them are obviously culture specific.

There is general agreement that much of the mass media material distributed is highly likely to violate local cultural values. Lees and Ojha (1999) have shared their experience of this violation while working with street children of Mumbai (Bombay), "dispensing" videos that were made by an international organization.

We began our work in India charged with making use of two video productions on HIV and drugs, putting them in the hands of adults working with street children in Bombay. Early on, the team of eleven of these children convinced us that it was important to move beyond interpretations of the videos, beyond AIDS and drugs. They convinced us that the real subject of our work was children's lives, and that sense cannot be made of drugs of AIDS without understanding how they fit into their lives. It became a question of meaning, what HIV means and what drugs mean to street children. Understanding children's lives meant asking the team to teach us how they interpret their own lives and how they understand their own behavior. It also meant learning how street children interpret the world of adults who they see every day (p. 121).

Essentially the children rejected the videos. The project then became one of enabling the children to develop their own media to use with their peers, to address their problems.

The model that has evolved from Jim and Sonali's experience, and similar ones from other sensitive development professionals like them, gives first consideration to the situation-specific factors of the cultural context. This becomes a driving force for applying participatory communication models in all aspects of action projects as well as in developing media messages focused on problem solving issues.

Preservation and Progress

A question that has been widely debated in development circles is whether it is possible to preserve cultural traditions and at the same time promote progress, modernization and change. The societal bonds of a common culture and pride in ones heritage can foster a powerful bond among people and be a stabilizing force in a community. Common bonds can often ease the stresses and strains of poverty. Cultural identity is nurtured through rituals, community festivals and a variety of celebrations. In rural communities it is these events that bring people together.

Preservation in no way needs to impede progress. It is possible that a focus on cultural preservation may in fact be the key to progress. Heritage provides a secure foundation for development endeavors that individuals and communities deem useful to their progress. The greater the cultural diversity in a community, the greater the effort to evolve mutually agreeable directions will be. As in any argument for diversity, the outcome is likely to be more creative and meaningful.

Vision and Challenge

The challenges for involving people in the participatory process are many and new ones will continuously evolve. At the same time the door to new opportunities and possibilities is open. Building human capacity is time consuming and progress can be excruciatingly slow. Successful projects in the future will recognize this fact and the goals set will allow a longer time span for accomplishment. In the future there needs to be recognition of the fact that projects need to be small and localized in order to allow participants a safer, more comfortable relationship with fellow community members. These "mini" projects can offer greater feelings of satisfaction and in reality, be more effectively managed and controlled. Small successes produce capacity, confidence, and courage to tackle larger, more complex development plans of action. Communication media—video, radio, and the Internet—will provide the mechanisms for linking and sharing the outcomes of these projects.

While local level action and control of projects is achievable and manageable, there must be mechanisms and programs that can move wider segments of the population toward shared goals. Undoubtedly, the role of a participation facilitator will become more crucial. Participant facilitators must, therefore, be competent. Greater challenges will require greater capacity and skills on the part of these persons to use the tools of technology and be able to apply transformation process skills effectively. These facilitators will need to understand the interface of culture and development, and be sensitive to the cultural diversities that at times may divide people. Most importantly they must understand "process" as a "product." Chapter 3 discusses this in greater detail.

Probably the greatest challenge for development facilitators lies in allowing people to grow and develop in ways that they themselves see important and useful. Imposing expectations and personal values must be avoided. Facilitators will need to conduct ongoing self-assessments to keep their process facilitation role free from personal bias.

Development projects will become more sustainable in the future because of people's involvement in the process. There will be local "buy-ins" from the beginning and more formalized "signing-on," making a commitment to participate. Facilitators will increasingly respect and seek out indigenous knowledge and involve indigenous people in participatory planning, participatory research, participatory project implementation, and participatory evaluation. Participatory communication, message-making, and use of media tools will under gird all of those participatory processes.

The vision? If it is to be sustainable, development will become increasingly localized, participatory, relevant and appropriately situated in order to make necessary linkages to regional and national development support systems that can lead to acquisition of resources.

Notes

1. Website Addresses: http://www.fao.org, http://www.worldbank.org
2. FAO, (2002, p. 1).
3. World Bank, (2002, p. 1).
4. Gumucio-Dagron, (2001).
5. Nair and White (1999) presents a useful analysis of the roles and characteristics of the Catalyst Communicator.
6. In Nair and White (1994) is a complete explication of the Cultural Renewal concept.

References and Select Bibliography

Alexander, K.C. and K.P. Kumaran (1992). *Culture and Development: Cultural Patterns in Areas of Uneven Development*. New Delhi: Sage Publications.

Colverson, K.E. (1996). *Women's Access to Agricultural Information in Honduras.* Ph.D. Dissertation. Ithaca: Cornell University.

Crabtree, J. (1988). 'Mutual Empowerment in Cross-cultural Participatory Development and Service Learning: Lessons in Communication and Social Justice from Projects in El Salvador and Nicaragua.' *Journal of Applied Research*, 26(2), pp. 182–209.

FAO (2002). *Participation: Our Vision.* (On line) http://www.fao.org/participation/ourvision/html

Freire, P. (1970). *Pedagogy of the Oppressed.* New York: Seabury Press.

Gumucio–Dragon, A. (2001). *Communication for Social Change: The New Communicator.* (On line) Communication Initiatives, http://www.comminit.com/review_alfonso.html

Lees, J. and S. Ojha (1999). 'Listening, Respect and Caring: The Heart of Participatory Work with Children.,' in S. White (ed.), *The Art of Facilitating Participation: Releasing the Power of Grassroots Communication*, pp. 121–47. New Delhi: Sage Publications.

Nair, K.S. (1994). *Participatory Video for Rural Development: A Methodology for Dialogic Message Design.* Unpublished paper. Rome: FAO DSC Information Division.

Nair, K.S. and S.A. White (1987). 'Participation is the Key to Development Communication.' *Media Development*, Vol. 34(3), pp. 36–40.

——— (1994). 'Participatory Development Communication as Cultural Renewal,' in S.A. White, K.S. Nair and J. Ascroft (eds.) *Participatory Communication: Working for Change and Development.* New Delhi: Sage Publications.

——— (1999). 'The Catalyst Communicator: Facilitation without Fear,' in S.A. White, K.S. Nair and J. Ascroft (eds.). *Participatory Communication: Working for Change and Development.* New Delhi: Sage Publications.

Narayan, D., R. Chambers, M.K. Shah and P. Petesch (2000a). *Voices of the Poor: Crying Out for Change.* New York: Oxford University Press. (Published for the World Bank) (On line) http://worldbank.org/poverty/voices/reports.htm#cananyone

Narayan, D., R. Patel, K. Schafft, A. Rademacher and S. Koch–Schulte (2000b). *Voices of the Poor: Can Anyone Hear Us?* New York: Oxford University Press. (Published for the World Bank) (On line) http://worldbank.org/poverty/voices/reports.htm#cananyone

White, S.A. (1998). *Participatory Communication: a Concept in Crisis.* Unpublished Paper presented to CIIFAD Seminar. Ithaca: Cornell University.

——— (ed.) (1999). *The Art of Facilitating Participation: Releasing the Power of Grassroots Communication.* New Delhi: Sage Publications, pp. 35–51.

White, S.A., K.S. Nair and J. Ascroft (eds.) (1994). *Participatory Communication: Working for Change and Development.* New Delhi: Sage Publications.

World Bank (2002). *Key Concepts.* (On line) http://www.worldbank.org/participation/keyconcepts.htm#ccd

3

Participatory Video: A Process that Transforms the Self and the Other

—————— ✳ ——————

Shirley A. White

Over the past two decades video has distinguished itself as a tool for social change and development. Video has matured as a communication medium in its own right, separating itself from broadcast television and demonstrating unique qualities which surpass television as a powerful tool to support individual learning and human resource development. This chapter intends to expand your meaning for participatory video as a process, looking beneath the process for linkages to social and psychological factors that relate to transformation and renewal.

Participatory Video as a Process

Participatory video as a process is totally self-involving. I tape myself. I tape others. We tape each other. We watch alone. We watch together. We react to and think about what we see. We discuss and reflect. We share with others. It is a useful process.

Through video, anyone can express ideas, articulate their view-points or voice opinions of importance with no barrier of status or consequence. The person who is reluctant to talk about their thoughts and feelings can be heard when they have something to say. Video grants the permission to speak and the power to express one's self. It also grants permission to share those expressions in a more public forum, addressing concerns that affect others in our "life-space." Video has the permission to emblazon meaning in the minds and hearts of those who experience the power of its images and words.

Participatory video as a process is a tool for individual, group, and community development. It can serve as a powerful force for people to see themselves in relation to the community and become conscientized about personal and community needs. It brings about a critical awareness that forms the foundation for creativity and communication. Thus, it has the potential to bring about per-sonal, social, political, and cultural change. That's what *video power* is all about.

It should be pointed out that not all *participatory video* (PV) is process-oriented. That is, what people are labeling "PV" is focused on the context for interaction, sharing, and cooperation with an outcome of individual and group growth. But some PV may, from the beginning, be focused on simply involving people in a meaning-ful way from start to finish in producing videotapes to meet a spe-cific communication goal. Therefore, it is important to know the purpose of involvement in the participatory process as it relates to use of video technologies.

Process vs Product

It is necessary to make distinctions between the *process* and the *product* of *participatory video*. On the surface, this may seem a pretty simple difference. But in reality, it becomes a complex prop-osition. The traditions of video, as we experience them through commercial television, have produced a firm mindset about the medium, even in countries that only recently have had access to TV. In some cases exposure to video *a la* videocassettes for home view-ing has proceeded broadcast television but the videos played are those produced in "TV" quality and mode. The prospect of having technological tools—small cameras, simple editing systems, video monitors—available for "hands-on" use presents a totally new video concept. When there are no rules that need to be followed, as is usually not the case with broadcast TV, the medium can virtually become what a person, or a group, or a community wants it to be. Add to this the emphasis on the interpersonal interactions in the communication/learning process, then the only limiting factors become consensual thinking, imagination, creative utilization of the medium and resources.

Video as process is simply a tool to facilitate interaction and enable self-expression. It is not intended to have a life beyond the immediate context. We have control over the "life" of a tape to meet our unique purposes. Once those purposes are achieved, the tape itself is no longer relevant. Preservation of the tape as valuable documentary evidence is an exceptional case.

What is the primary intent of the participatory video process? The intent is to promote self/other respect, a sense of belonging, a feeling of importance, a claim to an identity. Each person is acknowledged as valuable. Each person's voice is heard; their views are of equal worth and validity, irrespective of status, class or ethnicity. When we talk about the *process* we are talking about the total context of the experience of using video for self-defined purposes:

♦ To develop personal skills in use of video technology.
♦ To team up with others who also wish to learn how to use video technology.
♦ To enter into a dialog with group members and reflect on interpersonal interaction so as to improve relationships.
♦ To interact with teachers who view their role as that of a "co-learner."
♦ To modify personal behavior and strengthen individual identity.
♦ To define goals and outline courses of action for self-development.
♦ To construct messages focused on specific communication objectives.

Video as a product places high value on the videotape, which is to be produced. When it is produced through participatory video approaches however, there is involvement and interaction of both the individual and the organization that wishes to communicate a message via video. They know the point of view of the "audience" in regard to what they wish to communicate. This is a highly interactive situation which exists while the videotape is produced.

Viewed strictly as a product produced in a nonparticipatory manner, video is a passive entity. I watch myself. I watch others. What I see, I interpret for myself. I may watch with others, but unless the images serve to stimulate dialog, what I interpret is my own internal response. I have no control over the images as they present themselves. I have no control over who sees the video. I have no control over the messages of the video. I can choose to watch or not to watch the video. I have no expectations beyond the message moment, for others or myself. But in both cases, once the "product" is completed, it becomes an artifact of community and culture, for posterity. It can be cataloged, accessed and archived for present and future generations. The content hence becomes historical fact.

PV: A Tool for Self-definition and Empowerment

Seeing ourselves as others see us can initially be a big shock but is proven to be powerful in establishing a strong sense of self. A person views his/her own image and can objectify what is being observed. My viewpoint is that this is the essence of video power as an instrument for self-definition and empowerment. The act of seeing ourselves can join the links of self-observation, establishing a clear identity that may have been nonexistent. Identity and self-definition are necessary prerequisites for personal empowerment. Many examples of this phenomenon are evident in other chapters of this book. Shaw and Robertson (1997), in discussing ways video can facilitate individual growth through the group process, note that: "Video acts as a mirror. Playing back the recorded material can promote reflection and develop a sense of self." They point out that:

> Recording ... experiences and ideas ... assists a process of self-definition. Video acts as a mirror.... Videoing someone can be

a valuing process in itself. A focused camera picks them out from the crowd recognizing them as an individual.... (They are) equally valued. This boosts confidence that they have something worth saying, and helps them develop thoughts and form opinions. The positive feedback they receive increases their self-esteem and they become more able to express their ideas fluently (p. 21).

PV: A Tool for Education and Training

In extensive, long-term projects FAO groups have put together comprehensive learning packages that integrate video, dialog, print materials and fieldwork. Judging from documents I have examined, it appears that video has emerged as the medium of choice in FAO projects, including use with participatory farmer training. Unequalled by any other medium, its "immediacy" with instant replay in the field is valuable in checking and documenting project details. With video, commentary can be added in local languages. State of the art equipment enables quick and easy editing and tapes can be shown anywhere, anytime. Batteries or generated power can be used in locals where electricity is lacking.

One of the most powerful, yet most simple uses of PV is simple video feedback. Videotaping the individual learning a new procedure or skill such as applying pesticides, conducting an interview for participatory research, conducting a sample training session and then playing back the tape is a very effective learning experience. As the tape is viewed the person can engage in a self-analysis, ask for comments from observers, or have a more structured micro-feedback analysis with one's trainer or facilitator.

PV: The Role of ParVid in Community Building

The very roots of participatory video are in community building. The Fogo Process emerged from the context of community development. The early use of film/video to record the perspectives of Fogo islanders about their problems and take them to community leaders and officials led to community action. By sharing perspectives and points of view, the islanders validated their problems and were able to communicate their needs. Through the video process, the islanders themselves became more cohesive and gained confidence that in a partnership with government, solutions would be found.

The prime purpose of participatory video is individual and group development. Through the strengths of this process, trust, cooperation, and cohesive relationships develop. The group develops an identity and strength through the bonds that develop, creating in them a desire to communicate issues to the community. Just by working together they develop the nucleus of a new community—a community of shared interests.

When community members become proficient in using video, some members of the group will find opportunities to reach out to the community. Often, this results in the production and distribution of issue-oriented, or culture-oriented videos for private viewing. Or, it results in the establishment of a community broadcast station. This is evidenced in the many independent video organizations that have sprung up all over the world. These local level broadcasts serve to draw the community together. In many cases, video presentations have motivated community action. Ideally, community video is the community "speaking to itself" (Tomaselli and Prinsloo, 1990).

Participatory Message-making with Video

It is important to note that a distinguishing characteristic of participatory video is its focus on the outcomes of the process of "doing video." Nair and White (1994) presented a transactional model of participatory development and a typology of participation as a conceptual frame of reference for development communicators who seek to employ participatory approaches. They note that transactional communication is a "dialog, wherein sender and receiver interact over a period of time, to arrive at shared meanings." This implies that the communicating parties are "tuning in" to each other in an ongoing interaction with constantly shifting roles of "sending" or "receiving." This is quite a different model from the top-down, one-way persuasion models employed in earlier development endeavors. It could be viewed as a "two-way" persuasion process.

Participatory message development involves the grass roots stakeholders of development in the process of constructing and delivering messages. It becomes a blending of external and indigenous sources of knowledge. Stakeholders are full partners in all phases of the process: defining the message, designing the message, producing the message, and evaluating the message. The transactional model identifies the characteristics of the interaction of the development communicator and the grass roots stakeholder in each phase. Nair and White conclude:

> The goals of participation are clear. When a participatory approach is established, it can become a norm, thereby providing continuity and stability, thus increasing motivation and self-reliance of the participator. Given that the necessary information is available, participation in message development should lead to increased information seeking, thus decreasing the knowledge gap between the rich and the poor.
>
> Whatever adjustments must be made by the development communicator in order to accommodate participatory approaches, the transformation is worth it. He or she is likely to have greater satisfaction, since the participatory approach helps break the social and cultural barriers to acceptance of new ideas and practices at the same time preserving cultural identity. That is important for meeting the goals of development. But even greater satisfaction will be realized when one enables "grass-roots" people to develop their own communication competence to access and blend indigenous and exogenous knowledge to facilitate change on their own terms (p. 357).

White and Patel (1994) later applied this model to developing video messages in a comparative experimental study in a village in India and a county in the state of New York.[1] They found that the researcher as a person was an important variable in the Participatory Message Development (PMD) Process. That is, the personal style and competencies of the researcher to interrelate with people affected research outcomes. Several critical variables emerged during the process of operationalizing the PMD model:

♦ *flexibility* of the process (i.e., willingness to adapt and change directions),

- ability of the development communicator to play the *facilitator role,*
- the necessity of effective *interpersonal communication,*
- the *joint analysis/teamwork or spirit* among the researchers, development communicators and the intended receivers, and
- recognizing that the participatory process is an *educational process.*

Variables, which related to the role of video in development, were:

- video as a *reflection of reality,*
- video as a facilitator of *horizontal communication,*
- video as a promoter of *visual literacy* as functional literacy,
- video as an *attractive entertaining medium,*
- video as a *facilitator of shared experience and discussion,*
- video as an *initiator of community actualization,* and
- video as a *source of power.*

The important **outcomes** of the research were:

- It was possible to successfully operationalize the Nair and White Participatory Message Development Model using video with some changes in the model.
- The characteristic and potential of small format video, as a development tool, is an ideal medium of communication when using a participatory research approach.
- Operationalization of the Participatory Message Development Model is flexible and can be applied for any development issue, whether it is in a developing or a developed nation. The model serves as a guideline, not a recipe.
- Video as a development tool allows people to become involved in the process of decision-making and change in their community, which is an empowering experience.
- The presence of video in the community takes on a new meaning in that its evolution will move from a form of entertainment to a means of serious communication, dealing with and trying to find solutions to day-to-day issues.
- Finally, the process of participatory message development can be readily taught both to development communicators,

students of development communication research, and the intended receivers (pp. 382–83).

While these conclusions are general, it was our conviction that these two studies have established a process for using the Participatory Message Development Model. This process is useful and can be "taught." The precise behaviors of a development communicator who is in the position to use the model cannot be prescribed. It is clear, however, that the "professional" development communicator is the gatekeeper and initiator of the participatory message development approach. The "grass roots" development communicator in concert with the professional becomes the key person in implementing the approach and ensuring its success in contextualizing messages that address significant issues.

Motivation to Participate

What then are the incentives for involvement in a participatory video effort? Probably the biggest motivator is an expectation of personal gain that can lead to change that could significantly impact one's family or community. Thus, in many development contexts, women are enthusiastically embracing participatory video.

In a small experiment conducted by the Deccan Development Society in Hyderabad, India, facilitators sought to access video to disadvantaged rural women so they might express themselves. They were motivated by their own reasons for wanting to learn video production:

♦ We would like to let our issues be known outside.
♦ Our news must go outside.
♦ We are working on a gene bank in our villages. We can record information without depending on outside people to do it.
♦ We want to communicate with people in other *Sanghams*, to share our events.
♦ To photograph marriages, etc. (personal interests).
♦ When big government people come to our village, we would like to record what they tell us (as a document).[2]

This points out the important consideration for motivation to participate. Each woman in the training had a specific reason for wishing to develop skills in video production. In fact, in the first training session the facilitator had an open discussion among the women to exchange their reasons for participating and for being enthusiastic about learning how to "do video." Their discussion suggested that the women were eager to engage themselves in the community and video would give them entry into public forums where women would ordinarily find it difficult to have a "voice."

Video as a Claim-maker and Mediator

One of the earliest uses of small format video was to document issues, events, situations or claims. This remains a major use for participatory video. I recall the first tape, *Hivare–A Village in Maharashtra*, which was produced for the University of Pune project of which I was a part. Two distressing scenes were taped. The first was the image of a young man who had experienced a leg injury in an automobile accident and had developed gangrene. The local witch doctor had tied a peacock feather around his leg to promote healing. The second was an image of an unfinished water tower, which the villagers said had been left in that condition by government officials who had walked away from its completion. The two scenes made indirect claims that there was lack of appropriate medical treatment for the young man and that the unfinished water tower accounted, in part, for the severe water shortage the village was experiencing.

Interestingly, the video was shown to the Pune Rotary Club as a part of a presentation that explained the Development Communication Research Project. There were several individuals in the audience who expressed great concern over the two situations shown in the tape. Within a week, these individuals took action. The injured young man was brought into Pune for medical treatment. The government department responsible for completing the water tower project was made to do so and quickly. Claims, whether made systematically by design, or whether made indirectly, as was the case in the Hivare tape, can be effectively documented with video. By documenting the "realities," situations can be confronted, and subsequently remedied.

In my earlier experience with participatory video one of my graduate students experimented with video to mediate a conflict.[3] She was from Maine and had grown up in blueberry country. For several years blueberry growers and local residents there were locked in conflict over the use of chemical pesticides for the control of the blueberry fruit fly. Guthion had been used extensively by blueberry farmers, and it was applied through aerial spraying. The blueberry farmers said Guthion was necessary to meet federal regulations and consumer demands. Protestors countered the farmers with the belief that Guthion posed a serious health risk. The conflict resulted in violence, arrests, and ultimately economic damage for the blueberry farmers. There appeared little hope for any face-to-face resolution of the conflict.

My student knew many people on both sides of the issue and was a respected member of both communities. She approached both groups to work with her on an intervention for resolution of the Guthion issue, using video. Before entering into the process, a formal contract was drawn up between the groups by a lawyer outlining the rules and guidelines for the procedure. This protected the cooperating parties and was a constant reminder for the "video intervenor" of the agreed plan of action. Through this research mission, my student was able to use video as an intervention and mediation tool.

In the beginning an assessment of each group's "perception" of the Guthion problem was conducted. She then met with the protestors and videotaped their points of view. After the taping she sat with the group and made decisions vis-à-vis the edits to be made on the tape. Next she met with the farmers, showed them the tape made with the protestors, and then videotaped their reactions and point of view. She involved the farmers in decisions regarding any edits they wished to make on their tape. The farmer tape was then shown to the protestors. The reaction of protestors was videotaped and shown to the farmers. This video dialog was thus informative for both groups.

At this point, four months had lapsed since the "video intervenor" entered the scene in June. She edited a 30-minute version of the conflict resolution process from all the raw footage she had shot over the summer. This new tape was shown to both groups, after which they participated in a postperception assessment. Admittedly, the issue was still not resolved. The video intervenor however did feel that the hostilities had been softened through this mediation process. In June, protestors had been shooting at the helicopter sprayers and irate citizens were threatening physical harm to the protestors. By November on the other hand, the hostility had been diverted and the two conflicting parties were listening to their respective points of view. Video had in a sense provided a balance of power through equal access.

This project is highly relevant to the current development scene. It did not depend on a complicated process for the video mediation exercise. It was simple and straightforward. The conflicting parties in Maine were indeed rural people and they were not savoring the awkward positions they found themselves in. It was clear that they prefered to harmonize their differences if possible and be more congenial to one another. In most cases people in conflict would feel more comfortable if they saw a resolution. Participatory video has the potential to do this, but it still has to be fully explored.

Unexplored and Underdeveloped Potentials

A sampling of the diverse applications of video in development are reviewed in Chapter 17. The frontiers of the unexplored potentials lie in the interface of video and the Internet. The extent of this exploration, however, rests in the fact that Internet access is still a dream in many parts of the world. The Internet certainly could become a major teaching and training resource through the access and exchange of image materials on a worldwide basis. Local websites could tailor that information to local situations and develop their own, more effective, visual presentation for distribution to training centers via Internet connections. This however still requires relatively expensive hardware, software, and mindware.

The underdeveloped potentials of video are vast. There is no question that video use is open-ended and limited only by the imagination and the resources available to users. There are innumerable, well-reported pilot projects, which are waiting to be replicated in other settings. There is a need for knowledgeable professionals and practioners to pull together information on these projects with some evaluative assessment of them. A "Video Idea" book or website where one could make ideas more accessible would be useful. I would suggest that you try your hand at searching the Web. Just enter the keywords "*participatory video*" and you will be surprised at the extent of material assembled there for your use.

Transformation and Renewal

> *Life is not primarily a choice: it is interpretation. Outcomes are generally less significant—both behaviorally and ethically— than process. It is the process that gives meaning to life, and meaning is the core of life.*
>
> **J.G. March**

A Transactional Communication Perspective

In actual interpersonal communication situations, messages flow freely in a two-way pattern. Rarely can once distinguish "a sender" or "a receiver." Everyone is engaged in sending and receiving messages at the same time. As this occurs, each person is affected by the other. Both verbal and nonverbal feedback is simultaneously given in this process. This characterizes a *transactional communication perspective*.

This "transactional model" differs from an "information transfer" model where it is assumed that information and its meaning rests with one person and will be transmitted to another. As a transaction, the focus is on mutual reception of messages and particularly on the construction of meaning in each person's mind. The notion of "reflective feedback" or "reflective listening" is important to this perspective. The objective is to bring about shared meaning. The expression, "Meanings are in people, not in words" is often associated with the transactional approach.

It is the transactional communication processes that are pertinent to transformation and renewal as we are considering them in this chapter.

Transformation vs Renewal

There is a difference between transformation and renewal. Transformation is the process of moving from one state of "being" to a new state of "being." Renewal suggests reexamination of ones state of "being" and identifying ways to refresh or restore it to an original or improved state. These are complimentary concepts and when used together are more useful. In human resource development an individual, by entering into a series of involvements, acquires new knowledge and skills, which in turn engenders intellectual, emotional and functional personal growth.

Whose Transformation?

Initially, transformation must take place within *individuals*. Only through increasing the capabilities of the people can *communities* transcend their present conditions and move toward a new vision. Individuals in the process of transformation are open to experimentation and collaboration that can collectively move the community toward its development goals.

Transformation is inextricably intertwined with *the goal of empowerment*. Basically, this goal is knowledge acquisition. New knowledge is in itself empowering. It enables a person to think, to learn, to gain new skill, to reflect and analyze, to recognize relationships and causality, and ultimately to complete understanding. Knowledge provides the foundation for respecting one's self-worth, for formation of one's own points of view and opinions, and for building confidence to pursue one's goals. It builds the capacity for gaining control over one's own life and life space. It is at the heart of transforming situations and moving toward better quality life.

The combination of participatory message-making and disseminating those messages via the Internet, is unequaled as a means to empower individuals and communities. This combination could provide a flow of information that can be shared across communities. Information could be cross-checked from different sources enabling informed points of view. Cross-community discussions could be encouraged as they could ultimately lead to more enlightened, mutually beneficial decisions.

Transformation Process Skills

If transformation and renewal are expected, then we must look closely at the *process skills* of the facilitator and the individuals who are aspiring to work together. *Process skills* are those abilities of the facilitator which foster constructive interpersonal encounters using a variety of techniques. That through interaction everyone will be raised to a higher level of motivation, achievement, and "morality" is the process goal. This entails recognizing the worth of each person's contribution to the group, and at the same time nurturing skill development and knowledge acquisition that would contribute to personal transformation. These *transformation process skills* include: encouraging interpersonal encounter, promoting dialog, reflective listening, reconciling differences, reaching consensus, dealing with prejudice, conflict management, and fostering cooperation (see Figure 3.1).

- Encouraging Interpersonal Encounter
- Promoting Dialog
- Reflective Listening
- Reconciling Differences
- Reaching Consensus
- Dealing with Prejudice
- Conflict Management
- Fostering Cooperation

Figure 3.1
Transformation Process Skills

Interpersonal Encounter

Facilitating a constructive and satisfying *interpersonal encounter* provides the foundation for success in a working group. In order to do this, the facilitator needs to have significant information about the participants. Constructing exercises or situations where 1:1 interaction can take place, and guiding participants through fact-finding, and getting to know one another, is a first step. Through these encounters participants begin to identify common interests and differences. Recognizing personal behaviors that are engaging or offensive is also necessary. Using the video camera to provide feedback on exercises, gives participants a "real time" look at these interactions and behaviors. The facilitator faces a delicate task of enabling constructive discussion and creating a supportive climate for participants as they seek to reflect upon and understand their encounters.

Promoting Dialog

While dialog is a part of the interpersonal encounter, I would like to talk about promoting dialog as an "inter-human" relationship— where focus is on the shared experience or event and the deeper level responses that are made. Whatever dialogical exchanges take place, they will constantly focus on how the individual is reacting emotionally when confronted by the point of view of another person. (It is clear this requires reflective listening.) There is a pendulum-like motion within the person who seeks confirmation from another person. This motion shifts back and forth between revealing the imagined and the real self. Issues of the *self* will be discussed later in this chapter.

Promoting dialog that will put people directly in touch with each other is impacted by the perceptions they have of one another. Perceptions will change as participants interact over time, as will the nature and content of their dialog. Perceptions are a kind of "imagining" that acknowledge the uniqueness of individuals and enables more in depth contacts with the individual's feeling and thinking. Perceptions allow the "inter-human" relationship to unfold, without imposing ones own thoughts and feelings on the other or interference from a third party. One principle that should be kept in mind is that increased interaction will produce either increased "attraction" or "dis-attraction." Supporting these 1:1 dialogic explorations encourages each person to connect fully with every other person in the group.

Reflective Listening

Reflective listening is a technique in which the listener endeavors to clarify and restate what another person is saying. The intent is to better one's understanding, clarify thoughts and feelings, and to assure the other person that the listener is paying close attention to the person's point of view. A reflective response communicates empathy—identifying with another person's feelings and thoughts, and acceptance of the other person. By trying to fully understand the person, the listener is more likely to take appropriate action. Reflective listening requires a firm commitment to listen, which is hard work and takes time and energy. This is a skill that must be understood, taught and practiced because it does not come naturally to most people.

Reconciling Differences

Talk of *reconciling differences* suggests that we can identify what these differences actually are. It also suggests that people will "own" those differences and be willing to talk about them. The notion that to have differences is normal and expected is the key to reconciling them through constructive dialog. Respecting differences is a part of the process. Once differences are acknowledged, then one can determine whether their existence matters, insofar as accomplishing goals in task relationships is concerned. When people must work together, they must know that they are not expected to change, but they are expected to cooperate. If differences do interfere with relationships, then either the structure of the group or the definition of the task must be altered.

Reaching a Consensus

Consensus doesn't necessarily mean that everyone agrees on an issue, but it does mean they can be committed to a decision that is reached through dialog in which each person has been able to freely express an opinion on that issue. The process is one in which alternatives are identified, each person has stated their position and the reasoning behind their thinking, and a collective decision on a course of action is identified. This is not a speedy way to reach decisions because it requires that each person modify their point of view and merge it with that of others. The dialog presents the facts, brings in all perspectives and gradually rules out some courses of action. The final question is: Will you go along with this? The expectation is that once a decision is reached each person is committed to it and will do his/her part to carry it out.

Dealing with Prejudices

Recognizing prejudices and handling them is an easier task than it has been in the past simply because there has been so much public discussion on equality, human rights, religious freedom, and rights to race, ethnicity and sexual identity. Nevertheless, prejudices are a real factor in bringing together diverse groups in communities. Social class, sex, religion and caste have heavy bearing on interpersonal relationships. In working groups, these differences must be recognized early and head on. Bringing these differences up for discussion and constructing social situations where people can relate as equals can create an open environment for reconciling differences. Open discussions as to how people may have developed their prejudices, and why they feel they do can in some cases, but not all, be instrumental in diffusing or even eliminating those prejudices.

Fostering Cooperation

Cooperation is an absolute necessity if a group is to work together to achieve common goals. The environment for cooperation is characterized by sharing of ideas, thoughts, values and beliefs, concern about the learning advancement and well-being of others in the group, and a sense of ownership of the outcomes of working together. A goal-based model of collaborative sharing—space, information, work tools, responsibility—is required.

An environment that fosters cooperation would minimize competition. If conflicts arise, they would be negotiated in a cooperative manner with each person demonstrating the desire to resolve the conflict amicably and equitably so that mutual satisfaction is achieved. It is not expected that every person will be the perfect cooperator. It is not unusual for people to have to learn how to cooperate—recognize the behaviors that are perceived as cooperative, how to recognize conflict, and learn negotiation skills for resolutions. Bringing about cooperation is a task requiring considerable skill on the part of the facilitator within the group. In addition, the task of the members is to be supportive of the facilitator's efforts to

create an environment for cooperation. Bear in mind that cooperation, conflict, and negotiation are interrelated and it is virtually
impossible to separate their dynamics or their effects.

Conflict Management

Conflict is inherent in human relationships. When we talk about
"transformation," meaning recognizable personal change, it will be
accompanied by conflict. There is no change without conflict
whether it be interpersonal conflict or conflict within one's self. It is
evident that when individuals feel strongly about their differences
and defend them, there will be conflict. It is apparent that conflicts
will arise when people with seemingly incompatible goals try to
gain an advantage by giving priority to their own goals. When
diverse people and groups come together in one place to participate, the potential for a wide variety of conflicts is omnipresent. It
is therefore imperative that facilitators are equipped with the necessary tools to bring about *conflict management*.

I have used the term *management* rather than *resolution*. It is
unrealistic to believe that conflicts can be avoided or always resolved. However, it is realistic to believe that conflicts can be negotiated in positive and constructive ways through mediation and
management. Developing an individual's conflict-management skill
is a matter of developing communication skills. While not all conflict results from ineffective communication, all conflict management does involve communicating. Conflict does not have to be
disagreeable even though there is disagreement. Conflict is actually healthy because it helps move relationships out of a rut and
can result in new visions and renewed confidence between conflicting individuals. When feelings and positions are brought out
into the open, the door is opened for genuine interactions, and more
enlightened decisions.

Pathways to Self-actualization

Self-actualization refers to a person's aspiration "to be all that I can
be." The concept is drawn from Abraham Maslow's theory of motivation.[4] He had a positive perspective on human behavior: one that

believed that human beings embodied freedom and dignity as their driving force. People are basically good: trustworthy, honest, self-valuing, and self-governing. He held that an individual could achieve exemplary qualities like those of persons like Abraham Lincoln, Florence Nightingale, or Albert Einstein. He regarded the "dark side" of individuals—deceit, violence, hate, murder—as aberrant behaviors that occur when human needs are unmet.

Maslow's hierarchy of human needs has been referred to frequently in development literature. He regarded the four lower level needs—physiological, safety, love and esteem—as "deficiency" needs. These must be met before an individual can meet the "being" needs which constitute *self-actualization*—knowledge, understanding, meaning in life, beauty, peace and self-fulfillment. The "being" needs of *self-actualization* are not hierarchically ordered nor are they completely fulfilled by an individual. But as Maslow's theory suggests, it is the attempt to meet these higher level needs that keeps an individual reaching for higher levels of human attainment.

From my point of view it is this humanistic approach to human behavior and motivation that provides the frame of reference for participatory approaches to development. In examining the processes of participatory video communication, I find that being aware of and understanding the basic ideas embodied in the theories of self-development and interpersonal communication is critical for effective facilitation.

The *"fully-functioning"* self, a concept articulated by Kelley (1977), furthers our understanding of self-actualization. When a person is fully functioning, he/she must look at the self and feel that they are capable of performing the task at hand. An experiential background of success is helpful:

> (S)He needs to see process, the "building and becoming" nature of ... self. This being so, (s)he will see that today has no meaning in the absence of yesterdays and tomorrows. In fact, there could be no today except for both yesterday and tomorrow. (S)He must like what (s)he sees, at least well enough for it to be operational (p. 108).

This suggests that individuals are molded by their total life experience. Facilitating persons can further assist in the process of building, helping people realize their potential for change and improvement.

Kelley describes the *"fully functioning"* self:

◆ *The fully functioning personality thinks well of her/himself.*
This accounts for the "can-doness" of a person and the ability to assess what is realistic in terms of past experience. Positive self-regard gives the courage to launch out on unexplored territory as well.

◆ *(S)He thinks well of others.* When a person thinks well of themselves, they will think well of others. "The acceptance of others opens a whole world with which to relate. It is the opposite of the hostility which results from non-acceptance of self."

◆ *(S)He sees a stake in other.* When a person recognizes that other people intimately affect them, the responsibility for the quality of the self–other relationship becomes evident and self–other interdependence is acknowledged. "Coming into the awareness of mutual need modifies human behavior. (S)He comes to see other people as opportunities, not for exploitation, but for the building of self." Also accompanied with this stake is concern for the opportunities of others who have complementary needs and goals.

◆ *(S)He sees ... self as a part of a world in movement—in the process of becoming.* The idea of changing one's self carries with it the expectation that those with whom you interact will also change. "The person who accepts change and expects it behaves differently from the person who seeks to get everything so that it will be fixed from now on." This person expects each day to bring new challenges and new problems to be solved and greets the differences with anticipation. This person sees the value of mistakes, knowing that while treading new paths mistakes will be made. However, the evolving person can only go forward and profit from mistakes by reflecting on them as learning experiences.

◆ *(S)He knows no other way to live except in keeping with personal values.* A fully functioning person who has well established values, has no problem with consistency in behavior and does not have to constantly ask, "What did I say last week?"

When a person is functioning fully, their creative forces are consistent and ongoing. Kelley concludes that life to this person "means discovery and adventure, flourishing because it is in tune with the universe."

To build on Kelley's perspectives, it is useful to examine the concept of "*self*" which is based on our social relationships with others. The two aspects of *self*, according to the early theorist George Herbert Mead, is the creative "I" which is the inner person—a relatively unpredictable side of the human being—and the more predictable, restrained "me"—that side of the person that is social and shared with others. The restraining side sets the parameters of interaction of the creative side. The creative side of the person is the driving force of our behavior and the restraining side guides those forces. As one might expect, this is a dynamic interplay and is never totally fixed, often presenting an ongoing balancing act for a person.

Because our *self* is shaped by our relationship with others, the experiences we have with others account for the kind of person we become. Thus, if the *self* were constantly changing, one would expect the *self-concept* to be constantly evolving. It would also suggest that we should be concerned about the impact that interaction with others—engaging in shared activities. dialoging about innermost thoughts and feelings—might have on our *self-concept*. Understanding the dynamics of interpersonal interaction is important to the facilitator who brings people together in a social, goal-oriented process of learning.

However, *self-concept* or one's image of *self*, is who a person "thinks they are" and is not necessarily the *real self* that others see. This presents a complicated interaction picture. This self-estimation is important to the kind of change and personal growth that can take place. Another complicating factor is that individuals construct a meaning and expectation of the *other* based on their own sense of *self*. When transactional communication and partnerships in dialog shape the social context, a mutuality of meaning results. This does not mean that "group think" is an outcome; rather, that the context will honor diverse interpretations that can coexist.

But human beings are creatures of free will and in open environments they will be in control of how much *self* is shared and disclosed. *Self-disclosure* is the act of sharing either verbally or nonverbally those aspects of yourself that would not be readily recognized or understood if you did not dialog about those aspects. You make available the information about how you think and feel about issues, what governs your choices and personal experiences that have impacted your points of view, and how you behave toward others. It is important to see *self-disclosure* as a process that can have a positive effect on the communication transaction. It can be risky, in that disclosure could be met with rejection or condemnation. A person must assess the "good will" of the other, and gauge the extent and appropriateness of *self-disclosure*. When 'good will' is demonstrated it says that you will seek ways to "do good" to me, rather than ways to destroy.

Self-esteem and *self-confidence* go hand in hand. We need to have a clear view of ourselves but we also need to like what we see and believe in what we do. According to Griffin (1994), self-esteem is made up of four inner feelings:

♦ *A Sense of Competence. Self-esteem* balances two opposing factors—competence and expectation. "Self-regard is raised either by getting better at what we're doing or by lowering our expectation."

♦ *A Sense of Self-determination.* We are in control of our outcomes rather than yielding control to fate or the "powerful others." When people feel they have no say in their own destiny or are not in charge of their lives they probably don't have high self-confidence, or high self-esteem.

♦ *A Sense of Togetherness.* This refers to the "consistency of our beliefs, emotions, and actions." When our actions do not match the inner convictions that are rooted in our values, *self-alienation* is a likely outcome. A state of unrest will persist within a person until there is balance between action and conviction. Confrontation is necessary to achieve this balance.

♦ *A Sense of Moral Goodness.* In spite of living in environments where the presence of ethical and moral degradation is evident, people do aspire to ethically approved action (Griffin, p. 111). (There are, of course, exceptions, where what is approved and acted upon may be morally offensive, even physically and psychologically damaging.)

Building *self-esteem* and *self-respect* requires a basic process whereby individuals can examine, assess and modify their existing concepts, attitudes, and behaviors. Questioning the assumptions one makes about their own actions or beliefs often forces a person to modify their *self-concept* in order to maintain *self-esteem*. This mode of thinking is called *critical reflection*. It fits into the cycle of "decision-making–action–reaction–reflection." It simply suggests that a person understands a decision, thinks about what they are doing, observes the reactions to what they do and checks out the relationship between actions and observations. Our knowledge and experience enables us to challenge our actions, evaluate them against a predetermined set of assumptions, and alter future decisions based upon the resulting understandings. These understandings can be the basis for necessary changes and restructured courses of action.

Critical reflection is not self-condeming, or self-depreciating. It is a constructive process that enables ongoing improvement for the individual. It can be an important tool for reaching higher levels of competence. This process embodies risks, but when undertaken in a climate of trust and mutual support, individuals will be comfortable in taking them.

Trust Building

Trust, openness and risk-taking are omnipresent on the path to self-actualization. When new interpersonal situations present themselves, an individual will take one of two paths:

- ♦ If you believe that people are basically "good" and mean you no harm, then you will trust them until you have a reason not to.
- ♦ If you believe that people are basically "bad" and mean to do harm, then you will distrust them until they have proven themselves worthy of your trust.

These two counterpoint perspectives result from early experiences with people who have been harmful or helpful, or from living in an environment which is dominated by actions that prove harmful or helpful. In order to facilitate a trusting interpersonal climate, fears of betrayal or personal rejection must be eliminated. Over time, a history of interpersonal relationships that are built on social and task trust will produce strong bonds among people and high commitment to shared goals. However, there is always a possibility that trusting relationships will be violated. When this happens, it is extremely difficult to confront and rebuild a shattered confidence and commitment to work together.

An important element in trusting is *congruence* between the self and the action. For example, we sense people who always seem to be operating behind a screen, doing what they think is "politically correct," playing a role, saying things they think someone wants to hear. On the other hand, we sense other people who present themselves in a consistent manner, who can be expected to "tell it like it is," and who are genuine and consistent in their response to situations. They have an openness about themselves, which quickly establishes a comfortable rapport. They are *real*. "Being real" means being able to recognize your own thoughts and feelings and honestly and accurately expressing them to others in a nonjudgmental fashion. In order to do this one must be in constant touch with the flow of experience happening within oneself—a flow that is complex and continuously changing. In a sense you are transparent: nothing is hidden from others.

For development professionals, *personal credibility* is extremely important. It is an important dimension in the trust building process. Credibility is closely correlated with the congruence between how you present yourself and what you do. A part of personal credibility is information-bound and part action-bound. In a helping or consulting relationship, accuracy of the information you give and the reliability of your sources of information constitute meaningful and useful knowledge acquisition. People then come to rely on you for help and believe you will do your best to deliver accurate and relevant facts for use in your decision-making and to guide what you do. Repeated success with the assistance you give increases your personal credibility. When credibility is exploited or abused, it quickly erodes and trusting relationships vanish.

So much of the trust building process is a process of *sharing thoughts and feelings*. Sharing creates open, deep and enduring relationships, but over time can also create fragile relationships. Breaking confidences, doing something that offends the other person, or seemingly shifting alliances or backing off on loyalties and promises are some of the purposive or perhaps unintentional acts that can result when sharing becomes a norm. When this happens there must be a confrontation of the disruptive influence and open discussion on how to repair the relationship.

To maintain the optimum trust level among members of a group, sharing needs to be balanced with considered action, i.e., judging what is to be shared, and to what extent. Appropriate timing of the sharing process is also a consideration. One doesn't share just to satisfy personal desires; the reason for sharing is to facilitate relationships. Thus, there must be a willingness to "hear" what is shared; that which is shared should be appropriate to the situation at hand. Appropriateness is a matter of emotional content, relevance, and situational issues.

When the sharing process centers around *established mutual goals* it tends to be focused and pertinent to those goals. There is an understood frame of reference within which members tend to operate. They gauge the appropriateness of their own personal behavior in keeping with the goals of the group. These boundaries decrease the possibilities of unintentional acts that disrupt the trusting relationships among members of the group. As people experience positive and trusting interpersonal communication, they understand each other better and there is *reciprocity* in the working environment. Everyone is getting something from the experience and giving to the experience. Over time, there are fewer chances for negative experiences to have deteriorating effects on interpersonal linkages of the group. The risks of remaining with the group become far less when the level of trust is built over time and group members have learned how to confront differences and offenses.

Trust is the foundation upon which *relationships* are built. If effective team building or coalition building is to take place, then building trust becomes a priority on the action agenda. *Sensitivity, regard, and respect* are key elements in that building process. *Legitimacy, authenticity, relevance, appropriateness and reciprocity characterize self–other relationships.* It should be kept in mind that most clientele for development programs have a history of dependence, disappointment, distrust, disdain and despair rooted in extreme poverty and human need. Therefore, the road to positive self-regard, trust of others, a sense of individual independence and understandings about the benefits of *interdependence,* is a long and arduous one.

The Communication Environment

The key to transforming and renewing processes lies in the communication environment. When video technology becomes central to the activities, the nature of the environment is animated, active and full of opportunity. This is real, not imagined, space within which unique personalities interact not only with each other but in relation to video images which are a source of ongoing feedback. The people who move about in this space and relate within this space are confronted with ongoing "situations" which require action or reaction. The notion of situations suggests complexity, ongoing change and experimentation. People are within rather than outside these situations, thus unable to have objective knowledge about them. This creates a communication environment alternately offering opportunity and threat as personal interests, goals, strategies and patterns of relationships evolve. Figure 3.2 visually depicts the communication environment.

Interacting Situations are framed by elements of culture that impact on openness to opportunity and the process of interpreting opportunities in relation to other personalities with whom they are interacting. Situations change, people's expectations are constantly changing, and attitudes toward others are altered simultaneously. This sifting and shifting accounts for a dynamic environment for communication. Transformation is three-way: individuals change as their goals are transformed, the situation structure shifts, the patterns of interpersonal interaction change in relation to the situation. The cultural forces provide the base for extracting meaning of transformations in relation to the actions of people and the situations themselves. These forces define the parameters for sense-making, appropriateness, and mutual obligation.

Fostering a Creative Communication Climate

Interacting in a group work environment can be highly creative when people are surrounded by supportive members from the same group. The absence of personal rejection, threats or performance pressures releases individuals, enabling them to take risks and chances with their own capabilities. The first step toward this creative climate is building relationships of mutual trust, support, and respect. Such relationships free the person to leave their defenses behind and launch out to inquire, learn, and apply their knowledge.

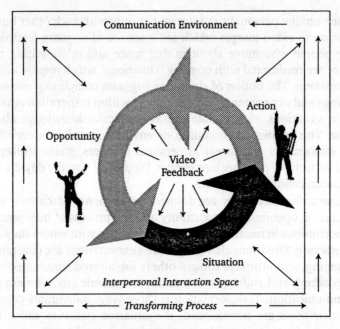

Figure 3.2
Communication Climate for Transformation and Renewal

This suggests that our focus must be on the communication linkages, patterns and systems that enable individuals to extract meaning from their environment. Individuals must adapt and learn to cope with the communication flow within their environment. *Adaptation* implies that we engage in examining the contradictions and discrepancies observed in the flow of communication; we test new ways of understanding it as well as ourselves, and we create new conceptual frameworks that enable us to adapt. If we cannot adapt to or change the communication environment, then we become defensive. *Defensiveness* is a natural reaction to a situation in which we wish to protect ourselves and the stability we hope for. Defense systems are not necessarily negative, they are needed as weapons of protection when the environment becomes disruptive and when it is not possible to facilitate changes which restore our personal balance. Defense mechanisms include reactions such as rationalization, denial, avoidance, identifying bias and prejudice, or projecting our reactions on others. At times these are useful mechanisms.

Supportive communication climates are necessary for individuals to adapt well to their environment and become productive within it. This increases their willingness to take risks and try things that they have not done before. It is rather like the cheering section at a cricket match or a football game. "Yea! Go team! Do better! Do something more spectacular!" Recognition, reward, reinforcement and practice are important.

Jack Gibb (1961) early on characterized the importance of supportive communications in organizations. His theory has survived the test of time. He emphasized the importance of openness of relationships in organizations and the importance of a person's willingness to become involved and responsive to others. He contrasted the supportive and defensive climate of the organization. He characterized a supportive climate as:

♦ a *descriptive* one where information flows freely with no expectation of specific responses in contrast to an *evaluative* one, e.g., blaming, judging;

♦ where there exists collaborative problem identification and problem-solving in contrast with *control* of others;

♦ where there is *spontaneity* of response free from hidden agendas or dishonesty, rather than *strategy* or manipulation of others;

♦ where there exists *empathy* for others, identifying with their needs vs *neutrality*, which implies lack of concern;

♦ where there exists *equality* accompanied by mutual respect and trust vs *superiority* or inclinations to dominate; and

♦ where there is *provisionalism* which withholds judgment or seeks more information upon which to base decisions in contrast with *certainty* accompanied by dogmatic behavior and the need to win or be right.

Gibb provided substantial clues to the important elements of creating supportive communication climates.

A Personal Experience

Last summer I had a renewing experience with video that reinforced my theories and my knowledge about the power of video

images and their potential to transform and renew those persons intimately involved in the process. The personal experience I'll share along with my reflections about renewal and transformation. But, in order to put it these views into perspective, I will unfold a bit of the background that has shaped my own thinking and belief in the powers of small format video.

In my early days as a journalist we were led to believe that "a picture is worth a thousand words." My constant companion those days was a completely nonautomatic, not so lightweight, press camera. My skills with it were substantial, including loading the 4 × 5 film into the holders and developing my own negatives. When I began my adventures into television technologies in the early 1950s, I was struck by how much additional information we could communicate through that medium. TV/video images have demonstrated a far more powerful ratio than that of 1:1000, i.e., the old saying, "a picture is worth a thousand words." The additional impact was the camera's ability to both record and transmit sound and image simultaneously. There was no question about its power as an intimate communication medium.

There was also no question that carrying around a portapak was not for the "weak." Portable it was, but easy to lug around, it wasn't. The quest for powerful images and to do one's own "creation" overpowered all obstacles. The power of the new media was immense. Indeed, there was another highly important element present in use of the media—control. There was freedom to choose the stories to be told, freedom to tell those stories in personal terms, and freedom to use those stories to reach a goal that was intimately defined and publicly shared. It was a medium that could transform people's thinking and behavior, especially when it involved looking at one's own image. It was a medium that had the potential to renew and refresh ideas, relationships, and abilities. In addition, it had tremendous power to deliver information for knowledge and action.

My first few years with video was television broadcasting in its formative years. I was fully involved with the "process." I made final decisions on content, staging, and presentation of programs. I sat by the director's side making joint decisions about sequencing, camera angles, lighting—all aspects of elements necessary for a final "product," the live broadcast. If the cameraperson wasn't framing the images just right, in our "run through," I took over the camera and showed him/her how I wanted the subjects to appear on the screen. It worked. There was high involvement of everyone in the process, from the content specialist to the cameraperson. They were a part of the team and as actively involved as I was in the decision-making and negotiations. It was a remarkably congenial, cooperative, connected flow of activity from origin of ideas to the actual broadcast. Not only that, but we made a systematic effort to get feedback on information needs, program effectiveness, and the usefulness of the program to our viewers. We were conscientious about what they had to say and altered future presentations on the basis of their feedback.

Those, however, were the "early days." We all know how technically sophisticated, role specialized, and highly produced, not to mention competitive, television broadcasting as mass media has become in its lifetime of over 50 years. It was no surprise when in the late 1960s there was a call for video to return to its early potential of control, intimacy, and interaction. The small handheld cameras came along to answer that call. But, it wasn't that simple. The concepts and theories that had evolved with television technologies, became the *rules* for use of small format video. The "experts" who came along with the new, smaller, user-friendly technology carried their rules–governed notions with them and laid out the guidelines for the use of small format video. They expected it to be "mini-television" or "toy television" mimicking the broadcast mentality which was firmly rooted. *Images were images. Or were they?*

Fortunately there were a few "free thinkers" who got their hands on the small cameras, and "alternative video" was born. My first exposure was through a colleague who brought the first small format video system to my university through a small grant to the Library Media Center. He was an audiovisual librarian. He was not a "television person" and therefore didn't have baggage from that experience. He was a visual communicator, a bit of an artist, part poet, and highly creative. He set the pace for a "no boundaries" approach to the use of the new technology. We teamed up to explore the power of video and to set up a training center for those students and faculty who wanted to explore the new and refreshing "do-it-yourself" video media. We made a trip to Canada to learn more about the *Challenge for Change* programs that were opening up people's participation in media. Our philosophy of "telling one's own story" was evolving, a video verite with space for imagination and interaction.

There are many stories regarding the faculty who were enthusiastic about using video early on. I will share briefly one positive and one negative outcome, from my early experiences of putting video in the hands of the "non-professional image maker." The university's extension forestry specialist participated in one of the first training sessions held in the field for extension staff. He immediately saw what images could do to assist him in his job. We had stationed a portapak in the regional office and he was first in line to check it out. He took it into the forest and gathered images about the problems and practices there that needed to be known by legislators who were passing laws to protect those forests. He took the videos to the officials and showed them, firsthand, what was happening. At the same time he gave them his recommendations. It worked. Very quickly, the specialist wrote a proposal, which was subsequently funded, and which enabled him to have his own camera. The camera became his primary tool for communicating. Whenever I saw him, he always had a new success story to narrate vis-à-vis his video ventures.

In contrast, a highly motivated dairy specialist, who was a frequent client of our video lab that checked out video cameras took the video training. He successfully produced tapes to use in his fieldwork. He was making fantastic progress until the day a colleague harassed him about video being a lowly activity for a professor. He asked the dairy specialist if he was unable to afford a grad assistant to do menial tasks like lugging video equipment around. The dairy specialist was embarrassed. Feeling the pressure, he immediately bowed out of his use of video, his enthusiasm and his confidence shattered.

Of course, there are many more anecdotes about our early experiences. In the early days technical and logistical problems abounded, which was inevitable as we were operating on limited resources. Human error was frequent with this new communication adventure. I recall a memorable but critical incident. One Friday evening I delivered a last minute edited tape to a county extension director 50 miles away. He breathed a sigh of relief when I arrived, since his annual public meeting for which he had made the visual report of the year's work was about to begin in two hours. When we put the tape on the player, it was the wrong tape. I made a speed demon trip back to the video lab to pick up the correct tape, changing a flat tire enroute. Happily, the videotape was delivered in time for its slot on the program, and the county agent breathed a big sigh of relief.

Since I had grown up with the early television experience, it was not at all difficult to encourage a novice to take control of the camera. The excitement of portable cameras, which one could actually carry from place to place to record whatever images one deemed important, was exhilarating. It was especially exciting when we launched a project in Buffalo, NY with low-income people living in a public housing facility. We had three sessions of training for women who were eager to improve their living environment. There were many problems in the public housing area, one being bad roads. During the training several images of the living conditions showed up on the participants 'image gathering' exercises. We left a portapak in the hands of the women of the housing development for several weeks. When we returned, we found that they had documented their horrific street conditions, and had taken the recorded tape, monitor, and portapak to the mayor's office, insisting on a "hearing." The mayor watched the video with them and listened to their stories. He found the conditions (of which he was unaware) unbelievable. The streets were soon repaired. The women proved to be good guardians of the university's video equipment, and they made maximum use of it while it was in their keeping.

The personal experiences that surrounded the early days of small format video were full of stories of memorable ups and downs. As I reflect upon this dimension of the medium, it reaffirms my conviction that it is the process of "doing video" that makes it powerful. The 10 years of experience I have had with "hands-on" video in India during the '80s and '90s were filled with many experiences and incidents that paralleled my early work in the 1970s with extension agents and rural people in New York. In the development context, a lot of time has been invested in the use of video, dealing with those ups and downs inherent in the "process." I am always amazed at the current extent of video use in development efforts all over the world.

Fortunately, technology continues to become more "user-friendly" and mechanically dependable. However, it should be remembered that poorer and more remote parts of the world are still effectively using what we term "obsolete" equipment. Digital technologies and video that interface with computer technology are still sophisticated systems that for many are not affordable. While this is rapidly changing it is likely that today's obsolete equipment will continue to be useful for another decade.

My Recent Experience

Regarding my recent personal experience with video, let me first say I am still using my decade-old VHS camera and editing system. While I have taught video for over past 25 years, I have not, in this time, put together as many "productions" on my own. My time has been spent guiding students through their learning process. Even internationally I have found myself assisting professionals to realize their own aspirations to employ video in their extension work. Another important dimension of my relationship to video is that I have taught *participatory video* methods since the mid-1970s. Picking up a camera and doing something on my own, for my own purposes has been a luxury that I have been enjoying since my retirement. Video, for me, can now be a personal medium as well as a professional one.

My new video adventure began last summer when our youngest, though not so young, son planned to get married in Sturgis, South Dakota, the venue of the annual International Motorcycle Rally. Such an unconventional wedding, particularly when it involves your own family, seemed like a "must" for documentation. I dusted off my camera, checked to see if the editing system could still handle the task, and packed up my gear for South Dakota. The rally in itself was a unique experience for me. Experiencing a "motorcycle wedding" was even more unique. But I was determined to document the event and emblazon it on everyone's memory through powerful images. I put my participatory process to work. Everyone got involved in creating a story line for *"Tying the Knot"* and identifying images to be recorded. After quick instructions, some even handled the camera to gather images (maybe even more shaky than mine). But we documented two days of activity and we captured two hours of interesting images—some quite powerful.

Input into the editing process was limited to the feedback I could get from my husband. I must say he did have distinct points of view.

He looked at the video from an entirely different perspective. So, I made several editorial changes. I did however manage to make a narrator out of him where necessary. The video was truly a participatory production.

Reflecting on the Process

As I was thinking about this book, it struck me that my experience in documenting "Tying the Knot" embodied many of the elements that give video its power. Critically reflecting upon my experience, this is what I find:

♦ In *documenting the event*, the video gave us snatches of real time that emblazoned the total marriage experience on memories. Although photos serve this purpose, video has become a frequent addition to still photos. For the couple, the first look at my edited tape was amazing. They saw a new dimension of their "big event," that is, many of the images were of situations and interactions which happened around them but of which they were unaware. They saw themselves as others were seeing them, and they saw behaviors of others that they had not personally witnessed at the time. Their wedding became a "bigger than life" experience through the video. They not only had a mental image of what happened, but also a record of images that went beyond the memory.

Through looking at the video, several times I might say, their big event became more powerful. They thought they should look at the video at least on every anniversary to renew their commitments to each other. My feedback from those who were directly involved in the wedding ceremony is that they relived the total experience, not only what was documented on the tape, but all aspects of their personal involvement with the couple's marriage decision, before and after the ceremony. When interested family and friends who were unable to attend the event viewed the tape, the impact of the tape was less. They appreciated seeing the tape and felt as though they had actually been there. However, they did not have the "reliving" experience that made the video powerful for those who were present at the event.

♦ The videotaping *activity altered the normal process* of wedding preparation. In the natural course of events, individuals would ask that certain images be recorded. For example, in setting up the reception table with the cake and decorations, special care was taken to see that we got a video of what each person thought was, or wasn't important. The arrangements were changed to make "better video." The scenes in the cottage where everyone was dressing for the wedding was full of: "Hey, you've got to get this on your tape." or "Please don't shoot me like this." Both camera shyness and camera "eyeness" became a factor in the collection of images that were videotaped. It is extremely difficult in video documentation to keep the presence of a camera from altering the course of action or natural flow of events. This can become a positive or negative factor in reaching the implicit goals of documenting an event.

♦ Video presence invariably *conscientizes personal behaviors.* What I observed in this situation was that the movement of the cameraperson provoked unlikely interactions and remarks. However, as the day wore on the camera became a fixture or a normal part of the environs, becoming obscure and less influential on personal behaviors. But when the video was viewed, individuals suddenly saw themselves as others see them. Evaluative responses were triggered within individuals. This is an element of the video process that can often alter behaviors.

♦ Video presence many times *catalyzes conversation* among people who ordinarily do little talking to one another. The camera at times triggered conversations and at other times ended them. This suggests that video serves to initiate dialog among persons who, on their own would not engage in dialog. At the wedding event, there were many people who were totally unknown to one another. The camera on many occasions prompted people to talk to one another, relieving them of their personal feeling of awkwardness, perhaps.

♦ It also appears that the process of videotaping *increases the individual's observation of the event.* Something is worthy of the camera's attention, it also becomes worthy of the on-looker's attention. Observation and careful listening seem to become more acute when the camera is selecting images.

♦ The person behind the camera feels a *responsibility for relevance*. Documentation is generally done with a specific purpose, for a specific clientele. The videographer has that purpose in mind as images are identified for recording. Relevance becomes an important consideration. For example, in the wedding context, the bride could well request that specific people or specific situations be taped. This is challenging when you want to be as participatory as possible in the production process to make sure that specific requests are honored. All parties to the participatory process deserve equal consideration.

Personal Outcomes

This personal situation was an excellent opportunity for me to renew my knowledge and enthusiasm for video, and to rethink the realities of managing *participatory video*. It reawakened my empathy for the individual who aspires to develop or sharpen his/her skills in putting together meaningful video production using participatory approaches. In addition, it inspired me to do more with the media I love so much. I have since updated my video camera, mostly because there was a mechanical problem with the old one that cost as much to repair as replace. My new camera is compatible with my old editing system, which is like an old friend.

Most of all, this personal experience confirmed my belief in the power of images and the unlimited potentials of the video camera. It is indeed kaleidoscopic and is responsive to the hands in which it is held. Its limitations are imposed only by a lack of respect for video power and a lack of understanding of its complexities as a technology and as a participatory communication tool.

Power and Potential of Participatory Video

The intent of this chapter has been to put the *participatory video process* into a broader framework of participatory communication and to discuss what I consider important dimensions of the power of video to transform individuals and environments. While video is a tool, it becomes more than a tool when used within developmental conceptual frameworks such as self-concept, reflective listening, dialog, conflict management, or consensus building. It then becomes a vital force for change and transformation of individuals and communities. It has unlimited potential.

Understanding the dimensions that lie beyond the tool is imperative for facilitators who make the decision to use video with a focus on the participatory process. The brief discussion of the elements of the *transformative process skills* in this chapter, for example, are just clues to the different kinds of theoretic and practical knowledge that needs to provide a base for the facilitators' capabilities. I see several areas of academic focus that provide the underpinnings for participatory theory and practice in development: cultural anthropology, social psychology, adult education, interpersonal communication, information and communication technology, and community development. This suggests that facilitators need broad academic exposure, or informal training in these areas. Experience gained directly from field level mentoring is invaluable.

Fortunately, we can learn much from development facilitators who now have years of experience with video in development. As you will learn from accounts narrated in Chapter 17, some projects have used video for very specific purposes and the experiences of every one of them has a unique aspect that makes them powerful in a certain context. While video can perhaps be about anything you want it to be, if the power of the image and the process are to be optimized, the "structure" for learning and media management must be carefully planned and executed. This is not a simple task, nor one for facilitators who lack adequate competencies and courage to put together creative, supportive communication environments for designing these structures and implementing programs.

Notes

1. White, et al. (1994). For details, see Chapters 15 and 16.
2. Sateesh (2000, p. 11).

3. Gay (1980).
4. See Griffin (1994, Chapter 10). This book is an excellent reference for basic information on Communication Theory.

References

Gay, G.K. (1980). *The Use of Video as an Intervention Tool in an Issue-Oriented Community Conflict.* Unpublished MPS Project Report. Ithaca: Cornell University.

Gibb, J.R. (1961). 'Defensive Communication.' *Journal of Communication,* Vol. 11(3), pp. 44–49.

Griffin, E. (1994). *A First Look at Communication Theory.* New York: McGraw-Hill, Inc.

Kelley, E.C. (1977). 'The Fully Functioning Self,' in J. Stewart (ed.), *Bridges Not Walls: A Book About Interpersonal Communication* (2nd ed.), pp. 106–17. Reading: Addison-Wesley Publishing Company.

March, J.G. (1991). 'How Decisions Happen in Organizations.' *Human-Computer Interaction,* Vol. 6, 95–117.

Nair, K. and S. White (1994). 'Participatory Message Development: a Conceptual Framework,' in S.A. White, K.S. Nair and J. Ascroft (eds.), *Participatory Communication: Working for Change and Development.* New Delhi: Sage Publications.

Sateesh, P.V. (2000). 'An Alternative to Literacy: Is it Possible for Community Video and Radio to Play this Role?' *Forestry Trees and People Newsletter,* No.40/41, pp. 9–13. Rome: FAO.

Shaw, J. and C. Robertson (1997). *Participatory Video: A Practical Approach to Using Video Creatively in Group Development Work.* London and New York: Routledge.

Tomaselli, K.G. and J. Prinsloo (1990). 'Video Realism and Class Struggle: Theoretical Lacunae and the Problem of Power.' *The Australian Journal of Media and Culture,* Vol. 3(2), pp.11–28. Also available online at http://www.fas.umontreal.ca/anthro/varia/beaudetf/Media_Autochtones/9-questions/pdf/Video_realism_Tomaselli.pdf

White, S.A. and P.K. Patel (1994). 'Participatory Message Making with Video: Revelations from India/USA Studies,' in S.A. White, K.S. Nair and J. Ascroft (eds.), *Participatory Communications: Working for Change and Development.* New Delhi: Sage Publications.

4

Participatory Video that Empowers

———————— ❊ ————————

Renuka Bery

Armenian folklore has it that three apples fell from heaven: one for the teller of a story, one for the listener, and the third for the one who "took it to heart."[1] In this chapter I have tried to show how all these elements are intertwined and without one, the others cannot exist. For without a storyteller, there is no story. Without listeners, who hears the story? And for the story to have meaning, people must be able to act. Participatory video is a special kind of storytelling that ideally involves the community in telling a story, listening to the story, interpreting the story through its own lens and being empowered to retell and change it to create a community—a political reality—that matches one's desired condition.

Participation motivates individuals to work collectively to take action. Empowerment involves personal growth and taking risks, and video is a medium through which to share stories. The convergence of these philosophies with a practical tool sets the stage for participatory video that empowers. The participatory video context becomes a relatively safe environment in which to tell risky stories that are powerful enough to inspire change.

Participatory video engages two different sets of people: producers and viewers. Producers are those who get involved in creating their own communication. Often, when producing a video for the first time, the video producer is in charge, making decisions, and finding his or her own voice. Producers identify the issues that are important to them and their community and wield the power to control the manner in which stories are told. Since the visual medium is a powerful tool that engages the viewers, these video producers, who once were like anyone else in the community, now have a skill that conveys the impression of power. Indeed, the viewers, too, gain access to a new type of power by internalizing the stories, redefining the issues and uniting to challenge old stereotypes and traditional power concepts. This central dynamic of participatory video helps to rearticulate the locus of power within individuals, communities and ultimately politics.

Empowerment

Those who do not have power over the stories that dominate their lives, power to retell them, rethink them, deconstruct them, joke about them, and change them as times change, truly are powerless because they cannot think new thoughts.

Salman Rushdie

Traditionally, power is an expression of dominance. But gender theorists have tried to present alternative power relationships that stress the power within individuals who can use the collective power of people and groups to harness the power to create change.[2] Using this framework, empowerment is an individual growing process—an inner awakening—that transcends the limits of society and culture and propels not only an individual, but a community and a society into new territory.

As a multidimensional process, empowerment incorporates four key elements: a psychological concept of the self that includes self-awareness, self-esteem, and self-confidence; a cognitive understanding of the power structures and one's placement within the existing systems; economic independence that gives a person or community the freedom to think, explore, and take individual risks; and, political analysis and the will to change the systems themselves.[3]

In essence, becoming empowered is a process of discovery that is unique to each person. The process is neither linear nor circular, but more like a spiral that moves up and down. Because the path of empowerment is a journey, people on that path do not stay the same or ever return to the same spot. One's consciousness and interaction with the social, cultural, and political structures is forever changed. In the development context, however, key elements of empowerment are: identifying a problem, critically assessing potential solutions and identifying one's role in the solution, taking personal risks to make the necessary changes, and finally involving others to ensure those changes are lasting and sustainable.

Empowerment is closely linked with identity and context. Gaining control of one's life, making one's own decisions and being able to influence the context in which one lives are essential elements of empowerment. In situations where they do not have power, people might not even recognize the ways to participate. Local people are often occupied by the struggle for survival. So, they do not have the time to engage in thinking about themselves, who they are, or what role they can play in the community. They are preoccupied with obtaining enough food for the family, paying school fees, or making sure that their small patch of land is sown and harvested. It may not occur to them that they have rights or that they can actually make choices.

Empowerment requires the ability to think for oneself and to be able to articulate those thoughts in the larger community. Too often the poor, the illiterate, the disenfranchised do not sense that they have the ability to participate actively in making decisions for themselves and for the wider community. And they have never exercised their voice. They have never had the opportunity to make choices and they have never tested their own abilities.

Examining Participation

There are no recipes or formulae, no checklists or advice that describe reality. There is only what we create through our

engagement with others and with events. Nothing really trans-
fers; everything is always new and different and unique to each
of us.

Margaret Wheatley

Participation does not mean the same thing to all people. Indeed, circumstances demand different types of participation depending on the individuals and the social and economic conditions involved. Thus, trying to define participation with labels and systems can only freeze the movement that continues to adapt in response to evolving priorities, realities, and contexts. However, Berengere de Negri, et al. (1999) have developed a useful framework to categorize various forms of participation that places these gradations on a continuum. Because participation is fluid and changing in various contexts, understanding these differences can be useful.

Equalizing the Power of the Process

We inhabit a world that is always subjective and shaped by our
interactions with it. Our world is mpossible to pin down, con-
stantly changing and infinitely more interesting than we ever
imagined.

Margaret Wheatley

Participatory communication defies definition because it can change to suit the environment and the need. Its value is its variety and looseness. Participatory video is a tool that supports education, cultural identity and preservation, organization, and political participation.[4] Indeed, participatory video has been used to raise deep cultural issues that most people do not question.

Participatory video is a tool, not a prescription for empowerment. Empowerment must be derived from within. By itself, participatory video is not enough to empower people. The participatory video process puts communication tools into the hands of ordinary people who have something to share. The strength of the tool, however, is only as powerful as the person using it. These communicators learn to use the tools and then plan and shape the content, perspective,

Table 4.1
The Participation Continuum*

Mode of Participation	Involvement of Local People	Participatory Video Applications
Co-option	Token representatives are chosen but have no real input or power.	Outside video producers meet with certain community members but decide the important issues and make their own program. Local audiences may or may not see the final product.
Compliance	Tasks are assigned with incentives; outsiders decide agenda and direct the process.	Community members conduct research. Outside video producers decide the important issues and make their own program. Local audiences may or may not see the final product.
Consultation	Local opinions are asked; outsiders analyze and decide on a course of action.	Community members share their thoughts and opinions about important issues, which outside video producers consider when developing their program. Local audiences may or may not see the final product.
Cooperation	Local people work together with outsiders to determine priorities; responsibility remains with outsiders for directing the process.	Community members and outside video producers develop the script together. The outsiders make the video. Local audiences will generally see the product but they are not the main target audience.
Co-learning	Local people and outsiders share their knowledge to create new understanding and work together to form action with outside facilitation.	Community members and outside video producers discuss the issues and develop the script. The production is made jointly with an outsider directing the process. Local audiences will see and have access to the product and so as to share it with other communities.
Collective Action	Local people set their own agenda and mobilize to carry it out in the absence of outside initiators and facilitators.	Community members determine the important issues, develop the stories, and make the video themselves. The purpose of the video is for use in the community to raise the stature of the issue and to advocate change.

*Adapted from DeNegri et al., *Empowering Communities*, p. 4.

and impact of the stories they wish to tell.[5] Through this process, local producers learn to identify issues and to articulate them clearly. However, participatory communication can provide local people with new opportunities to gain self-confidence, to think for themselves and to speak out, which in turn, nurtures the internal spectre of empowerment. Participatory video is also a tool that enhances a video producer's status in the community, often reinforcing the internal confidence building that has begun to take place.

Internal changes are crucial in building empowerment. External constructs are also significant because they enable the person engaged in the participatory video process to take on a visible role, often for the first time in their life. For example, Tuli, a Bangladeshi village woman who had become a video producer, was making a production at a local *mela* (fete). She was videotaping speeches of local candidates because she wanted a record of their campaign promises. Finally, one official chided Tuli, saying, "Why do you have a video camera? This is not the work of a woman." Tuli explained what she was doing and then went on to add, "If I had not had the camera, you would not even have noticed or talked to me." Thus, participation is inextricably linked with empowerment—an enabling factor that can help empower people.

Participatory video programs are often started through local non-governmental organizations have an established presence and role in the communities they serve. Members of these organizations are trained in participatory video and challenged to use this tool to bring changes within their communities. Their vastly differing backgrounds and experiences allows each participatory video producer to use this modern communication medium to tell stories and raise issues in a variety of new and creative ways. Indeed, a framework evolves through this participatory communication process that enables the individual to examine his/her self-identity and build his/her self-confidence. The individual can articulate new, transforming thoughts without fear and implement changes, for themselves and within the surrounding community. Finally, interacting with outside forces brings about change in the social context that ultimately shifts the dynamics of power over political will and processes.

Defining Self

As noted earlier, participatory video engages producers and viewers in a process of self-definition and identification. People's experience of the world is shaped by who they are and how they fit into
their cultural context. Those from different cultures or with various
levels of education, economic opportunity, and social status all
have differing relationships with power and society that influence
their frames of reference. A man will tell a very different story from
a woman within the same household or community. Adolescent
perspectives of the world are distinct from those of adults because
they have a narrower worldview and range of experience from
which to draw. An urban dweller will experience life, politics, society, and culture very differently from a villager. These constructs
color one's perceptions, one's sense of self and, as such, are the keys
to determining one's identity in the social fabric of the community.

Participatory video stories identify, illuminate and validate people's realities—often invisible in the larger communal or political
context. Participatory video's role is to create dialog and to encourage producers and viewers to exercise control over their lives that
may be unrecognized and untested. All people have the capacity
to be empowered but often have never explored it. The Self-
Employed Women's Association (SEWA) in India uses video to tape
trainees introducing themselves to their peers. This is sometimes
the first time these women have ever talked outside the home. One
video trainee interviewed a man on the street and came back to the
group full of pride because she had never talked to a strange man
before and it wasn't so scary or difficult after all. In fact, hearing
these powerful stories and watching them on tape enabled other
women in the group to think about the risks they could take by
doing things outside the "cultural norm"—to think for themselves
and to think "new" thoughts.

Learning to think for one's self is a process that feeds into becoming empowered. When someone is able to make decisions and
express them, that person is no longer under the control of someone else. It can be a difficult transition, because suddenly the person has to take ownership of his or her decision—for better or
worse. Self-doubt can plague the process as can the lack of support
from others who may have something to lose from this new found

independence. But for the person undergoing this transformation, when the strings of control are suddenly cut, the freedom to dance and move in whichever way they choose is a heady feeling. Suddenly everything becomes possible.

Hassina, a Bangladeshi woman who had been abandoned by her husband, transformed overnight when she discovered the power she could wield as a participatory video producer. Despite openly hostile criticism and taunts from the men in her village as she made her video, Hassina persevered and completed her story. When she realized that taping women's testimonies would give them a voice in the community and serve to prevent or mitigate violence and abandonment, she sought out these women's stories in all the neighboring communities. For the first time, Hassina saw herself as an active part of a solution to violence against women.

Building Self-confidence

Participation in this process brings a new perspective to one's life and situation. While this can be a fearful exercise at first, participation almost always gives the doer a sense of pride and ownership in the process and the outcome. With this, comes confidence. As a person's self-assuredness increases, he or she starts to explore further, outside the initial confines of their context.

The education program at Tostan, a Senegalese NGO, is based around the philosophy that literacy skills are not sufficient to prepare learners for active participation in the social, political, economic, and cultural decisions related to developing their communities and country. Members of the program illustrated the importance of active participation in focusing power. When these women got together, they were able to reflect on issues and practices that they had previously accepted. When as a group they began to question these cultural practices, one woman explains, "The Tostan program gave us a certain amount of confidence that we never had before, confidence that we could change things if we wanted to."[6]

In the participatory video process, the subject and producer share similar experiences and serve as equals in documenting the stories. In Egypt, one participatory video group was afraid to be seen carrying the camera and recording a program outside. They started recording programs inside and gradually moved outdoors into the community as they became more confident and competent. As Neama Mohamed said, "The video project increased our self-confidence. We couldn't be shy when we had to address the whole community."[7]

Once recorded, the videotape becomes a tool to bring these experiences to others and to invite reflection so that the viewers can seek to experience their own reality in ways that they, too, had never imagined. These audience members will internalize the viewing experience uniquely and will consider, perhaps for the first time, their ability to influence their own lives and the role of their community. In this manner, the viewing experience empowers people's lives and enables them to think for themselves about their situation and how to take control of their lives and make changes where possible.

The viewers can identify strongly with stories and issues that are central to their lives, which can open their minds to thinking in new ways. As a visual medium, video is particularly powerful. A video program produced by SEWA in India sought to teach people, women in particular, about the importance of being counted in the census. Traditionally home-based work was not considered "work" and thus an entire economic sector was undercounted. The video, which was broadcast on local television and shown in many communities, reached out to women and their families and encouraged them to take political action—to make their voices heard in the greater community. In addition, the video and the association with SEWA validated their work and gave them the confidence and collective strength to negotiate for better working conditions.

Exercising One's Voice

Language is a key element in expressing one's identity. How you speak, where you come from, and how you tell a story all define who you are and what your reality is. Oral tradition posits that people who tell the stories have the power,[8] and that oral tradition changes over time in response to changes in society and culture. Getting one's voice heard is an incredible challenge for those who are traditionally marginalized from the formal systems of power, indeed, those who have been socially or culturally silenced.[9]

Important topics affecting the well-being of the community cannot be limited to the classroom and need to be presented by the participants themselves for public debate and deliberation. But participants need skills for discussing important issues. Personal testimonies are powerful ways to open the door on an issue—suddenly more and more stories come out. The presence of outsiders often hinders the openness of discussions.

Another Tostan participant remarked that: "The education sessions woke us up. We received information that we never had before and the new knowledge has given us a voice in our community. For the first time when we speak, everyone listens because what we say is based on objective facts."[10] These subtle but critical shifts in society pave the way for sustained changes at all levels—from family to politics. Indeed, as civil society advocates point out, societal changes at the macro (national) level will not happen until and unless these shifts have occurred within the family.

Participatory video focuses on who is communicating—people from inside the community—not outsiders who insert their own values and cultural constructs into the communication. Participatory video producers are not communication experts, journalists, broadcasters, or academics knowledgeable in communication theory, but rather community participants who know and understand their situation, tell their own stories, and share them within their own context in an attempt to create positive change. Often this is the first time these storytellers exercise their own voice as often have often been disenfranchised, economically, politically, culturally or socially before.

In Nigeria, young people at Action Health Incorporated (an NGO) have been using participatory video to highlight their own reproductive health issues—to share information with their peers, to educate parents about the need to communicate better with their children, and to convince stakeholders that the adolescent community has a voice that needs to be heard and issues that need to be addressed. Participatory video has given young people this opportunity to express themselves genuinely; they write the scripts, handle production, and edit tapes with minimal supervision from adults. The adolescent teams play back the tapes within and outside their community to raise consciousness about young people's perspective and view of reality.

In Bangladesh, Shameema, a village video producer and member of the organization, Proshika MUK, wanted to make a tape about a neighboring village that made bamboo handicrafts. When questioned as to why she wanted to make this tape, she said, "In this village women weave the bamboo, not men. I want to show my sisters in other villages that they can do this kind of work too." Thus, from the outset, this tape was designed to empower viewers to expand their horizons and to "think out of the box." Using the Proshika video equipment in her village, Shameema and the video team made a tape about these women.

Central to this medium is the development of dialog. Indeed, in the postviewing discussions of Shameema's tape, women gathered around the producers leading the discussion asking questions about how they could start a bamboo business, until they realized that they had the capacity to start any kind of business. This excited and energized them and they began exploring all sorts of possibilities to become involved in areas that were traditionally male dominated. Just watching this tape and talking among themselves afterward was enough to unleash the power and confidence that often lingers just below the surface. But, continued dialog is necessary to keep the dreams alive—to motivate the members of the community to act on these dreams.

Effecting Change

Sometimes what is missing is not the voice, but the public space that accepts and values these voices.[11] *Once things are documented—written down in words or pictures—they become static and can be interpreted, rather than created anew. The power of participatory communication is its two-way nature. "The beauty of participatory communication is that it can adopt different forms according to need and that no blueprint model can impose itself over the richness of views and cultural interactions.... It is kaleidoscopic because it changes its color and shape at the will of the hands in which it is held."*[12]

There was a time when video technology was bulky, complex, and expensive. However, over the past 20 years, as technology has miniaturized and become easier to operate, opportunities have grown for non-experts to use technological tools in new ways to advance their own agendas. Typically, participatory video producers use handheld video equipment and often edit their programs in the camera so external editing equipment and additional training is not necessary.

The end product, however, is not the objective; generally, the finished tape marks the midway point in the process. An essential part of the participatory video process is showing the tape within the community and using it as a starting point to advocate change. This instant playback characteristic of video is one of its most empowering qualities because those who are the subject and those who operate the technology collaborate as equals.[13] As Nils Bohr said, "We are both spectators and actors."[14] Take the case of Shameema: she identified an issue (nontraditional work) that she wanted to highlight in order to empower others. Viewers not only watched the program, but they also interacted with the producers who were their neighbors. These interactions highlighted the possibility that people just like them were also engaged in nontraditional work.

Participatory video many times requires the whole community to participate in the process. This involvement creates an ownership and pride within the community. Video can be used in iterative cycles of shooting and screening to tell stories and create dialog that unfold over time in response to the changes that occur. This process enables those telling the stories to communicate them in the way they think is most appropriate.

Participatory video documents ideas that people have adopted and then blends the freshness of oral tradition to elicit new thoughts from the viewers through playback discussions. In this participatory video context, both the producer and audience are powerful actors since the producer gains the power to tell a story and the viewers internalize the stories during playback sessions and gain the power to take control over and change their lives and the structures of the society in which they live.

Maneno Mengi, a community development organization in Tanzania, uses video as a tool to "strengthen local organizations and to give a loud voice to previously unheard people."[15] During a 1997 cholera outbreak, communities used video to conduct a situational analysis and to engage in participatory planning that resulted in communities developing their own action plans to prevent cholera. Similarly, villagers in Mali produced a tape on hygiene and water sanitation practices and shared it with several neighboring communities. One year later when a serious cholera epidemic swept through the country, the villages that had screened the tape credited the few cases of cholera to the video program because the villagers had changed their behavior after watching the tape and discussing the implications.

Video in Bangladesh has been used successfully as a deterrent to expose wrongdoing in certain communities in an effort to change the behavior of community members involved. In communities where men have abused or abandoned their wives, Banchte Shekha producers have videotaped testimonies of these women. The men, faced with exposure on video often return to their wives and stop the abuse rather than suffer the shame of "starring" on the video-tape. In the meantime, recording their testimony helps the women realize that they have and can exercise their fundamental rights. Thus this process serves to empower another section of society. Finally these testimonials, used as evidence in village courts, help ensure that the community acts as a fair mediator.

In Tellal Zenhom, Egypt, participatory video producers have gained new visibility in their communities as spokespeople and leaders. They have engaged their community in participatory video and as a result, community members, the local council and officials are raising issues that participatory video could address. The team's video programs are being used to "spark discussion and promote the search for local solutions."[16]

In Senegal, a women's literacy project became a vehicle for national policy change. Women studied human rights and learned that each woman has the freedom to decide for herself what she does with her body—a revelation because it contradicted the cultural tradition of circumcising female children. But as one woman explained, the village's decision to stop the practice of female circumcision, "brought us other advantages too. We became aware that we could make a difference in the world ... and we go from neighborhood to neighborhood to facilitate discussions with the other members of our community: men, women and young people."[17] As these women began to think critically for themselves, they also learned the power of open dialog in bringing about political change.

Influencing the World

Who decides what voices are heard, and what stories get told, is critical. Too often stories are not told because those controlling access to media channels do not understand or give credence to local stories. In West Africa, for example, many "beat" journalists have been trained to improve their health reporting. Despite the training their stories rarely appeared in the media because the editors, who held the power, did not think health was an important issue. However, when these gatekeepers—the editors—learned how to communicate with and involve health workers in developing stories using evidence-based data that were critically important to the community, they started changing their perspective and practices. One empowered editor in Mauritania risked his job to publish an extensive story on adolescent sexuality and reproductive health in this heavily Muslim country because he wanted to start a debate on the subject within the community. This risk paid off: since then this editor has covered every seminars on women's issues, written extensively on HIV/AIDS and produced a special series on the education of girls.

As the above example shows, advocates are made, not born. Participatory video producers learn to be, and to find, leaders who can act and nurture change. They are using media to spread their message and they have learned to build constituencies and networks of concerned people. The transformation from speaking out to building external support for sustainable changes is a critical element in the participatory video process. Neama Mohamed became an outspoken advocate for educating girls and eliminating the harmful practice of femal circumcision after becoming a participatory video producer. She has been a successful advocate for not circumcising daughters, including her own, and is working to change the practice in her community.

As the Proshika producers in Bangladesh became more adept at participatory video, they began to explore new ways to influence the local political scene. "We could record candidates' campaign speeches so that when they are elected we can hold them to their promises," said one producer. Though these techniques may not change the actions of elected political leaders, the producers were empowered to think that they might, and that with such visual advocacy tools, the politicians might indeed be held accountable by the electorate.

In India, some video producers used their skills to create a program about vegetable vendors who were banned from selling on the street where they had sold for generations. When the producers showed the tape to the commissioner in private, he was able to see for himself the results of his action and reversed his decision. The collective voice of the vendors captured on videotape was a strong message—delivered in a nonconfrontational way—that enabled the commissioner to hear and take action. Such events send strong messages to the producers and the community about their own power.

The Association for Rural Education and Development Services, an NGO working in South India introduced participatory video to extension workers and village facilitators there. They produced a series of video dramas that focused on issues of literacy, landlessness, nonformal education, collective action, and political participation. These dramas depicted the collective struggles of people's experiences in the community, yet highlighted the need for continued action and change.[18]

The Kayapo, an indigenous population of the Amazon, learned to use video as a tool to preserve their culture from the ever-encroaching outside world. As a community, they wanted to record their rituals for their children, to document cultural memory. Yet, as they mastered the medium, the Kayapo understood that visual representations of their culture could be used politically, to achieve recognition and to protect their rights to resources, land, and dignity.[19]

Participatory communication sparks an internal dialog that ultimately challenges the traditional specters of power. Active storytelling through video helps the producer and the viewer to look within themselves, sometimes for the first time. This definition of the self is powerful and sets the stage for seeing the self in relation to others, which sparks an examination of the power concepts that exist. The accompanying self-confidence leads participatory video actors to question these traditional power relationships and provides new avenues to redefine the power structures. Ultimately, participatory communication becomes the force that people use to influence the external world to bring about change to the broader social and political contexts.

Transformation

*Never doubt that a small group of thoughtful, committed citizens
can change the world. Indeed, it is the only thing that ever has.*

Margaret Mead

Advocacy is a deliberate process which brings about change, and
one in which change takes place incrementally. Thus, individual
empowerment is perhaps the first step to political transformation
through collective advocacy that signifies the empowerment of
whole communities. Advocacy requires a conscious effort by those
involved to research an issue and its context, identify a strategy to
bring about change, and finally take direct action. Success in advocacy usually involves various factions uniting to exercise power
and influence where necessary. Lasting success however is only
gained through raising consciousness about the larger fabric of
society and culture. Empowerment must occur at the individual
level before it can sustainably affect society. If a woman doesn't
have a voice in her family, she cannot exercise it effectively in the
community or the larger political context.

The use of video is generally just one piece in the advocacy strategy,
but visual images can convey powerful messages. The participatory
element ensures that these messages come from the individual and
community and are not an outside force imposing its ideas and
conventions onto the issue. Moreover, inserting participatory video
into the advocacy process empowers the community and its producers to take charge, to seek alternatives and to take responsibility for improving their lives, and for creating new expectations
within the larger social and cultural context—in effect creating a
new paradigm for those in the future.

Once the local community members learn the skills necessary to
communicate using video and the knowledge of their own power
as agents of change, they can become advocates—seeking stories
to tell as well as serving as magnets for others in the community, to
raise issues that can be developed effectively as visual stories. As
these examples illustrate, video can mobilize and empower a large
group of people—such as being counted in the census, or advocate
to an audience of one—such as the commissioner who regulates
vending licenses.

Visual Literacy

As globalization marches onward, the world keeps shrinking. Mass media has penetrated even the most remote villages throughout the world and visual images tell a story even when the spoken dialog doesn't translate. Viewers who live in a media-saturated world expect fast-paced images to grab their attention and draw them inside quickly. If the images do not resonate immediately, the viewers tune out and walk away. Moreover, the rise of the information superhighway makes access to voice, text, and images quicker than ever before.

But seeing is not always believing. Visual literacy comes with critical viewing skills. Essential to understanding the visual medium itself is the need to recognize what is behind the information and the pictures—who is in control, who is communicating, and why. With mass media, the storytellers are often hidden as are their motives. As storytellers, they are not linked to the community. So whose story is being told? The reporter's or the community's? Viewers have a responsibility to ask these critical questions rather than sit passively and accept the information they see as truth.

Despite the fact that the mass media has shaped people's taste for information, particularly visual information, small media continues to flourish because it shows a social reality that television cannot. In participatory communication the community is involved in the process—both as producers and as viewers. In participatory video, language is both oral and visual and the story serves as a takeoff point for inspiring change. When villagers hear and see people who sound and look just like them on video, they can relate to the program and the issues raised. After all, the people they see on screen seem to be exactly the same. As two adolescent video producers in Nigeria note, "The participatory communication strategy is a good mirror of society. It uses 'real' people with whom the audience can relate their experience, thereby making the video more believable and effective for attitude change."[20]

Conversely, while watching a tape about a foreign community may inspire envy or emulation, the story will not resonate so strongly or trigger such a powerful response so as to spur action and change. Participatory video evolves slowly, relying on the power of the story and the strength of the storyteller to inspire a new paradigm that motivates the viewer to act on the new ideas presented through this medium.

Acceptance of a New Paradigm

I had always thought that we used language to describe the world—now I was seeing that this is not the case. To the contrary, it is through language that we create the world, because it's nothing until we describe it. And when we describe it, we create distinctions that govern our actions. To put it another way, we do not describe the world we see, but we see the world we describe.

Joseph Jaworski

Participatory video producers can adapt the medium to meet their needs, whether it is used to expose current reality or to weave a narrative that brings the changing world closer to the viewers. Different styles of participatory video have emerged around the world that address the specific context and needs of the communities it serves. In Nigeria, adolescents have used drama to convey powerful changing realities. In Bangladesh, village women have used video testimonials to unite women in the fight against violence. In Brazil, the Kayapo people have used video to reaffirm their cultural values and to represent themselves to the outside world on their own terms.

As we have seen, participatory video is truly empowering. It opens up new avenues for telling stories in ways that will build strong individuals and communities. These stories are strong enough to identify problems and to make necessary changes in order to improve lives and to transform societies in ways that value the individual and recognize the unique contribution and dynamic of every interaction.

Notes

1. Willard, 2001, p. 9
2. Miller, p. 5

3. Adapted from Stromquist as cited by Scherl, 1996.
4. Gumucio–Dagron, 2001, p. 20
5. Stuart and Bery, 1996, p. 305
6. Tostan, 1996, p. 46.
7. Gumucio–Dagron, 2001, p. 316.
8. Riano, 1994, p. 48.
9. Hochheimer, 1999, p. 246.
10. Tostan, 1996, p. 46.
11. Riano, 1994, p. 124.
12. Gumucio–Dagron, 2001, p. 8.
13. Stuart and Bery, 1994, p. 3
14. Winifred Moore, 1961 p. 30.
15. Gumucio–Dagron, 2001, p. 285.
16. Gumucio–Dagron, 2001 p. 314.
17. Tostan, 1996, p. 48.
18. Fabel, 1995, p. 212.
19. Gumucio–Dagron, 2001, p. 91–96.
20. Gumucio–Dagron, 2001, p. 184.

References and Select Bibliography

Allen, D., R. Rush, and S.J. Kaufman (eds.) (1996). *Women Transforming Communications*. Thousand Oaks: Sage Publications.

Bery, R. (1995). 'Media Ethics: No Magic Solutions,' in *Power, Process and Participation—Tools for Change*. London: Intermediate Technology Publications.

———— (1999). 'The Discovery Principle: A Participatory Approach to Training,' in *The Art of Facilitating Participation*. New Delhi: Sage Publications.

CEDPA. (1994). *After Cairo: A Handbook on Advocacy for Women Leaders*. Washington, D.C.: The Centre for Development and Population Activities.

De Negri, B., E. Thomas, A. Ilinigumugabo, I. Muvandi and G. Lewis (1999). *Empowering Communities*. Washington, D.C.: The Academy for Educational Development.

Fabel, E. (1995). 'Video II: Demystifying the Technology,' in *Power, Process and Participation—Tools for Change*. London: Intermediate Technology Publications.

Fugelsang, A. (1982). *About Understanding: Ideas and Observations on Cross-Cultural Communication*. Uppsala: Dag Hammarskjold Foundation.

Gumucio–Dagron, A. (2001). *Making Waves*. New York: The Rockefeller Foundation.

Hochheimer, J.L. (1999). 'Planning Community Radio as Participatory Development,' in S.A. White (ed.) *The Art of Facilitating Participation*. New Delhi: Sage Publications.

Miller, V. (2001). *Politics, Power and People: Lessons from Gender Action and Analysis*. Boston: Just Associates.

Moore, W. (1961). *The Roots of Excellence*. Burlington: The Lane Press.

Riano, P. (ed.) (1994). *Women in Grassroots Communication*. Thousand Oaks: Sage Publications.

Scherl, I. (1996). *Participation and Empowerment*. Unpublished manuscript. Ithaca: Cornell University Department of Communication.

Servaes, J., T. Jacobson and S.A. White (eds.) (1996). *Participatory Communication for Social Change*. New Delhi: Sage Publications.

Stuart, S. and R. Bery (1994). *The Power of Video in the Hands of Grassroots Women: Video SEWA—A Case Study*. Unpublished manuscript.

——— (1996). 'Powerful Grassroots Women Communicators: Participatory Video in Bangladesh,' in *Women Transforming Communications*. Thousand Oaks: Sage Publications.

Tostan, (1996). *Breakthrough in Senegal: Ending Female Genital Cutting*. Dakar, Senegal.

White, S.A. (ed.) (1999). *The Art of Facilitating Participation*. New Delhi: Sage Publications.

Willard, N. (2001). *The New York Times Book Review*, (February 18, 2001). New York: The New York Times.

5

The *Fogo Process*: Participatory Communication in a Globalizing World

———— ✳ ————

Stephen Crocker

In this chapter Stephen provides an overview of the genesis of the Fogo Process in Newfoundland and its export to other places in the world. He also comments on its sociological significance for thinking about the status of community in a globalizing world. He situates the Fogo Process within the history of endeavors to use film/video media to promote social change.[1]

The National Film Board of Canada's (NFB) *Challenge for Change* program in the late 1960s pioneered the use of interactive film and video as a tool for social change and empowerment in remote, underdeveloped locations. The promoters of this project at the NFB and Memorial University of Newfoundland (MUN) gave film and video equipment to isolated communities so they could create a collective image of themselves and their social problems. This locally produced televisual image would then become a medium for communication with distant decision-makers, such as governments and financial institutions. The *Fogo Process* (so-named because it was first developed on Fogo Island, Newfoundland) created a very effective televisual public space for addressing social and political concerns. The process was embraced by development agencies around the world and is now widely regarded as the forerunner of many more recent developments in participatory communication and subject generated film and video.

The early media experiments in Newfoundland, which were later carried on in the United States, Africa and Asia, offer a unique opportunity to understand how notions of location, community and public space change in the current globalizing world. Today there is a popular belief that real-time technologies such as video and digital media destroy our sense of place, because they give rise to a world of instantaneous communication where distances between places cease to matter. It often seems that the whole world resembles a single monoculture of capitalism, mass society and consumer culture. The *Fogo Process*, on the other hand, provides real evidence of how people who have been marginalized by the economic and political structure of the world system can renew and empower their local communities and transform conditions of uneven development.

The Documentary Tradition and the Problem of Globalization

Developments in participatory media such as the *Fogo Process* should be understood in light of the social and cultural problems created by the globalization of economic and social life. Globalization separates political and economic forces from the life-worlds they regulate. This often makes it difficult for communities to represent, through examples of local experience, the abstract global social processes that effect everyday life. From its very beginning, film has been used as a device for addressing this problem, rendering intelligible the dizzying complexity of modern social experience. In its simplest form, it has served to present information about distant places to help define and contextualize local experience.

The Lumerire brothers, the inventors of movies, popularized their cinematograph in the 1890s by traveling around the world's major cities and displaying "actualities" which presented visual evidence of everyday life in other parts of the world. The Russian filmmaker Dziga Vertov thought it would be possible to develop a universal film language (kino–Pravda) that, unlike print-based media, would not be bound to particular languages or communities, but would speak a universal film language intelligible to any viewer anywhere. Vertov's *Man with a Movie Camera*, which documented life in Russia was made with real people on the street. Later, Italian "neo-realist" filmmakers like Roberto Rossellini and Vittorio de Sica began to film live action in the streets based on scripts that addressed real social and economic problems.

During the period of colonialism and empires, the European nations used film both to provide information about the native populations they controlled, and to present information about the British in the colonial world. *Mr. English at Home*, for instance, is a wordless film made by the British Colonial Film Unit in 1940 to show the Africans what a typical day in the working life of an English family[2] was. *Southern Rhodesia: Is This your Country*, on the other hand, was designed to attract European colonists to Africa by showing them the resources and lifestyle available to them in Africa.[3] These are all instances of the attempt to use film for sociological purposes, by providing information about distant social and political forces that affect local social experience.

Canada's documentary tradition from which the *Fogo Process* was derived is an important milestone in this development. For John Greirson, who coined the term documentary and also started the NFB, the documentary's function is more sociological than aesthetic. Greirson saw the documentary as a tool for creating a more democratic world. Under the influence of the American sociologist Walter Lippman, Greirson believed that "because the citizen, under modern conditions, could not know everything abut everything all the time, democratic citizenship was therefore impossible."[4] This problem only becomes more pronounced through the century. As the social and political centers of power become more distinct from the places they control, it is difficult for anybody to acquire the information necessary to make informed decisions. Film, with its powerful ability to present aggregated details in a way far more immediate than print and other media, presented itself as a means of producing better informed citizens.

Film Activities among the Poor: The Genesis of the *Fogo Process*

The *Fogo Process*, which is the focus of this discussion, is a more complex phenomenon than any of the documentary traditions that preceded it. Not only was the finished product important, but the process of filmmaking itself was employed as a powerful tool of social change. The development of the Fogo project represented a significant change in direction for the NFB. The initial purpose of the NFB was to make films about social problems that would make Canada better known to Canadians. In the 1960s there was an increasing feeling that films should not only document social issues, but also be involved in them.[5] Instead of an outside film industry making top-down films *about* people, films might be made *by* the people about their own social problems. The *Challenge for Change* program at the NFB grew from this movement and represented the emergence of a new kind of socially engaged film. More specifically, the *Challenge for Change* program proposed three new kinds of films: films for the departments and the general public explaining a problem, films for social workers and change-agents, and films planned and produced by the poor themselves.[6]

The 1966 NFB film, *The Things I Cannot Change,* was one of the first films made in this new program and is often thought as a fore-runner to the films created on Fogo. It was a film meant to explain the social problem of poverty to a wide Canadian audience and documented the trials and tribulations of a family in Montreal, caught in a cycle of poverty. When it appeared, it caused the family great embarrassment and they became the subject of ridicule in their own neighborhood. *The Things I Cannot Change* did not achieve its goals but it provided a valuable lesson for all future film activities among the poor: if film were to enable a source of empowerment it would not only have to be *about* the poor but *by* them as well.

Producer and director Colin Low who headed the Fogo team wanted to give the people of Fogo Island the opportunity to define and represent their social problems. Instead of simply using the community as material for a film, Low wished to place the tools of *filmmaking* in the service of the collective expression of the community.

In Newfoundland, Low worked with Donald Snowden, a community development worker who directed the Extension Service of Memorial University of Newfoundland. This was an outreach branch of the university that helped to promote social and economic change in rural Newfoundland. Both Low and Snowden cite the appearance of the 1965 Economic Council of Canada's *Report on Poverty in Canada* as a direct catalyst of their work on Fogo. The Council's report was essentially a document on urban poverty in central Canada that simply projected its findings onto rural Canada. It defined poverty as a net income of less than $4000. Snowden said that it displayed the distance of the central bureaucrats from problems of rural Canada. In rural Newfoundland, Snowden recognized many other dimensions of poverty not mentioned in the report. These included what he called "poverty of information and organization." Snowden suggested to Bob Phillips, head of the Privy Council of Canada and the Trudeau era War on Canadian Poverty Program, that they sponsor a series of films that would explore the reality of poverty in rural Newfoundland. A year later, the NFB decided to begin its proposed film activities among the poor in rural Newfoundland.[7]

Colin Low, who was chosen for the project, was widely regarded as one of the most talented young filmmakers at the NFB. Low toured Newfoundland with Snowden and together they eventually chose Fogo Island as the site of their initial experiments. Fogo was chosen for a number of reasons. It was an island composed of several small fishing communities, which were slated for resettlement to a centralized mainland community. Here, fishery was in a state of decline and the inshore technologies with which the fishermen plied their trade were becoming obsolete. More than 60 percent of the population depended on welfare. Apart from material poverty, Fogo, like many other Newfoundland communities, suffered from what Snowden had termed the poverty of information and organization, 5000 people lived in 10 communities in relative isolation from each other, further divided by religious denomination. These communities had neither a common voice amongst themselves, nor an effective channel of communication with the government.

Colin Low initially intended to make a documentary on poverty, and in the process teach young Newfoundlanders the art of filmmaking so that they could then make films themselves. He, until then had not yet envisioned any of the feedback techniques of participatory communication for which the *Fogo Process* would become famous. On Fogo, Low and Snowden worked with a community development officer or "social animator" Fred Earle who had been working in the island for Memorial University for over a year, well before there had been any talk of a film project. His job was to help the community identify and define social problems about which they needed to communicate with each other, and with the government in St. John's. The field-worker spent time in the community getting to know the people and their problems. He sought to determine the kinds of information or resources the people required, and a good spokesperson for a given community.

When the NFB arrived on Fogo, it was Fred Earle who helped introduce them to the community and helped the community decide what social problems would be the subject of their films. The field-worker was thus a mediating link between the filmmakers and the community. This role was quickly recognized as a central, defining element of what became known as the *Fogo Process*. For example, when films were screened in communities it was the field-worker who helped lead discussion. In fact, in subsequent "Fogo" style projects it was not the filmmaker but the field-worker/ social animator who assumed the role traditionally assigned to the director of documentary films. It was the field-worker who helped focus and guide communication on the part of the community, and it was hoped that field-workers might in turn bring films (and later videotapes) to other isolated communities so that people could recognize and reflect on common problems.

Colin Low produced more than 25 short films on Fogo. The titles give a sense of the kinds of material they covered. These included: *The McGraths at Home and Fishing, The Founding of the Cooperative, Citizens Discussions, Tom Best on Cooperatives, and Discussion of Welfare*. In addition to films that dealt with difficult social problems, there were also more lyrical films such as: *The Songs of Chris Cobb, Jim Decker's Party and The Children of Fogo*.

Low and Snowden learned to intersperse screenings of uplifting, affirmative films such as *Children of Fogo* with the more somber and difficult topics of cooperative, or fishermen-welfare relations. This, it was thought, would help initiate community discussion and dialog after the films were shown. Above all, they wanted to avoid bombarding people with too much serious material that might deaden the atmosphere.

Community input into the editing of material and feedback between the community and decision makers are now recognized as key ingredients of the *Fogo Process*. However, neither of these was originally intended when the NFB arrived in Fogo. After several months of shooting, Low decided that it would be nice if people could see some of the material produced. He screened it for the communities and received feedback. Only one short film on education in Fogo was cut because people objected to the tone of the interview. Nevertheless, the precedent of community feedback and control of the image that became a hallmark of participatory film and video was born.

The development of a "feedback loop" between the communities and government was also fortuitous. Originally, the film project was co-sponsored by the NFB and Memorial University. When the material was first screened for Lord Taylor, the university president, and the board of the NFB, Taylor expressed some concern that it would not be well received by the government and might cause problems for the university. A screening was eventually arranged for government officials and university academics. The material *was* well received. A film was made of the fisheries minister's response to the films and when this was shown on the island, the feedback that would become hallmark of the *Fogo Process* was in place.

The people of Fogo eventually resisted the government attempt to resettle them and formed their own successful fishing cooperative. To what extent this can be directly attributed to the *Fogo Process* is questionable. However, it cannot be denied that the filming process played a large role in opening channels of communication both among island communities, and between the island and the government.

Film as Process and Product

In many ways the uniqueness of the events that transpired on Fogo was that the process of filmmaking became more important than the actual films produced. What was empowering or emancipating was the sense of community and cooperation necessary to make the films. In fact, it is clear that the importance of the process of community involvement and empowerment had a direct effect on the kinds of films that were produced. Low maintained that the Fogo films were structurally different from most documentary images. He claimed he made "vertical" films. He noted that most documentary film had a "horizontal" structure that consisted of a montage of scenes from different situations crosscut together to give an overall effect. They were based around an "issue" for which they collected evidence from several sources. Low thought that the horizontal structure was less effective for the kind of socially engaged process that they hoped to promote on Fogo. In the traditional "horizontal" structure an individual's story tended to get swallowed up by the larger story, which might not be what the interviewee intended at all. Low's "vertical" film avoided techniques of crosscutting and montage, and consisted of a single film based on a single interview, an adaptation of the mise–en–scène technique. Instead of making one or two regular length documentaries that cut back and forth between various settings and speakers, Low made separate films about individuals whose opinions were representative of more widely shared positions in the community.

In all he made 28 short "vertical" films, each about 10 minutes long. He explains:

> When I went to Fogo I thought that I would make one, or perhaps two or more films. But as the project developed, I found that people were much freer when I made short vertical films: each one the record of a single interview, or a single occasion. In the end I did not do any intercutting at all, because if you intercut people on the basis of issues, what usually happens is that you get one person who is all wrong, one person who is partly right, and a third person who is right. He becomes the smart guy, who puts the others down. This putting down can harm people within a community.[8]

It is clear that the process was driving the "product" or outcome on Fogo island, but it is not always clear exactly what that process was all about. Each context was unique and each individual was important, thus giving each process its own character.

Self-reflection and Empowerment in the *Fogo Process*

There are two different elements that we should distinguish in the *Fogo Process*. The first of these is relatively straightforward and concerns the establishment of channels of communication among isolated communities, and between these communities and distant decision makers. The creation of these networks of communication proved immediately effective in Fogo, throughout Newfoundland, and around the world in places where print and other media were relatively absent. Having effective communication links with governments and financial institutions is crucial as sources of power and capital become globalized, or simply more distant from the places they effect. Film is especially important in this respect in communities where the written word does not have the same currency it does in urban areas.

There is another element of the *Fogo Process* that is more complex, and that is often thought to be the more empowering element of the process. It seems that everyone who reflects on the *Fogo Process* has identified the empowering effects of seeing ones "life" on film, or to be more precise, on screen. The effect is said to promote feelings of confidence, self-worth, better self-image, all as a result of seeing yourself as others see you. This self-reflexivity, which may be the core of the *Fogo Process*, remains undertheorized and not clearly understood. Anthony Marcus, a psychologist who used the *Fogo Process* of video feedback as a therapeutic treatment of dangerous sexual offenders, explained the power of self-reflection by saying:

Confronting himself on camera gradually helps a person develop an internal image of himself.... Most individuals have difficulty communicating their emotional 'hang-ups' but video taping and the playback evoke a response on the emotional level. The simple device of reflecting an image magnifies the individual's self image. The emotional dilemma induced by the gap between the image on screen and the subjective feeling of the viewers, produces a crisis in which the person attempts to bring the two aspects into harmony, thus increasing his self-knowledge. He cannot remain aloof to himself and he is caught in the conflict between actual conduct and inner fear-fulness.... He confronts himself remaining at the same time less defensive than when someone else confronts him.[9]

In other words, viewing one's own image produces a division between what George Herbert Mead called the *I* and the *me*, i.e., effectively my own understanding of myself and my motives, and other people's image of who and what I am. It is necessary to recognize a distance between these two parts of the self. In the account Marcus gives, what is valued is a greater harmony of the two. But we could equally argue, as contemporary psycho-social theory does, that it is important that we be able to recognize a difference between these two elements of the self so as not to be swallowed up in the socially created images that others have of us.

At any rate, the psychological or even psycho-social explanation is compelling but it does not explain why the process seems to work better in rural places where there is little history of exposure to mass media. As a sociologist, what seems decisive to me is that individuals are able to overcome their isolation from one another and see a collective representation of their community. The creation of a sense of community depends upon the ability to project a collective image where none previously existed. I would suggest that the process of seeing oneself on film is empowering because it creates what Benedict Anderson called an "imagined community," which he claims is necessary for the formation of a sense of community that exceeds one's immediate geographical location.[10] Anderson traces modern nationalism to the emergence of 18th and 19th century European-American newspapers and novels that present information from distant places, all thought to be part of a common national experience. In reading the newspaper, for example, people in one geographical place feel the presence of others and feel that together they constitute a community—an imagined community. The effect is quite powerful. The nation is an imagined entity but one that is quite real, one of the few things, in fact, that people are willing to die for.

In Fogo and rural Newfoundland, film and video had played an analogous role. The social and political organization of rural Newfoundland mitigated against a strong sense of collectivity. People were geographically isolated and the "truck merchant credit systems" pitted community against community, and even family against family.[11] When communities needed to react against centralizing forces that treated a region or community en masse, as happened at Fogo, people had no collective sense of themselves to draw upon. The Fogo films were unifying both at the level of process, in bringing the communities together through the auspices of the extension/community worker, and by providing a collective representation of the community. Through film, isolated communities could imagine themselves as a part of a single common community. Thus, the films created an external "virtual community" that could act a reference point for people to given them an image of themselves. This not only aided in the development of long-term community strategies, but also in smaller and important matters of community organization. For example, in Lord's Cove on the Burin Peninsula the process of self-reflection had dramatic results:

> Its instant impact was particularly evident at a community Council meeting in Lords' Cove on the southern tip of Newfoundland where playback of the meeting provided those present an opportunity to view the appalling lack of participation and to look at their own apathy. As a result of this realization the meeting was rescheduled, received greater participation and resulted in a new election of officers.[12]

In Deep Bay, Fogo extension worker Stan Kinden found something similar:

> The people in Deep Bay wanted to organize an improvement committee meeting but they couldn't get anyone to stand up and speak. So they asked me to organize a five-night workshop on public speaking, and I brought along VTR. The first night only five people would stand up and say as much as "I'm John Jones from Deep Bay." I played the tape back and I think a lot of people were ashamed to see themselves sitting there not saying anything; the reaction was, "if he can do it, I can." At the end of the third night, the last people got up and said their names. On the fifth night, we organized a mock meeting. The person who had taken three nights to say his name was the one who offered to be chairman.[13]

In sum, the *Fogo Process* allowed people to form an ideal common image of themselves as a collectivity, something that their material conditions of life had made difficult to achieve.

The *Fogo Process* after Fogo

The NFB continued their *Challenge for Change* work in Fogo for a year and a half, after which they moved to other projects in Canada and abroad. In all, the *Challenge for Change* program lasted for about a decade. Indians rights and culture became a central focus. *You are on Indian Land* (1969) was produced by an all Native American crew and dealt with treaty rights on the US-Canadian border. There was also *Hunter of the Mistassini* (1974), *Our Land is our Life* (1974), and *Amisk* (1977). Later projects involved urban problems, prison groups and even, as mentioned earlier, group therapy with dangerous sexual offenders. In addition to the playback of videotape in small settings there were attempts to develop local cable community broadcasting services. These however were very different from the initial Fogo experiments since they involved broadcast to a wide anonymous audience, instead of the face-to-face discussion which characterized the original experiments in Newfoundland.[14]

Colin Low and Don Snowden also collaborated on several projects in the United States. They were asked by the U.S. Office of Economic Opportunity to carry out projects in Farmersville, California, Hartford, Connecticut and Skyriver, Alaska. These projects did not receive the same kind of enthusiastic response. Snowden believed that this was because these places had already been bombarded by images and sounds through television and film. This suggests, as Snowden often pointed out, that the *Fogo Process* works best in communities that do not have access to mass media and have only restricted access to important external information.

Meanwhile, the Memorial University of Newfoundland created its own film unit and continued the work begun on Fogo. Snowden remained director of the Extension Service that now devoted a great deal of its efforts to film and video work. Harvey Best headed the film unit of the Extension Service. Tony Williamson was head of the Community Development branch of the Extension Service. Paul

McLeod began to work with the group in various projects and later on many international projects. It was the Memorial crew who exported the process to African and Asia. In fact, while it was as a MUN/NFB collaboration that the whole project began on Fogo, it was the Memorial team who perfected the *Fogo Process* and eventually exported it around the world. Many of the techniques that had emerged by accident or good fortune on Fogo were now formalized by the Memorial unit as elements of an empowering use of media in social change.

The first post-Fogo project which set out to put the theory of the *Fogo Process* to work in new settings was on Port aux Choix on the Northern Peninsula of Newfoundland. It was now decided beforehand, for example, that everyone who appeared in the film would have editing rights before the material was screened outside the community. Snowden has described these projects as more "information oriented" than the Fogo films which he characterized as "impressionistic" and aesthetic in orientation, probably as a result of Colin Low's professional filmic influence. The Extension Service specifically downplayed the aesthetic or creative treatment of life and did not place any special emphasis on higher production values such as better cameras, editing and sound. It was believed that higher production values could take away from the informational character of the films and so, in order to elevate the hard information content of the films, it was best to downplay the aesthetic element. Indeed, the task now was not so much to "make films," as they had originally intended to do on Fogo, but to promote adult education and social animation.[15]

Video was the favored medium when it arrived in the form of the first portable "portapak" half-inch, lightweight video cameras and playback equipment. Video greatly aided the *Fogo Process* for it allowed for more immediate feedback between the community and its taped image. The remarkable results such as those mentioned earlier in Lord's Cove are only possible with the immediacy of video.

In addition to the actual creation of films the Extension Service also distributed the Fogo films to other communities in Newfoundland. This allowed other isolated and similarly impoverished communities to recognize the similar conditions and problems of organization and development. A field representative in Labrador, reported that screening the Fogo films there was a useful way of initiating group meetings and problem-solving. In subsequent years, the Extension Service created a videotape network that consisted of creating and distributing "information tapes" to remote centers at the request of their local field-workers. The whole thing worked something like an early version of the Internet. The idea was that people could exchange tapes and/or request tapes from other communities who had similar problems or solutions to problems.

Port aux Choix represented the first real attempt to put the "Fogo theory" to work.[16] The process was begun at the request of the local extension worker. The Extension Service worked with the Northern Regional Development Association to produce tapes that dealt with community organization, economic problems, the culture of youths and their future in the area. Port aux Choix's problems were very different from Fogo's. Fogo was a community, which the government had little interest in maintaining and developing. In fact, it was widely perceived that it was slated for resettlement. Port aux Choix, on the other hand, was a government designated growth center. It was a place to which isolated communities were resettled, and in which the government hoped to promote modern, wage paying jobs.

In Port aux Choix extension workers noticed an immediate impact of the *Fogo Process*. Local people complained about the lack of local consultation in the choice of location for a breakwater. Soon after the film was screened the government chartered a plane to bring in officials and consult with the community. It was apparent that participatory communication in Newfoundland was already having some important impact on government. It was the use of the *Fogo Process* in radically different cultural and social contexts, however, that proved that its techniques were not unique to Newfoundland. In fact, the concepts and techniques were portable and had global applicability, particularly in conditions of uneven development where there had been little exposure to mass media.

The *Fogo Process* Goes Abroad

By the early mid-1970s the *Fogo Process* was beginning to gain international recognition. An international conference on film, videotape and social change was held at MUN and gathered scholars and community activists from all over the world. Reading the transcript, one gets a sense of the shared feeling of being on the verge of something new and important that could make a real difference in community development.

In October of 1973, Tony Williamson, Director of the Extension Service, presented a paper on the "*Fogo Process*" and the Extension Service's work at the UNESCO meeting on the Planning and Management of New Communications Systems in Paris.[17] Five years later in 1978, Professor V.K. Dubey, of the Banaras Hindu University in Varanasi, India, came across Williamson's paper. He wrote to the Extension Service at MUN and asked them to share their expertise in India. Don Snowden and Paul Mcleod eventually visited India in 1979.[18] With Dubey, they began preliminary work for a project involving a cooperative at the National Dairy Research Institute in Karnal, Haryana. In the small village of Taprana they collaborated on a related projected, about which the film, *Eyes See, Eyes Hear,* was made. In this project, video was used to establish channels of communications between rickshaw drivers in Taprana and bank officials in a distant city. Because they had been unable to secure loans to purchase their own rickshaws, the drivers were forced to rent their vehicles at considerable cost. Using video they made a tape on which they spoke about what they found wrong with the bank's dealings with the village and why they believed they were good credit risks. The tape was shown to the bank officials who in turn made a tape inviting the villagers to visit them and discuss their finances. Eventually, the drivers were able to secure loans. In Bangladesh, a similar project was used to establish communications between physical engineers and social groups concerned with small-scale water control. Other similar small-scale projects were carried out in Uganda, Guyana, Nepal and elsewhere, all with great success. The seeds for all these projects lay in the experiments carried on Fogo.

In a paper he wrote prior to his death in India in 1984, Snowden summarized some of what he had learned about the process over 15 years of video based participatory communication all over the globe.[19] He suggested that video could function as a new form of literacy among populations who do not regularly practice reading and writing. It could facilitate the establishment of lines of communication within a village or area, and between the village and distant decision makers. Apart from its informational content, it could also be used to demonstrate processes such as the use of technology. The success of its usage would depend on the number of factors that proved themselves over time and around the world. Foremost among these are the use of a community worker, or social animator. Snowden suggested that the social animator get to know the community first before introducing video technology. The manner of its introduction will determine whether or not it is thought of as a part of the community, or as a foreign intrusion. Thus, Snowden suggested that the equipment first be set up in a central location that people will traverse in the course of their daily interactions. Villagers should be encouraged to handle the equipment, look through the camera so they would get used to seeing their image on screen. He pointed out that the showing of films should similarly be done in a familiar, common place where people are comfortable to congregate and talk about social problems.

But apart from the viewing of the final product, it is again the process that matters most. Snowden writes:

> The very presence of a community worker with this technology shows or provides a sense of caring and involvement which enhances the willingness of village people to become involved in new ways of learning and doing. The community worker and the video process bring people together for a common cause, create new information channels and insure a belief and confidence in self-help.[20]

Since these early experiments in participatory video, many other similar programs have developed, some growing out of the *Fogo Process* and some with their own independent history. Professor Dubey's National Council of Developmental Communication (NCDC) for example, continues to exist and is involved in media-based development projects in India.[21] But there is also the Village Video Network of New York started by Martha Stuart. Stuart's work has given birth to Video SEWA, part of the Self-Employed Women's Association, a trade union of rural Indian women founded in 1972. Stuart worked in India on projects using film and video to promote community health.

In 1984, at about the same time that Snowden, McLeod and the MUN team were invited to India, Stuart was invited to Ahmedabad to train SEWA in the use of video. Since then, SEWA has produced more than 400 films on topics ranging from sanitation and health to labor organization.

While many of these films have been screened at international festivals, and won awards, the process of filmmaking is, just as in the Fogo experience, still as important as the films produced. For example, in one instance rural "bidi" workers (women who roll tobacco leaves) used video to address their exploitation by traders who paid less than the minimum wage established by the government. The women were apprehensive about taking the matter to court because they believed that the courts would favor the traders and because they were unfamiliar with the legal process. The organization videotaped a moot court in which the women presented their cases. In this way they felt more confident about the process and eventually fought and won their cases.

More recently, the Indian and Italian governments have entered into a joint agreement to create a training production center in Calcutta called *Roopkala Kendro*. Gaston Roberge of St. Xavier College, who is consultant to the project explains that it is a unique project in that it aims to create a new breed of video filmmakers with a strong foundation in the social sciences and a commitment to participatory video production. "The hope is to train video filmmakers who would make educational films with the participation of the people for whom those films are made, " says Roberge.[22]

The Future of Participatory Communication

The *Fogo Process* emerged at a time when much of the world's population had not been exposed to film and television. Don Snowden often claimed that the *Fogo Process* would only work in situations where people have little access to mass media. The process was designed to empower these communities by giving them access to tele-technologies. Today public life is being transformed by the rapid integration of digital technologies, e.g., video, the Internet and cellphones. Greater speed in the production and circulation of images is also a factor. It often seems that the technological interconnection of the globe through satellite, Internet and other telecommunications is diminishing the whole idea of remoteness. Doesn't the spread of the Internet, for example, effectively mean that there are very few who are not connected? Who are the non-receivers of images and information about the distant places and decisions that affect their lives? In such an environment, what will be the future of participatory communication and how will that process change?

Of course, we cannot say now what the future of the Internet and digital technologies will be. It is clear at present though that its usage is unevenly distributed around the globe. The National Aeronautics and Space Administration (NASA) has recently published a map which is a composite picture of the world at night (at no time is all of the world in darkness). The map, which was circulated over the Internet, is a very beautiful picture of the earth composed of patterns of golden light against the blackness of the continents. However, what immediately strikes one is that the patterns of light are largely concentrated in the so-called developed world. Large strips of Asia, Africa and South America are relatively dark, while the Eastern Seaboard of the US, and the closely spaced cities of Western Europe dominate the night. A map of Internet usage follows roughly same the patterns, which suggests that talk of the end of remoteness or the global village is premature. If the *Fogo Process* thrives in places without mass media then it may still have quite a long future ahead of it. In short, while the Internet is relatively inexpensive, portable and easy to learn, access to it remains concentrated in the center of the developed world.

The greatest legacy of the *Fogo Process* may turn out to be its mode of integrating communication technology into daily life. The newer technologies like webcams, small digital cameras, desktop editing equipment and so forth, promise to democratize the means of communication and to be more accessible than film cameras, or early video equipment. But the evidence from places as different as Fogo, Newfoundland and Taprana, India is that the empowering capacity of media technology may lie less in its portability or efficiency than the way in which it is received by a community. In future, it may become easier to train people to be filmmakers, video technicians, or Internet browsers, but it will remain a challenge to help them become social animators in their own communities. For that reason, we still have much to learn from the *Fogo Process*.

Notes

1. For an analysis of the *Fogo Process* which situates it in the history of reality based media, see Janine Marchessault, 1995.
2. *Mr. English at Home.* British Colonial Film Unit: Great Britain, 1940, 35MM.
3. *Southern Rhodesia: Is this Your Country?* British Colonial Film Unit: Great Britain 1947, 35MM.
4. John Greirson, quoted in Philip Rosen, 1993, p. 78.
5. This demand for a new socially engaged cinema was not peculiar to Canada, of course. For a good overview of the history of the attempts to create "subject generated" or "participatory" film see Jay Ruby, 1991, pp. 50–67.
6. See Jones, D.B., 1981, p. 159.
7. For Snowden's account of the genesis of the Fogo project see Quarry, 1984.
8. Colin Low quoted in Gwyn, 1972, p. 5.
9. Anthony Marcus quoted in Gwyn, 1972, p. 34
10. See Anderson, 1985.
11. For understanding of the divisive effects of the truck credit system in outport Newfoundland, see Sider, 1986.
12. See MUN, 1972, p. 7.
13. Quoted in Gwyn, 1972, p. 10.
14. For a good overview of these developments see Wiesner, 1992.
15. See Quarry, 1984, and Snowden, 1984.
16. See Memorial University of Newfoundland Extension Service, (1972) p. 6; from Paul McLeod in a personal communication, October 2000.
17. See Williamson, 1973.
18. See Quarry, 1984; and Dubey, 1984. From Paul McLeod, personal communication, October 2000.
19. See Snowden, 1984.
20. See Snowden, 1984.
21. From V.K. Dubey, personal communication, October 2000.
22. From Gaston Roberge in a personal communication, October 2000.

References

Anderson, B. (1985). *Imagined Communities: Reflections on the Origins of Nationalism.* London: Verso.

Dubey, V.K. (1984). 'Don My Friend,' *Interaction,* Vol. 2(3), pp. 11–16.

Gwyn, S. (1972). 'Film, Videotape and Social Change,' *Seminar Report.* Extension Service, March 13–24. St. John's: Memorial University of Newfoundland.

Jones, D.B. (1981). *Movies and Memoranda: An Interpretative History of the National Film Board of Canada.* Toronto: National Film Institute.

Marchessault, J. (1995). 'Reflections on the Dispossessed: Video and the Challenge for Change Experiment,' *Screen*, Vol. 36(2), pp. 131–46.

Memorial University of Newfoundland Extension Service (1972). *The Fogo Process in Communication: A Reflection on the Use of Film and Videotape in Community Development.* St. John's: Memorial University of Newfoundland.

Quarry, W. (1984). 'The Fogo Process: An Interview with Don Snowden,' *Interaction*, Vol. 2(3), pp. 28–63.

Rosen, P. (1993). 'Documenting the Documentary: On the Persistence of Historical Concepts,' in M. Renov (ed.), *Theorizing Documentary*, pp. 58–89. New York: Routledge.

Ruby, J. (1991). 'Speaking For, Speaking About, Speaking With, or Speaking Alongside: An Anthropological and Documentary Dilemma,' *Visual Anthropology Review*, Vol. 7, No. 2, pp. 50–67.

Sider, G. (1986). *Culture and Class in Anthropology and History: A Newfoundland Illustration.* Cambridge: Cambridge University Press.

Snowden, D. (1984). *Eyes See, Ears Hear: Supplement to a Film under the Same Title.* St. John's: Memorial University of Newfoundland.

Wiesner, P.K. (1992). 'Media for the People: The Canadian Experiments with Film and Video in Community Development,' *American Review of Canadian Studies.* Spring, pp. 65–99.

Williamson, A.H. (1973). 'The *Fogo Process*, User-Oriented Communications Systems, and Social Development, The Canadian Experience,' Summary of a Presentation at UNESCO meeting on the Planning and Management of New Communications Systems, ' Paris, France, October 8–12, 1973.

Part 2

Video that Transforms

6

The Transformative Power of Video: Ideas, Images, Processes and Outcomes

———— ❋ ————

Mary Jo Dudley

In today's era of television, film, home videos, and the Internet, few would debate the potential for the combination of visual images, words and sounds to influence our view of ourselves and our world. As consumers of images designed to entertain, shock, move or inform us, most of us are aware of the power that these images have in shaping our worldview. Through video, many of us have experienced the beauty of places we have never visited, the fear of dangers far from our homes, and the joy of reunions that took place on the other side of the globe. While we may acknowledge that these images have changed us in some way, it is unlikely that we contemplate how these creations have the power to influence and transform those who produced them.

The introduction of low-cost video technologies has ushered new actors into the video production arena. Just as the amateur video of police violence against Rodney King brought protesters to the streets in California, video cameras are being used by indigenous leaders, children, domestic workers and others to rally public viewers around their concerns. The ever-growing access to inexpensive video cameras has led to a new genre of video productions, permeating the boundaries that traditionally limited media access to professional journalists. Increasingly, grass roots organizations and development practitioners are experimenting with video to document their realities and to shape how they are being presented to others. Moreover, women, youth, indigenous people and others are using video to present new or hidden aspects of our lives and our world.

It is through this process of producing videos that local communities are learning the art of constructing messages to communicate their concerns, describe their successes, or share their dreams with others. As the examples in this book illustrate, video has the potential to deeply affect audiences and producers alike. As traditional communication forums have become more open to grass roots productions, videos are being developed to uncover injustices, to give visibility to the needs of isolated or marginalized groups, and to tell stories of how everyday people overcome adversity. In doing so, new actors have entered social and political spheres through visual media, and the ideas, images and messages they create are being used to influence and transform power relations around the globe.

- How can video be used to document, produce, and challenge one's reality?
- How does this tool empower those who control it?
- How does the process of constructing one's own public image provide new opportunities to analyze the structures of power in which one is embedded?

Video is a powerful medium and the dissemination of video messages through television broadcasts can have far reaching consequences. In the examples I present ahead, the video production process required a group to closely examine the issues they wanted to raise, to decide upon the potential audience, and to identify those who could influence their reality. In each case, the video producers hoped to challenge existing power structures through a combination of uncovering wrongdoing, constructing alternative messages, publicly questioning the plans of those in positions of power, and/or by assuming power through access to technology. These examples demonstrate the transformative potential of video.

Uncovering Injustices: Making Wrongdoing Visible

Film and video have frequently been used to illustrate injustices, abuse, or suffering, particularly when calling upon national and international entities to respond. Documentary films on suffering or injustices such as those caused by war, famines, natural disasters, and physical or emotional abuse have provided the crucial documentation required for the enactment of national and international laws and regulations to protect the defenseless.

Historically, documentary films have played an important role in highlighting injustices and violations of human rights. In the 1960s and 1970s, documentary films such as *The Battle of Chile* brought the stark realities of the brutality of Pinochet's military dictatorship to audiences around the world. The powerful images of soldiers shooting into the crowds of defenseless students, the burning of piles of books from the university library, and the dragging of union leaders from their homes were so strong that the film was forbidden in many Latin American countries.

Images of the dead students at Kent State, the aerial spraying of napalm on Vietnamese women and children, and the long lines of black body bags being loaded into government airplanes were instrumental in raising consciousness and building opposition against the US involvement in Vietnam. Depictions of war and destruction have been used to both support and dispute the actions of those in positions of power. Nonetheless, the power to create such images and the decision on what should be included in or excluded from the media has traditionally been in the hands of a few producers, editors and media owners. The allegiances between politicians, businessmen, and others that have occupied positions of power and those who control the media have been well documented.[1]

More recently, television and radio stations have been pressurized to provide spaces for free expression. As individuals and communities are seeking new ways to communicate their changing needs to those who have the power to determine their fates, they have increasingly turned to the media to influence public opinion. The introduction of community access television and community radio has provided opportunities to illustrate some of the less visible injustices of people around the globe, and to provide forums for those whose voices have been absent or silenced. When certain members of society become isolated or marginalized due to a severe imbalance of power, and their economic, political, social or physical survival is threatened, they may seek relief by bringing their concerns to the forefront through the media. One of the most powerful tools has been the use of video by local communities and development practitioners to express concerns, explore alternatives, and eventually communicate this information to policymakers. Increasingly, video cameras are being used to document injustices and wrongdoings, and these videos are being shown to call for assistance and change. By using video to bring images of these injustices to new public arenas, traditional power relations are being challenged and contested.

Video production can also provide a catalyst for analyzing how power structures influence certain groups. While producing a video with Colombian domestic workers (see Chapter 13), the discussions about potential audiences began with an examination of the power structures that keep women from being fairly remunerated for their work. The women returned to this conversation on structures of power on numerous occasions as they adjusted their video production goals to meet the needs of the group. During the process of using video to learn about their individual and collective histories, they became aware that a contributing factor to their sense of powerlessness was the use of physical violence and sexual abuse. The group was transformed by uncovering this shared experience of physical and emotional abuse.

While the women were uncertain of their possible success in advocating higher wages, they were confident that society would not condone physical abuse of private employees (in this case domestic workers). The public response to questions being recorded on a video camera brought a taboo topic out into the open, and in so doing provided a window for the women to begin to establish a public dialog to address the issue. This experience raises important questions about the relationship between bringing injustices to the fore as a first step to empowerment. How is "empowerment" accomplished? How can the sexual and physical power of men over women be challenged and transformed?

The very act of breaking the veil of silence surrounding the topic was an important first step to contesting the vertical relationship between domestic workers and their employers. Furthermore, the public discussions of sexual abuse uncovered a new arena of abuse of power and the impacts of such wrongdoing. By analyzing their social location the domestic workers were able to develop a strategy to challenge mistreatment by their employers, and consequently to increase their capacity to influence and control their own destinies. In this example the video camera was the catalyst for both the examination of power and the development of an approach to publicly confront unfair treatment.

Media as a Construction

Much can be learned from the decision-making process involved in constructing our reality through video production. One important lesson that emerged as part of the process of producing a video with domestic workers was an understanding that media images and messages are constructed. Video offers the possibility for allowing the producers to deliberately select what information needs to be included or omitted. The discussion about the "message" we planned to convey through the video prompted an extensive discussion about power dynamics between the women and their employers. This analysis of these relationships formed the basis for a deeper examination of possibilities for influencing those in positions of power. For example, the women were very interested in conducting interviews with their employers because the mere act of conducting an interview might cause the female employer to rethink her treatment of the domestic worker. At the same time, if the general public heard the opinions of typical employers, they might be persuaded to reexamine how they think about domestic workers. Through deliberate efforts to challenge stereotypes, the women replaced depictions of domestic workers as "victims" or "servants" with new positive images of domestic workers as working women to be respected. The recognition that media messages are created empowered the women to develop new video messages to address social injustices (employment discrimination), and to make wrongdoings (sexual and physical abuse) visible.

How does the Process of Constructing a Video Message Empower the Producers?

In the case of the domestic workers they were able to tell their story and describe their role in society from the perspective of an employee, rather than through the typical presentation of their reality as viewed from the perspective of the employer. For those who have been socially isolated it is this possibility of gaining access to a public forum that has encouraged groups to arm themselves with camcorders and develop their own videos as vehicles for expression. For example, an association of independent video makers in Bolivia helped a group of shoeshine boys to make a documentary about their lives.[2] Through a video forum the boys discussed their understanding of their role in Bolivian society, and how being employed gave them a sense of purpose that they were not able to find through education. The fact that people were interested in producing a video about their lives gave them a sense of pride in their work, thus reinforcing their sense of belonging. In this instance, the *process* of making the video (coincidentally entitled *Making Waves*) was far more important than the final video *product*.

In Ricardo Gomez's description of the *Magic Roots*, a children's oral history project, he also emphasizes the relative importance of the process over the product. Similar to the experience of the domestic workers and the shoeshine boys, the children by sharing stories, learned about how media is constructed and the importance of both form and content (see Chapter 9). Through video letters, the children documented their history, their reality, and their imagination and eventually shared their stories with other children throughout Latin America. Through this process the children were able to articulate their individual, as well as collective identities. Gomez emphasizes that the most important outcome of the project was the "increased sense of self-esteem gained by the children."

How are Empowerment and Increased Self-esteem Related?

A documentary about a group of working class drag queens entitled *Butterflies on the Scaffold*, raises awareness about the daily lives of gays and transvestites in Cuba. By constructing a message of how they understand their role in Cuban society through performance, the participants presented their collective identity. Using video to challenge the constructs of machismo, through the presentation of alternative male images, the actors were able to establish a protected space and consequently reinforce their right as different.

The understanding of media as a construction has led others to pick up video cameras. Video has taken on a new importance in development efforts as we document events and realities, construct messages, and transmit these messages to various audiences. The possibility for videos to be used as advocacy tools has brought new actors into the fore, and these actors are using video not only to create but also to resist the authority of those who wield unfair power.

Questioning Authority

The video camera scanned the gray horizon as the indigenous leader described how the area had once been fertile fields that produced the fruits and vegetables that formed a central part of their daily diet. All that could be seen was a flooded plain. He went on to describe how all the trees were now underwater and how the people who had lived for centuries in the river basin were forced to relocate and leave their ancestral lands. As he described their hour-long boat journey to buy food in a regional market, he warned: "Don't let them do this to you. The river spirit is out of balance."

In Brazil, the video of the flooded lands of a neighboring Amazonian tribe spurred the Kayapó into action against a dam project, which if implemented would also flood their lands. Incensed by the possibility of a similar fate, the Kayapó cameramen documented the impact of the dam and showed their video of the flooded area to all the members of their community. The video showings stimulated discussions regarding the potential negative effects of the dam proposal on their livelihood and access to their traditional lands. To avoid becoming dispossessed of their homeland they developed a strategy to challenge the Brazilian government's proposal for a World Bank loan for dam construction. Aware of the power of media images, Kayapó leaders arrived at a meeting between the Brazilian government and the World Bank in full war regalia to contest the development plan. The images of a visibly angry woman shaking a spear at the officials appeared in newspapers and on televisions across the globe.

Ten days after the meeting, the World Bank announced that they would not make the loan for dam construction, and that the funds would be made available for conservation purposes only. It wasn't a mere coincidence that the Bank decided against funding the dam construction, despite their spokesman's claims that the confrontation in Altamira had no influence on their decision.

What Role did the Media Images of Angry Kayapó Play in the Decision-making?

The Kayapó's brilliant use of the media to draw national and international attention to their concerns has resulted in both political and financial support for their causes, and moreover it has provided them a forum through which to express their views on plans that would seriously affect their futures. Terence Turner is an anthropologist who has undertaken field research in various Kayapó villages since 1962 and collaborated on Kayapó video productions. He points out that one of the most successful aspects of the series of dramatic Kayapó political demonstrations and encounters with the Brazilians (and other representatives of the western world system such as the World Bank and Granada Television) has been the Kayapó's ostentatious use of their own video cameras. They recorded the same events being filmed by representatives of the national and international media, thus ensuring that their cameraperson would be one of the main attractions filmed by the other crews.[3]

The dam construction was halted, at least for the time being, and their resistance strategy succeeded. For most people that is where the story ends. However, internal dynamics among the Kayapó have been severely altered by the events surrounding the widely publicized action at Altamira. Turner notes that when putting video cameras into the hands of community members, the social and political location of the recipient of the camera matters. By giving the technology to an individual, the relationship between the individual and the group may be altered, and for this reason special attention must be given to how evenly knowledge and access to the technology is being transferred.

Power through Technology

As video equipment has become less expensive, more portable and more accessible to the general public, the "camcorder revolution" has resulted in an explosion of new video productions—from amateur documentaries, art and music videos, to highly structured video messages. Combined with the expansion of the Internet, visual images and texts are shared across the globe. In many developing countries, video technology continues to be relatively expensive, but nonetheless it has become within the reach of a growing sector of the population.

There are many examples of how communities that had previously been "subjects" of videos have taken ownership over the shooting and editing of videos about themselves, their communities, and issues of concern. The process of gaining some control over the images that are presented and how groups are represented can be facilitated as the members learn how to use technology to that end. In the case of the Colombian domestic workers and the Kayapó, their ability to manipulate the camera and make editing decisions allowed them to control the content of the edited videos.

While video technology continues to be primarily in the hands of those that have the financial resources to maintain it, there is a growing movement of popular video producers and networks that provide video equipment to local groups to produce videos on social issues. Non-governmental organizations (NGOs) such as the Brazilian Center for Indigenous Education and Documentation (CEDI) have been involved in making video technology available to a broader public. For example CEDI's *Video in the Villages Project* was founded in 1987 to give indigenous communities control over their own images. By promoting grass roots video production among

Amazonian groups, they facilitated the sharing of information among indigenous communities. In Vincent Carelli's documentary *The Spirit of TV*, Indians discuss how video has helped them preserve their stories, beliefs and rituals, connect with other tribes and communicate their messages of protest to the government.

Visual anthropologists and media scholars have begun to examine some of the larger social issues imbedded in giving video cameras to local communities for the purpose of self-documentation. Terence Turner comments on the social effects of indigenous media in indigenous communities. He says that as video takes on political and social importance in an indigenous community, which member of the community assumes the role of video cameraperson matters. The person who makes the important journey to the alien city where the editing facilities may be located plays a prestigious role. These become issues fraught with social and political significance, and consequently, social and political conflicts having a cumulative effect on the internal politics of a community and the careers of individuals.

Turner emphasizes that the Kayapó have used media such as video to establish contacts with other indigenous groups, governmental agencies, NGOs and other nonindigenous groups.

The purpose of such temporal and spatial connections for indigenous groups like the Kayapó has not been to insulate themselves from contact or engagement with the outside world but to engage more effectively with their ambient national and global systems, draw upon their resources, and take part in their politics in order to increase their power to control their own resources and determine the social and cultural terms of their own lives (p. 472).

Turner argues that it is precisely this engagement in determining how the events are "represented" that includes the process of filming to "become an integral part of the event that is being recorded."

How does this Example Illustrate how Power is Being Transformed?

Since Kayapó camerapersons are able to film important meetings and events, they have the power to influence the public perspective on these by providing their own footage to media outlets. In one case the Kayapó leader alluded to how power relations had changed when he noted that instead of the Kayapó traveling to the city, the governmental officials came to them making the arduous and somewhat dangerous journey through the jungle. In this sense the Kayapó had relocated the stage for negotiation over their futures from the urban capital literally to Kayapó territory. In part they were been able to accomplish this because they had access to technology that could challenge the relations of power by gaining public support for their position as they had in the negotiations of the construction of the dam.

Conclusion

I have presented here examples of how grass roots organizations have used video technology to provide public visibility for their concerns as a first step to contesting unfair practices. In the case of the domestic workers, the Kayapó and the shoeshine boys, video provided a vehicle for them to advocate their needs and desires outside the traditional confines of literacy. By engaging in a process of elaborating messages through video, the participants were forced to examine their social, economic and political locations to devise an approach that would allow them to influence the status quo. In each case, the process of developing their arguments proved to be extremely enlightening and in some instances more important than the final video product. By gaining access to video technology, the actors were able to partially level the playing field and begin to interact with media producers on a more even ground. While these reflections provide a window into how some groups have begun to use video to transform power relations, there is much more to be learned. Perhaps these observations on how video is being used to uncover wrongdoing, to construct alternative messages, and to publicly question the plans of those in positions of power will inspire others to arm themselves with video cameras to address injustices.

Notes

1. See Edward Herman and Noam Chomsky's *Manufacturing Consent: The Political Economy of the Mass Media*.
2. For more on this topic, see Karen Ranucci's documentary, *Making Waves*.
3. See Turner's, *Defiant Images: The Kayapó Appropriation of Video*, p. 7.

References and Select Bibliography

Dudley, M.J. (1996). *Uncovering the Invisible Workers: Using Participatory Video and Feminist Methodologies to Challenge Distorted Images of Colombian Domestic Workers*. Unpublished manuscript. Ithaca: Cornell University.

Ginsburg, F. (1991). 'Indigenous Media: Faustian Contract or Global Village?' *Cultural Anthropology*, Vol. 6(I), pp. 92–112.

Gramsci, A. (1992). *Prison Notebooks*. Edited by Joseph Buttigieg. New York: Columbia University Press.

Herman, E.S. and N. Chomsky (1988). *Manufacturing Consent: The Political Economy of the Mass Media*. New York: Pantheon Books.

Turner, T. (1992). 'Defiant Images: The Kayapó Appropriation of Video', *Anthropology Today*, Vol. 8(6), pp. 5–16.

———— (forthcoming). 'Representation, Polyphony, and the Construction of Power in a Kayapó Video,' in Jean Jackson and Kay Warren (eds.), *Indigenous Movements, Self-Representation, and the State in Latin America*, University of California Press.

———— (forthcoming). 'Representation, Politics and Cultural Imagination in Indigenous Video: General Points and Kayapó Examples,' in F. Ginsburg, L. Abuu–lughod and B. Larkin (eds.), *The Social Practice of Media: Anthropological Intervention in the Age of Electronic Representation*. Austin: University of Texas Press.

7

Candid Thoughts on the Not–so–candid Camera: How Video Documentation Radically Alters Development Projects

❈

Barbara Seidl

The senior producer/director of a public television documentary series shares personal observations "from the road." Her work, profiling exemplary development projects worldwide, has revealed that the documentary process has the potential to radically alter the leadership, mission and priorities of the projects undergoing documentation. The author evaluates the changes that may occur in the project at each stage of the video documentation process— before camerawork begins, when cameras are shooting on site, and broadcast/screening of the finished product. Careful consideration is given to the positive and negative influence that the video documentation process can have on development projects—both intentional and unintentional. Firsthand accounts of development groups engaged in video documentation or 'stories from the road' illustrate these benefits and risks throughout the chapter. The hope in telling these stories is to provide those who are considering video documentation with information, which could help them maximize the benefits and minimize the risk of video documentation. The author then offers an alternative method of documenting development projects based on the lessons learned from these experiences.

The wizened Nepalese farmer in the colorful cap beamed a broad toothless smile at me and gestured toward the new saplings growing at the edge of the forest. "He's saying that those new trees mark the boundary between the community's land and Chitwan," his granddaughter translated, tilting her chin in the direction of the thick forest that was Nepal's Royal Chitwan Nature Reserve and home to one of the world's most studied cluster of wild tigers.

Because those new trees grow so fast, we don't have to go into Chitwan for firewood anymore. The wild animals that live in the forest have attacked fewer villagers—and there have been fewer revenge killings of animals. Because this new small forest is closer, we don't need to spend the whole day in Chitwan gathering firewood. There's more time. Some of the women have learned to sew and have started tailoring businesses for the tourists who come to see the animals. The women have earned a little money and that is helping with school fees for the children.

I was stunned. Here was a tree whose very existence was in some part responsible for the protection of an endangered species, creating an economic base for village women, and sending kids to school. I would have been more stunned except that I had been experiencing moments like these on sites of extraordinary development projects for over a decade. I was on assignment for a public television series that profiles the work of successful nonprofit organizations working toward positive social change. The crew and I had been sent to Nepal's Royal Chitwan Nature Reserve charged with the same mission that had taken us to 10 other countries: document the innovative successes of nonprofit organizations; find the stories of success, passion, and commitment that will inspire a public television audience to make a difference in their own backyards; discover why people commit themselves to taking on challenges larger than themselves and tell their stories so that we can inspire others to do the same; find out what happens when one person helps another. We got four days on the ground in Nepal.

The Influence of Video Documentation on Development Projects

The specific assignment in Nepal was to document the innovative mix of environmental protection, micro enterprise and community development that had been responsible for prosperity in the villages surrounding Nepal's Royal Chitwan Nature Reserve and the subsequent preservation of the endangered tiger population. This accomplishment was particularly extraordinary because it was being achieved at a time when other communities were committing revenge killings and poaching tigers for the traditional Chinese medicine trade. The killings had devastated entire ecosystems by removing its apex predator. As the senior trainer for the anti-poaching camps explained to us:

> We must protect the tiger from poachers because if the tiger dies, there will be too many deer. The deer will eat all the bushes and shrubs to the ground and then they will die. Then all the bugs and birds and animals who live off the bushes and shrubs, they will die. Without the bugs and birds, the other plants and trees will die. Soon the rivers and the streams, they will dry up. And where does man get his medicine? It will all be dried up. If the tiger dies, then man surely will die.

So, by saving tigers, this nonprofit was taking the critical first step in saving entire ecosystems. There was no question that this was a story worth telling.

The question for me was: what would be the cost, or benefit, to the very project we were trying to celebrate, document, and potentially replicate? How would my own choices and behavior help or hurt the project? What happened to Heisenberg's principle that the act of observing changes—what is being observed—in itself creates change? What happens when those "observations" are made by a four-member team of strangers through a very large camera lens, and then broadcast on national television? It was Heisenberg on steroids!

What follows is a personal analysis of the influence of video documentation on development projects. It is unresearched and unsubstantiated in the traditional academic sense, but is the result of years spent in the field with a crew and camera, working with nonprofit organizations. I could say that these are "stories from the road," but they are as often stories from the phone line and screening room because the work of video documentation begins to affect organizations well before the camera rolls and long after the documentation is complete. My hope in telling these stories is to provide those who would engage in video documentation with an understanding of the potential benefits and risks of the process so that they might use this tool to its full advantage.

As a means of synthesizing these stories, I have first addressed the personal and professional biases that were in place when they were gathered. I have then grouped these experiences into the three stages of video documentation:

- ♦ Before camera and crew are on site (the preproduction planning stage).
- ♦ While the crew is shooting images on site (the production stage).
- ♦ After the process is complete and the results are seen (the broadcast/screening stage).

Within each category, we'll consider the positive and negative influence—both intentional and unintentional—of the video documentation process on the development project. Real firsthand experiences with development agencies engaged in the process of video documentation will serve as examples throughout the chapter.

Bias in the Video Documentation Process

Bias is an unavoidable part of the video documentation process and it determines the filter through which we see images and take in information. I liken it to standing at the edge of the Grand Canyon and taking a photo. The photo will reflect your bias. You will capture whatever was important to you—be it the color of the rock, the depth of the crevice, or the expanse of the sky. Your bias determines what you select and what you reject. Similarly, a documentary about flaws in America's health care system is not likely to capture stories of happy customers anymore than the geologist at the Grand Canyon is likely to photograph the tourist information center. It's not heinous; it's inherent.

The key point to recognize is that every individual brings a bias to the process that may or may not be helpful. In all cases, the quality and relevance of the completed work will be effected because the bias dictates what is selected and what is rejected, or which part of the Grand Canyon you'll be photographing. For example, the experiences and observations that provide the foundation for this analysis were gathered under tremendous bias. The Public Television series that I work for has a clear and outspoken agenda, as do I as a producer/director.

The Series Bias

The documentary television series that sent our crew to Nepal and 10 other countries, has a clear agenda that seeks nothing short of a radical change in perspective. About to celebrate its 10th season of broadcasting on over 100 public television stations, the intention of the series is to change how we see ourselves as a people. By presenting the work of noteworthy nonprofit organizations and celebrating the power of ordinary people to accomplish extraordinary tasks, the series intends to inspire viewers to recognize their own abilities to create change. There has never been, and likely never will be, a presumption of traditional journalistic objectivity in the programs we produce. The marketing tag line is that we "seek to explore the magic that occurs when one person helps another." In operational terms, the series producers are committed to using positive images and positive emotions to tell the success stories of social service. The series itself is an experiment in the viability of media as a tool for social service.

This bias means that when we participate in video documentation of development projects, we are not trying to take a picture of the whole Grand Canyon. Our focus is on what is working well, what can be replicated, what our western audience will understand, relate to, and be inspired by. That frame excludes a large amount of potentially interesting and educational material. So our bias is immediately apparent in both our approach (positive images, positive emotions) and our content (success stories, innovations, stories of overcoming challenge).

The Producer/Director Bias

As the person orchestrating the video documentation process, I bring my own bias to the process. The producer/director is responsible for the documentation from the initial concept to final distribution. So, for all practical purposes, the director is the storyteller. I was not trained in the traditional journalistic cannon. Rather, the bulk of my formative experience with video production, and storytelling is under this somewhat unorthodox model called "Participatory Message Development." This training routinely puts me at odds with my responsibilities to the series. Contrary to the investigative journalism model that is in search of quantifiable and demonstrable truth, this model dictates that the videographer has nothing whatsoever to do with defining truth. The Participatory Message Development model makes the videographer a vehicle for the telling of someone else's story. The medium is to be used in service of those who wish to be heard.

Operationally, this means that while documenting someone else's story that individual knows what is and is not important. Part of the documentarian/videographer/producer's job is to be quiet long enough to hear the story as told in the way that the people who lived it would have it told. It's not about quantifiable demonstrable truth, it is about relative truth. You are not on a search for facts that quantify the experience, e.g., before the new forest was planted, there were 10 revenge killings and this year there have been none. But the truth of the story is as much in the "retelling" of an actual experience. It's in the recounting of emotions and reactions. So, the story is as much about what happened to people as it is about the factual sequence of events. In the case of the Nepalese trees, the story is about what happens to a community when they control their own destinies.

These are the academic and conceptual roots of my work. They are routinely in direct opposition with my mandate to get the job done within four days of shooting and 10 hours of footage. They are often at polar opposites with the need to tell the story in a way that is entertaining for an American public television audience. But they influence every choice I make. When approaching a Grand Canyon-like project (and many good development projects are long-term multifaceted endeavors), I debate between taking the "photo" that my bias tells me to search for, or the "photo" the series bias requires.

Nepal: Debating How to Capture the Story

Do I spend half a day and three hours of my available tape stock sitting with the women's sewing circle listening to the challenges they faced in creating their own businesses and the impact it has had on their children's lives? Or do I identify one spokeswoman, preinterview her without a camera to identify the critical components of the story, and then profile her experience with her children? If I choose the latter, have I negated or dismissed the other women's work and held this woman's accomplishments as being more valuable than the rest? How much damage would I do by doing that? What's the alternative? What part of the story do I need to sacrifice in order to have the time and tape to sit with the women's sewing circle?

My primary objective in the field is to capture a powerful and compelling story in an accurate and respectful manner. But personally, there is also a desire to use the video documentation as an opportunity to congratulate, confirm, celebrate, and recognize the hard work of people who have been struggling to achieve change for many years against outrageous odds. I imagine that for a rural Nepalese woman who has spent the better part of her day gathering firewood in a forest, vulnerable to an attack by wild animals, my shooting her tailoring business or her children studying might make her feel good about her accomplishments. That conclusion is arrogant. It's paternalistic. It assumes that she doesn't already feel good about her accomplishments and she can benefit by some outsider taking pictures of her children. Its also one of my intentional uses of the medium. Whose life can I improve by pointing a camera their way and acknowledging their effort?

Summary

Bias is an inherent and unavoidable part of the documentary process. It behooves would-be participants in the documentary process to investigate each others bias in the earliest possible stages. The filter of bias defines what is of value and will have an immediate and direct impact on the quality and usefulness of the documentation. For example, the experiences that provide the basis of the analysis for this chapter were gathered under two primary sets of bias:

♦ *The Series Bias*: to profile the story of the development work as a source of inspiration for a public television audience.
♦ *Producer/Director Bias*: to solicit as much of the story as possible from the people who did the work and experienced its results, to use the process as an opportunity to recognize and respect those who have taken risks and achieved positive change through hard work and commitment.

These biases can come into play at every stage of the video documentation process.

How the Video Documentation Process Alters Development Projects

Video documentation has positive and negative influences on development projects at every stage of the documentation process. The person or people conducting the documentation deliberately orchestrate some of this influence; some is unintentional. At every stage there are benefits to be had and hazards to overcome. The *first stage* of the process is called the preproduction planning stage that occurs before the camera and crew arrives on the scene.

The *benefits* of this stage include:

♦ Focusing of mission.
♦ Clear identification of leadership.
♦ Clear identification of priorities.
♦ Increase in project productivity/workflow.
♦ Increase in organization's credibility/ stature.

The *hazards* of the preproduction planning stage include:

- ♦ Inadvertently changing the leadership structure.
- ♦ Discovering dissention/disagreement about the mission or objectives.
- ♦ Diluting the power of the story.

The *second stage* of the process is called the production stage and it involves capturing images on video or "shooting" at the site of the development project.

The *benefits* of this stage include:

- ♦ Increased exposure of the project in the local community.
- ♦ Creation of an opportunity to publicly recognize supporters, leaders and participants.

The *hazards* of the production stage include:

- ♦ Creation of a very visible and public forum for dissention.
- ♦ A radical drop in productivity because of the presence of the camera.

The *final stage* of the process is the creation and screening of a finished product. The benefits of this stage include:

- ♦ Increased awareness of the work outside the community.
- ♦ Greater outreach to those who can benefit from the service.
- ♦ Recognition/validation of those who did the work.
- ♦ Increased financial support.
- ♦ Increased organizational credibility.

The *hazards* of the screening stage include:

- ♦ The documentation becomes the accepted "truth" of the project.
- ♦ Successful documentation of one project often motivates documentation of others.

Stage One: Before the Cameras Roll

The work that happens before the crew arrives in the field is called *preproduction planning* and involves identifying who, what, where, when, why and how of any project. The ultimate goal or objective of preproduction planning is structuring the work so that the project can be completed with the time and financial resources available. In my opinion, it is as critical to success as good camerawork, clean sound, and creative editing.

Why is Preproduction Planning Necessary?

The notion of going out into the field with a camera, rolling tape and assuming the story will just unfold in front of the camera requires either a very large benefactor or a very short story. Some productions are done that way. It is a rare and enviable storyteller who finds herself in that position. Once the story and characters have been identified, some producers will choose to use a less expensive format, a smaller camera, and/or a smaller crew in order to spend more time in the field with cameras rolling. This is one of the choices made in preproduction planning. Its a choice that can't be made unless you've done enough preproduction work to roughly know what your story is about and how long it will take you to document it.

Resources for video production are often clearly delineated between those that may be used before production and those that are available only for field shooting. One day in the field with camera and crew, for example, costs at least six times as much as a day of preproduction planning. Therefore, many documentaries adhere to the mandate of doing as much advanced planning as possible, while still maintaining flexibility for spontaneous events and an unexpected unfolding of the story. This process is necessary to create the framework or structure used to accomplish the task within the time and budget allowed. It can be a tricky dance and requires the cooperation of the organization being profiled if it is going to be effective.

Intentional vs Unintentional Influence on Development Projects

The intentional impact of preproduction planning on development projects is that development agencies identify project leaders, participants, the critical elements of what has been accomplished in the development project and how. Essentially, you are identifying the characters, locations, and the arc or progression of the story you are going to tell. The unintentional impact includes inadvertently neglecting some leadership groups or inaccurately focusing on a less involved group, refocusing project mission, revealing dissent about missions and objectives, stimulating an increase in workflow and productivity, and contributing to an organization's stature and credibility. I'll address the benefits and risks present in each of these situations and provide an illustration for each.

Intentional Consequences: Identifying the Who, What, Where, When, Why and How

The preproduction stage is very pragmatic. Together with the organization, the producer identifies:

♦ The main story.
♦ The main "characters" or people to tell that story.
♦ Any additional members of the community who play a key role in the story.
♦ Where the story takes place—which locations you will use and what is likely to happen there.

Focusing Mission, Leadership, and Priorities

It's important that the organization reach an agreement about project objectives, leadership, and priorities. As anyone who has done community organizing or development work will attest, reaching clarity of objectives, leadership and priorities is not a small undertaking. Without a clear agreement on those key points, the documentation can become a power struggle as differing factions vie for control of the shooting/production process so that their perspective can take prominence. The way to avoid these power struggles during the production phase is to create an opportunity for communication and debate during the preproduction stage. Some organizations I have worked with have welcomed the pre-production process as an opportunity to hone and reach a consensus on these issues. Some have needed to delay video documentation of their work because they discover large disagreements about their identity and priorities.

Honing the Mission: Getting to the Heart of "What"

The executive director of a children's village for war orphans and I had been struggling to identify what lay at the heart of their work. Were they about providing shelter? A refugee camp? A permanent home for homeless children? That sounded good but was a little pat. Before we could move much further in our storytelling, we had to figure out what the crux of the story would be. This would be the story of what, about what? Yes, there were the individual children's stories and the stories of the staff that would certainly be incorporated, but into what cohesive thought or conclusion or representation? Where were we going here?

We did not have a year or even a month to just roll on whatever happened and let the story evolve organically. We needed to, at the very least, narrow our focus to what was critically important and inherently valuable about the institution—not just momentarily compelling, i.e., a child who had emerged from a recently topical conflict. We tossed and turned around programs and departments, alumni experiences, stories of current children and staff, all to articulate something we couldn't express. All of these pieces were part of what bigger picture? The mission was essentially to provide a permanent home to children who had none. For decades the children's village had done that and more. The director and staff had been so fully engaged in doing the work that they hadn't had a moment (or the need or the opportunity) to wrap their heads around what the work really meant. The challenge made the executive director's brow furrow and my eyes squint, but I have to admit I was enjoying myself.

After a long preproduction meeting haranguing over the meaning of it all, the director found me at the breakfast table in the campus dining hall to say he had found the answer. It had all gelled in his head during the night. He then laid out a five-point plan of adolescent growth and development, community building, and self-empowerment. I thought of my audience absorbing a five-point plan while cooking dinner between ringing phones and crying children. I held my breath.

"No—that's not it" he said, looking stricken. "That's only 'the how' of what we do. These five pillars are how we do our work. It's not the work." I waited and watched the wheels turn.

"And we do that ... we do those five pillars so that they belong. The 'what' of what we do is that they belong—to something—to anything. Everything we do is so that this child, who belongs to nothing, now belongs—to a faith, to a community, to himself. That's it! That's what it's about. *To belong.* That's what this community is. That's what we've created here. Something they can belong to—that they will always belong to...." I waited again.

"Yes. That's it. I've never thought about it that way before. That's really it. Thank you."

Throughout the rest of the morning we bounced this conclusion off various staff—all of them beamed with the clarity and simplicity of it all. Yes, that is it, they agreed. The camera wasn't even in the country yet and the process had changed how they saw the meaning and mission of their work.

Focusing the Mission: When a Key Player is Left Out

On another occasion I was filling in for a colleague who, at the last minute, was unable direct the crew in the field. All of the pre-production work was done. The story, characters, locations, mission and priorities were identified. I just needed to follow through on the plans. I arrived on site to discover that one of the key leaders of the organization was threatening to sink the project. I met with him without the cameras in an effort to determine what his concerns were. I discovered that he had been left out of the entire preproduction process. We talked through the objectives of the project, the objectives of the series, and the manner in which the work would be conducted. He also wanted to know who I was and about my agenda. In the end, he agreed to participate and provided what I now view as one of the most powerful and moving interviews I have ever had the privilege to be a part of.

As I went to remove his microphone, he thanked me for my sensitivity and quietly said, "May I ask something of you?" Of course, I said. "Next time you want to do something on (this organization), ask us what we would like. Don't script it for us." Agreed, I said.

Unintentional Consequences of Preproduction Planning on Development Projects

We know that there can be "fallout" from the preproduction process. In the case of the children's village, preproduction led to greater clarity and commitment to a newly focused vision or mission. In the last example, it resulted in the unintentional disregard of a key participant. Other unintentional consequences include:

♦ Diluting the story.
♦ Creating an unintended shift toward a Western bias.
♦ Increasing organizational credibility.
♦ Increasing project productivity.

Potential Hazard #1: Disregarding the Contributions of Some Participants

By following our objectives for financially prudent preplanning, for the successful completion of the project, required the organization to say, "this story is important, this story is not. These people must be interviewed. These people need not." Video documentation can be a costly and rare opportunity for many organizations. Selecting which leaders will and will not speak is akin to holding an election—and there are often hurt feelings or political upheaval over who was selected "when the cameras came."

Nurses vs Board. We were in preproduction with a medical nonprofit that used an unusually effective treatment regime in which community interaction and self-perception were as important as medicine in recovering patient health. After many discussions about how the approach worked and what the key elements were for its effectiveness, the nonprofit and we agreed that the nurses, as well as a number of other key staff, be interviewed to articulate the process. We also agreed that the board of directors for the nonprofit would not be a necessary, on air component of the story.

While it may seem a small and obvious matter that story lines must be narrowed and that for every component that is selected another is rejected, such choices have the potential to cause damage to an organization if they are viewed as public statements of what is valued and what is not. If ignored, this situation is a quick way to lose a board member.

Potential Hazard #2: Diluting the Power of the Story

Sometimes the unintentional consequence of focusing the mission and narrowly identifying leadership is that we end up one step away from what really happened. When faced with the challenge of selecting one or two leaders from the dozen or so who may have been involved, many remote communities and organizations thwart the potential damage of this situation by selecting the best English speaker as the 'leader' or designated spokesperson for the village. It is then clear to the 'real' leadership and the rest of the community that this person was identified because of his/her language skills. This eliminates the delicate situation of selecting one or two leaders from the dozen or so who may have been involved. It also dilutes the power of the story as the story is heard from the community's best English speaker rather than someone who has been involved with the development project from the beginning and can speak more personally about its importance and potential impact on the community.

Potential Hazard #3: Designing the Story with a Western Bias

As you work with the organization, trying to figure out what the story is and how to shoot it, you are invariably drawn to stories that you believe your audience will find compelling. You look for stories that hold a particular visual appeal, or that have the interest or depth containing multiple components within one framework. For example, the story of economic prosperity in Nepal is more interesting if we can experience it's impact on an entire family or entire neighborhood as opposed to the same story of economic impact as seen through the eyes of one old man in the village. That old man may be the most important elder in the village, and for that reason alone you may chose to include him in the story of the development project. However, since you are ultimately preparing your work for a Western audience, the story will hold greater attention and impact and be perceived to be more important if it affects more people.

Bolivia: Telling the Story for a Western Audience

We were one month late for a seven-day shoot in Central America and e-mails were flying. The project coordinator/development officer on the ground had been facing her own challenges trying to get all the answers we needed. She was firmly committed to her role as facilitator and would not make any decisions about the project. She felt that the project and the story belonged to the community. As she saw it, she was just the person with the language skills and the e-mail. But if our limited time was going to be successful, we needed the community's help with advanced preparation.

We needed to know who the project leaders were. There existed the officially elected community leaders—who had had little to do with the actual work of this particular project. There were community members who were supposed to be in charge of the project— but in fact had not done much work on it. There were community members quietly going about getting the job done and motivating others to do the same. Then there was the person the community had identified as the leader—a young man who knew the community well but currently worked in the city. He spoke English. Who did we want?

This was where my educational bias ran smack into the series bias. Under this participatory research model, the videographer–as–technician is required to honor the community's choices. They know what's best—they know how they want to represent themselves. They wanted the English speaker who was living in the city. I wanted compelling television and wanted to gather the story from those who had experienced it. I e-mailed back that we wanted to hear the story from the people who were most involved in the project—the people who could tell us and show us how it had worked and what it meant to them to be doing it. They had to tell us who that person should be. In fact, they had already told us who it should be—I was simply asking the question again hoping to get a different answer.

The facilitator then told me a story about a woman in the village who was the treasurer of the water committee—how her two sons used to be sick all the time until the well project brought sustainable clean water source to the community. The new clean water source and the health of her children were a direct result of her work on the committee. Here, I thought, was a part of the story. It was a part of the story that would allow my western audience to grasp the value of the work. But the community hadn't selected this woman as someone who could represent the project. She was an elected treasurer of the water committee—I was the one who felt she was a more important, compelling, and interesting part of the story for my western audience rather than an English speaker from the city. I asked the facilitator to request that the woman and her children be available one of the days that we would be shooting in the village.

Potential Benefit #1: Increasing Organizational Credibility

Simply being selected to participate in a preproduction process has been known to raise the stature of some groups. We had just begun. We hadn't shot a single frame. We hadn't identified the main characters or even considered how we wanted to approach the story. We were all still at home in Boston when the organization we were going to profile contacted us to say that we had already aided their progress as an organization. Just being able to say that they had been selected to be profiled on a public televisions series was bringing additional recognition, support and credibility to an already prestigious group.

Potential Benefit #2: Increasing Project Productivity

It would be logical to conclude that video documentation involves turning on the camera and capturing what is there. In my experience, there is a tremendous amount of work that happens on development projects in anticipation of the cameras being turned on. Participants are strongly motivated to make as much progress as possible before their work is recorded. While I am not aware of anyone who has engaged in the arduous process of video documentation in order to generate this kind of accelerated productivity, it certainly is a useful side benefit.

Cleaning Up for Company

The crew had been up every morning at four to drive on unpaved mountainous roads to our shoot locations—remote communities in the Bolivian Andes where lack of clean drinking water and sanitation had resulted in rampant cholera and the deaths of a number of children. We were profiling a nonprofit that had partnered with local Bolivian NGO's to provide technical support and training for local communities interested in building wells, water tanks and sanitation systems.

This had been one of my first projects for the public television series and I was still unsure of myself. Subsequently I had the crew covering anything and anyone who stood still long enough. I had asked them to do way too much, they had been overscheduled, and we had already shot too much footage. This was our last day of shooting and the words of the organization's executive director were ringing in my ears.

> Seeing a whole community come together to build wells and water tanks is great visual stuff—but latrines are really one of the most important things we do in terms of health and sustainable living. I know latrines aren't sexy, and in a half-hour program you're not going to devote much time to it, but we really have got to get it in there somehow.

So that morning found me mumbling, "latrine, I need a latrine," as I made my way to the van. I shouted to the driver's seat and the organizations' in-country coordinator who had been with us since we arrived at the airport. "Paul said he wants us to be sure to get some latrine shots. You had mentioned that village near here where they have a project under way. Can we make a quick stop there?"

She turned in her seat. "Oh no. Really? A quick stop? They've been working so hard." Shifting back into her seat belt, she caught my eye in the rear view mirror and slowly started the car.

> See, we had a real warm spell and so these guys had been taking their own sweet time getting these latrines finished. But

when they heard that you were coming, we must have gotten ten latrines built in the time it was taking us to do two. It's just been incredible. The project is just about complete because they wanted it to be ready for the camera. I know you guys have a lot to do today but I was hoping we could spend more than just a few minutes there.

As we pulled into the village, Bruce, our director of photography, asked: "So how much of this do you need?" I thought I needed about two minute's worth. I needed some shots of people working on a latrine and a shot of a finished latrine. That was about it. But if I did that I'd feel like a dinner guest, stuffed after the appetizer. So I explained to Bruce that we didn't really need very much of this, but that these people had been working triple overtime to get all these latrines up and operational for us to see. And he said: "Right. One Big Deal coming up."

No earthquake, no election, no starlet has ever received such good coverage. There were even individual shots of villagers standing next to the latrine they had worked on smiling and waving into the camera—shots both Bruce and I knew I'd never use.

The Challenge of Involving the Organization in Preproduction Planning

Narrowing the story can be harrowing for organizations that are firmly committed to the value of each and every contribution— they would not leave out the janitorial staff and the lady who brings the sandwiches anymore than they would leave out their president.

I have profiled many field and development operations that expand and diversify their missions to meet local concerns. For example, an organization committed to providing accessible health care for rural women soon finds itself involved in everything—literacy, job training, day-care, domestic abuse counseling and micro-loan programs because that is what is necessary to keep the women in that community healthy. Everyone involved in the organization understands how the success of a prenatal care program and the subsequent decrease in maternal death is predicated by a micro-loan program that enables women to start small businesses which in turn gives them the bus fare to get to the clinic. "Obviously," the field development person might say, "of course you need a good micro-loan program for successful prenatal care."

So, when some producer/director who wants to bring a camera and tell the story of this organization asks, "I thought you were a health care organization. Why are you running a micro-loan program?" the question can be as challenging as someone arriving in your living room saying, "I thought you were an accountant but you are here playing with a child. Who are you?" The temptation is to answer this irritating, ignorant, time-drainer of a visitor who is preventing you from getting to your loan circle. "Never mind. We know who we are and why we do what we do. We don't need to explain it to anyone else." But, as nonprofit development agencies looking for support for both ongoing work and innovative successes, we do need to share our passions and beliefs with the outside world in order to ensure that the work continues and that we are of service to those organizations that could learn from our mistakes.

The challenge of any mission in the face of media is very similar to the earlier example of the demanding stranger in your living room. A nonprofit organization in the midst of ongoing development is asked to make the same choices about who they are—and the key word is choice. As much as every member of our crew would treasure the opportunity to take a more anthropological approach to their work, the financial reality of television production is that we are on the ground for four to seven days. Our story will be told in a tidy 24 minute package. A really huge complicated story will be told in a tidy 48 minute package. Nearly all fundraising videos are under 12 minutes; many are between three and five minutes. A news story is rarely longer than two and a half minutes—many are one to one and a half minutes. An organization's ability to focus it's content radically improves its ability to communicate with the outside world.

Bias in Preproduction Planning

My professional bias dictates that, in the process of preproduction planning, the story should come directly from the organization. I find it arrogant to think that an outsider who has done some homework and spent a very limited amount of time in the community would be in any sort of a position to determine what's important, powerful, or valuable about the work that is being done. But, I don't always walk that talk.

While that theory may make some intellectual sense, it may not always make good television. How, for example, do we visually articulate the concept of children "belonging" to a community, to a faith, to themselves, in a way that doesn't come out feeling, tasting, and smelling like pabulum? How do you then turn the concept into powerful and compelling television? You could sit with a camera for a couple of years and experience evolution with your kids. You could be there for a couple of years (off and on) and hope it unfolds in front of you. In the end, the budget for the Israel project would require that the story be shot in seven to 10 days and then edited into a tidy 24 minute package.

The community in Bolivia wanted us to focus on an English speaker. We went with a woman who had been central to the process because we needed a stronger story. In response, the community asked us to speak with a number of other members of the water committee as well. We did—including the gentleman who had first concluded that the children were getting sick from a contaminated water source. We never would have heard about him if we hadn't asked to speak with the woman whose children were now healthy. So preproduction is the opportunity to hear the whole story, consider all the possible options of how to tell that story, and then sort out which parts be told and how.

The opportunity for damage occurs if these choices or decisions are made in a vacuum. If the executive director of the children's village had reached his conclusion without input from the rest of the community, the consequences could have resulted in internal sabotage against the project as well as a larger long-term impact on the organization. If we had spoken with the treasurer of the water committee and no one else, we would have caused some damage to the work done there also.

Summary: The Impact of Preproduction Planning on Development Projects

In the preproduction or "before shooting" stage of video documentation, intentional impact is through the identification of project leaders, participants, and critical story components. If a participatory message development model is in place, the project participants determine all of the choices about what will be said and by whom. However, the financial and practical constraints of television production rarely support such full participation. The unintentional impact of preproduction varies widely and has been known to include alienation of some leadership groups and simplification of the story to include a more western perspective. Preproduction planning may also inadvertently result in increased credibility for the organization and/or increase productivity on projects.

Development agencies can and have been dramatically impacted by the video documentation process before the first frame is shot. We'll now examine how shooting in the field and the broadcast of the final program impact the work being profiled.

Stage Two: "ACTION!"

There are a number of benefits to be gained and hazards to be wary of at this *second stage* of video documentation. This production stage involves capturing images on video or "shooting" at the site of the development project, and is the most visible part of the video documentation process. As such, it brings the project to the attention of nonparticipating members of the community. This greater awareness has the potential to lead to greater support from a broad cross section of the community. The high visibility of this stage of the process also creates a forum to publicly recognize supporters, leaders, and participants.

However, the same level of high visibility that makes field shooting beneficial for development projects can also pose some potential hazards.

Potential Hazard #1: Work Stops

The most obvious hazard is that the presence of the camera routinely and unintentionally creates a radical drop in productivity that can last hours or days. It is important for those who engage in video documentation to be aware that, unlike the preproduction stage that seems to generate productivity, field shooting slows or stops productivity. Less will be accomplished on the project itself during this stage of the process.

Potential Hazard #2: Leadership Decisions are Extremely Public and Open for Scrutiny

Until the production stage, much of the video documentation work is conducted directly with participants and leaders—those directly involved with the project. When shooting begins, the documentation work is open to the whole community. While that has the positive potential of bringing awareness and credibility to the project, it also has the negative potential of raising dissent or attacks on the project or process.

Zambia: "What's the Point?"

The local chief's daughter had died of AIDS and we were videotaping the funeral. As the throngs dispersed and I made my way toward the van to join the remaining camera crew, the chief's eldest son stepped forward and blocked my path. "Can I ask you something, seriously now?" he demanded. The usual question filled my imagination as I tried to keep my face peaceful and composed. Would he ask me what I thought of Africa or why Americans were such violent people who hated their children enough that they would allow them to be adopted by strangers? Would he ask how to apply to a university in the States or inquire into the world famous promiscuity of white women? I nodded and waited.

"What's the point?" he spat. Of Aids? I thought. Of his sister's death? Of life?

"You film all this. You show people. And then what? Does anything happen? Does anything really happen? Tell me how we benefit from you filming this. What do we get out of it? I know what you get out of it. You sell it. But does any of it help us at all?"

I explained that if it didn't do any good at all, if it didn't have any benefit for the chief and his family, then I couldn't do it (produce the film). What would be the point, after all, as he had said? I explained that our hope and intention was to show how the chief had worked with the local hospital to create and train a system of volunteer home visitors who cared for the tribe's AIDS patients and AIDS orphans. His sister's funeral served to show that AIDS was prevalent in the community—that there was a problem—so people could understand the value and importance of the solution. He stopped me cold.

"How do you know she died of AIDS?"

It seemed a strange question in a community where AIDS had nearly wiped out an entire generation leaving scores of babies with their grandmothers. A simple question really—and I made a mistake. Feeling the need to reestablish the fact that I had become a part of this process with his family's permission, I explained that the family member who had been caring for his sister had told me she had died of tuberculosis resulting from AIDS. Mistake. Despite its prevalence, AIDS still carried the stigma of promiscuity and was a whispered diagnosis, rarely listed on medical charts.

"She did? She said that?? She said it was AIDS? So ... it was AIDS."

"Yes" I blundered. That was the reason we had asked his father if we could videotape the funeral. If I could tell this story about what his father had done when his village had started dying from AIDS, then maybe I could get money for the hospital to pay for the patients' medicines, or maybe I could inspire someone to start a similar system of their own. At the very least, I could recognize the chief and all the volunteers who were caring for the AIDS patients, for their success at choosing to stave off death to make life more bearable and beautiful for those who would eventually die. There might not be more money, I agreed. He was right. This film would not put money in his pocket—and for that I was sorry—it wouldn't put any in mine either. In fact, we would have to pay to put the story on television. So, I guess the point is to say: "Look. See. Something is working. There's death. There's AIDS and this community has figured out how to take care of their own. Recognize and honor their success. That's the point."

He nodded. It was the best I could hope for.

We were there to document the development process that the chief and his tribal leaders had undertaken with the local hospital to set up and train a cadre of volunteer home health workers. This one conversation with the chief's son meant our presence there would result in a number of unintentional outcomes. At the very least, we had added to this young man's hardship at the loss of his sister. Perhaps we had caused him to question his father's decision to allow foreigners into the village, potentially damaged the reputation of the family member who had shared the diagnosis with us. Or, we had unavoidably singled this funeral out as being more noteworthy than any of the hundreds of others that had occurred in that village in the past few years.

Intentional vs Unintentional Influence: "Take only memories, leave only Land Rover tracks."

There's a saying posted in some huts along the Appalachian Mountain Trail that reads: "Take only memories, leave only footprints." I see this as an ideal to strive for in documentary fieldwork. Once we show up with a camera and crew, our great hope is to impact the actual development process as little as possible. Since tremendous amount of negotiation and discussion occurs ahead of time, the plan is to show up, document what is already happening, speak with the people we would like to speak with, and capture the critical elements of the story in the most efficient manner possible. If I've been successful in my preproduction planning, I know roughly what lies ahead, whether or not it is important to the story, and how it all fits together. Then, of course, I have a personal and fairly paternalistic agenda of using the camera as a means of validating good work. I have to work hard so that that does not come in the way of getting the job done.

This is the essence of our primary objective in the field: to capture the most compelling story as completely and respectfully as possible, and in the shortest amount of time. It's difficult to know if you've taken more than the memories or left more than the footprints behind because so much of our influence is intangible. You may never know what you have taken from a group—privacy, dignity, self-image, position of power. Perhaps you have removed their pessimism, fatigue, boredom, or apathy, or left behind—a sense of pride, entitlement, celebration/recognition, or exploitation? You may never know unless they tell you.

African Aids Hospital: "This Helps"

I was interviewing the director of a hospital that was losing patients and staff to AIDS at a steady rate of five each day. Part of his responsibility was to help the hospital staff maintain their mental and emotional health while caring for patients in desperate circumstances. When I asked how he accomplished that he gestured toward the crew behind the camera and said:

> Well, this helps. Your presence here has bolstered us—enriched us in some way. You're here because you think our

community outreach program is something special. The fact that you have come all this way to talk to us about it, to make us part of a bigger global effort, something larger than ourselves and this hospital, that has boosted morale considerably. Just your being here has helped us somehow.

The reality is that, as invisible as we say we would like to be, four white people carrying a television camera and driving a Land Rover in sections of the world with no roads, cars, white people, or television cameras will unavoidably leave more of an impression than footprints. So our greatest impact in the field is our unintentional impact—what's really happening instead of what we would like to happen. I think we are fortunate to learn that some of that impact is positive.

Unintentional Influence of the Shooting Stage

Again, for the most part, we are unaware of the impact we create while shooting in the field. Occasionally, someone will tell us: "You know, because you are here, this has happened." I have listed here some of the unintentional impacts of video documentation.

♦ All activity comes to a screeching halt. Whatever was happening or important to that community before we arrived comes to an immediate standstill. Considerable energy is quickly committed to finding out and attempting to create what people think the camera crew wants to see. Whatever was happening is not happening anymore.
♦ Those not involved in the development project now become curious about what is so noteworthy that it has attracted a television crew.
♦ Local officials who were only tangentially involved in the process now step forward to present full support for the work.
♦ Project participants question the group's decision to participate in the documentation.

There are two more ways in which we unintentionally influence development projects. These are the influences about which I am most curious and have the least amount of information on. In the production stage, we capture small pieces of the story in order to put it all together into one big picture. I wonder how much of our bias is operational while emphasizing some aspects and de-emphasizing others on a development project. For instance, we chose to profile the director of the hospital rather than the chief of staff because the director's name was raised repeatedly as being the "rock" that everyone leaned on. I wonder about the conse-quences of that choice.

The other unintentional influence occurs simply by introducing a number of foreigners and foreign equipment into a community. How does that exposure change that community?

Fretting in the New Nepalese Forest

I looked at the tree—a tree whose existence protected endangered animals and enabled women to educate their children. I looked at Bruce Lundeen, our director of photography whom I had worked with for five years on four continents and more shoots than either of us cared to recall. I looked at Bruce looking at the tree. "Ya got the tree?" I asked. "Yup" he said. "Got the tree."

His pause was one of grand respect and diplomacy—hard learned after weathering too many canceled flights, lost equip-ment, and rained out shoots together. "It just looks like a tree, does-n't it?" I asked. He turned, smiled, and nodded. "Yeah. So far. So far it just looks like a tree."

I knew clearly that I was missing the heart of it all. But then how could I have expected to get the heart of anything when I was ask-ing Bruce to take a picture of a tree? Were we taking the simple story of this fast growing tree and making it more than it was? Per-haps we had granted it an inappropriately significant role in what was actually an extensive and complicated economic and commu-nity development program.

Without aggrandizing ourselves too much, was it possible that the people responsible for the forest project would become some-thing else because they were now the subjects of a television show that would be shown in the United States? Were they now more important in the village because of that recognition, or less impor-tant because they had chosen the spotlight and shared the commu-nity's secrets with outsiders? Had a lackard presented himself as a leader and our translator hadn't caught it, or did he have his own ulterior motives? What were the real consequences of mistaking the lackard for the leader? Why was the male project coordinator introducing us to only men? Were the women, who seemed to be significant beneficiaries, involved in this project? Should I just chill out, take some shots, get my job done, move on and not worry about all this so much?

A crowd of children began to gather around Bruce as he patiently waited for me to get my act together and wisely suggested I drink some water and get out of the sun. As I moved toward the van I saw Bruce showing the children how the camera worked by placing it on their shoulders and having each look at the others through the viewfinder. I knew that whatever our intentions and our ability to tell this story, this television crew was already having an impact on this community. The question wasn't *would* this video documentation effect the project and the community. The question was *how*. I wasn't confident I would ever know the answer to that question.

Summary: The Impact of the Shooting Phase on Development Projects

Production work in the field impacts development projects in a number of ways. It increases awareness of the project in the local community, serves as an opportunity to recognize leaders and participants, and provides the most visible opportunity for dissention and opposition to the project. Shooting in the field also seems to have the uniform impact of stopping everyone dead in their tracks, from a few hours to a few days. Little substantive work is accomplished on projects while shooting is taking place.

Stage Three: On Air

The *last stage* of production is the final creation and distribution of a completed product. I have mentioned, earlier in the chapter, that the series' intention is to motivate or inspire individuals to create positive change in their own lives and communities. We have never tried to measure that impact. There has been no comprehensive or evaluative survey of the viewing audience or of the organizations profiled. We have some figures that allow us to guess at the potential impact of the broadcast. For example, the series is broadcast into 10 million homes, viewed on over 100 stations across the country, our 1–800 viewer line receives upwards of 2,500 calls per year, etc.

Everything we know about the impact of creating these stories comes from the organizations themselves or from messages on our viewer line. The kinds of benefits that development groups report having received as a result of the final product include:

♦ Increased awareness of the work outside the community.
♦ Greater outreach to those who can benefit from the service.
♦ Recognition/validation of those who did the work.
♦ Increased financial support.
♦ Increased organizational credibility.

It's important to remember that these comments are from those who have benefitted from the program and are therefore uniformly positive. It would be rare for a viewer to pick up the phone and call us to say: "You know, that show really didn't do a thing for me." We only hear from those who are moved.

Resources Raised; Program Replicated Internationally

One of the first organizations ever profiled was an all volunteer group providing hospice like care for the terminally ill at no charge. No one pays and no one is paid. Their total annual budget was $60,000. Upon completion of the program about their work, they rented a bus and toured the United States showing the program to fraternal clubs, church groups and community organizations. They credit the program with increasing their budget six-fold and with inspiring the creation of similar programs in both the United States and in England.

The top executive of the organization expressed his point of view, saying:

> The value of the documentary ... is virtually inestimable. It has proven to be a valuable tool in a number of ways:
>
> ♦ in telling the (organization's) story to people who are learning about us for the first time; by attracting part-time and full-time volunteers;

- ♦ inspiring and orienting new volunteers;
- ♦ stimulating the formation of new, all volunteer service group endeavors;
- ♦ training new members of group homes;
- ♦ attracting individual, corporate, and foundation donors, who often are notable to visit (the organization) in person; and
- ♦ presenting aspects of (the organization's) "model" to local groups (e.g., churches and civic groups) and at national and international conferences.

The executive goes on to tell us: "There is a hospice in southern England that has patterned itself after (this organization)—being all volunteer, no paid staff and no fee for services. About three years ago the organizers of this hospice were inspired to create their hospice after viewing the documentary."

Mission Accomplished

A woman who lost her newborn child to a birth canal infection started one of the smallest organizations we have profiled. The infection is easily diagnosed and treated. If mandatory testing for the infection had been part of her prenatal care, her child would have lived. The finished profile was used as part of her efforts to raise awareness about the infection. The national guidelines for testing pregnant women have now been changed to include this test in a routine screening, and a vaccine is now under development.

Recognition for Hard Work: "No one Ever Hears that Part"

We had just completed a private screening of our episode about a hospital that used an alternative approach to treating mental illness. The approach involved an unusually high level of participation from other mentally ill patients and the entire therapeutic community. It was a very intense, demanding, and effective approach that took its toll on the entire medical staff. After the screening, a woman approached me with tears in her eyes. "You got it, " she said. "You really got it. The part where the psychotherapist talks about bringing yourself to the process and how you have to be

aware of what your own issues are—how they can affect the treatment—that doctors are not lofty beings who have answers but that
we are engaged in a relationship and that we bring ourselves to
that relationship. That's it. No one ever hears that part."

She then introduced herself as a psychiatrist who had been in the
field over 20 years and thanked me for expanding the story beyond
the patient's perspective.

From The Viewer Line

I'm calling from Tennessee and I just saw the program about
mental illness. My son has schizophrenia and we've tried just
about everything. I'm so relieved to know that there is a place
like this out there for people like my son. Even if he doesn't
end up going there, just to know that somebody can go there!
Somebody' s son is going there even if it's not mine—this place
is just a blessing. You have no idea how hard it is for parents.
Well, maybe you do. Anyway, I wonder if someone there could
please call me back and tell me how to get a hold of that organization. We're just at our wit's end over here.

More Exposure, More Funding, More Credibility

In a letter to the program's producer/director, the executive director of an organization writes:

The benefits to our program that have resulted form the production and airing of the documentary are far too numerous to
describe in this short letter, but I will attempt to summarize a
few. PBS stations in over a dozen cities where we operate
homes have aired the documentary. And in many of those cities local newspapers, network television news shows, and
other media have done stories on us because we were being
profiled by the Public Television series. In addition to increased
media coverage, we have seen multiple financial benefits,
although not from sources that you might expect. Viewers of
the documentary do not frequently contact us, and when they
do it is most often to refer a child or offer volunteer services—
both extremely valuable contributions to our organization.
However, numerous substantial financial rewards have come

from foundation and corporate giving officers who have viewed the film and been extremely moved. It is impossible to measure the precise impact the film had in their positive funding decisions, but many giving officers have specifically mentioned that the documentary moved them to tears.

Another remarkable story of how the film benefited us occurred during a licensing meeting in a city where we are planning to open a home this summer. Located in a state with extremely rigorous childcare licensing requirements, we arrived at the licensing office for our "stage two" interview. The licensing officer greeted us with a huge smile, and opened the conversation by commenting that she had seen the documentary about our organization on PBS the week before and was deeply moved. She noted that she was thrilled to have received our file the following week and looked forward to moving us through the licensing process and helping us to begin serving children in her community. Wow!

The director goes on to say that after seeing the film, one gentleman sponsored four years of private school tuition for a student in the organization's care.

Voicemail from an Organization Announcing Pennies from Heaven

Just wanted to call and let you know that we received a very large check today from a gentleman I have never met. He had never heard of us but we sent not him a copy of the show and some information—and he sent us a check. Thank you my friend. Hope you're well....

Recognition: "Thank you for Existing"

An executive director of an organization writes:

Over the past year we have been overwhelmed by the positive response the film has received. It has enhanced the mission ... in at least the following ways:

  ♦ Recruitment of both staff and new "guests" (clients).
  ♦ Staff and volunteer training.

- Public relations throughout our local area (we were honored by the Chamber of Commerce for being featured on PBS).
- Fundraising from individuals and foundations.
- Teaching the ... model to other social entrepreneurs.
- A renewed sense of purpose among members of our board and corporation.

It would be difficult to overstate the positive effect the show has had on our organization as a whole ... we continue to find new uses for it all the time. Perhaps the most altruistic result we have noticed is indicated in the letters received, not from potential participants or donors, but from ordinary people just thanking us for finally portraying mental illness in a way they could understand and relate to. So have thanked us just for being in existence these eighty-five years.

From the Viewer Line

Hi! I just saw your show about protecting wild tigers and I had no idea. It was just great. I watched it with my kids and they got to see what it was like to live in a Nepalese Village and see that, you know ... we were all part of one big planet here. It's all interwoven together. Those folks are doing some great work there. I just wanted to call and say hey, keep up the good work.

Summary: Impact of the Broadcast on Development Projects

Our understanding of the influence that broadcast/screening of completed video documentation has on development projects is inconclusive. We do know that the development agencies we have profiled have experienced a wide range of benefits. Some of those benefits include greater awareness of the social issue they are addressing, enhanced outreach abilities, considerable recognition of the value of their work as well as increased funding and credibility.

A Suggested Model for Video Documentation of Development Projects

While working in an Arab community in Israel, I learned one of the most bittersweet expressions I have ever known—possibly inspired by generations of alternating war and peace talks. In a region where the growing season for apricots was short, fast, and produced some of the most incredible fruits in the world, there was an expression: "Bokra, fee mish mish" meaning "Tomorrow, with the apricots." It was used to describe things unlikely, inevitable, and worth waiting for, and because it would be a long wait before the delicious apricots would eventually arrive, I interpreted it as the cultural equivalent of "When Pigs Fly," coupled with an aeronautical engineering course for pigs.

As I debated on how we would carry out the video documentation if we could anyway we wanted, I found myself muttering "bokra, fee mish mish" into my teacup—seeing my conclusions as both unlikely and inevitable. If the objective of video documentation is to document the work with the least amount of influence on the work itself, then some preposterous construction of clandestinely placed and remotely operated cameras can do the job of recording the actual physical work being done. But that would completely miss the story of what it all means to the people doing the work.

I think the most effective way to get the job done would be to marry the skills of a storyteller with the principles of the Participatory Message Development model. In my head, I envision training two or three members of the community who are working on the project to use and repair the camera, audio, light and editing systems; each inevitably recording a different perspective of the project. Their documentation should be long-term and comprehensive—from identifying needs and resources to project evaluation, replication and/or follow-up. It would result in far more footage than any television crew could afford to get. It would also, in all liklihood, be of lower quality than what a professional video crew would have recorded—but, arguably what you lose in quality you might gain in authenticity. These documentarians and community leaders should then work with a storyteller to synthesize the various perspectives into a cohesive and comprehensible representation of the work. This approach meets the objectives of getting the most accurate representation of the work while still experiencing many perspectives on the same project. It also diffuses some of the power struggle issues, such as of who was selected to speak when the television cameras came.

It is also impractical to place such a significant amount of time and resources on the video documentation of a project. It becomes an issue of priorities—is it more important to pay for expensive cameras and training or for tree saplings, well pipes or medical care? That's what got me mumbling into my teacup ... "bokra fee mish mish."

Flying Apricot-Eating Pigs

The unlikely and inevitable has arrived. While it was inevitable that video documentation technology would continue to advance, it seemed unlikely that it would advance in ways that made it appropriate—inexpensive, highly mobile, easy to use and repair—for long-term comprehensive documentation by nonprofessionals. The recent advent of easily operable, fairly accessible, highly mobile and fully integrated digital editing and shooting packages has made field documentation of projects much more feasible. The mobility of these handheld camera and laptop systems also allows for the creation of regionally-based media centers which could support the documentation of many projects simultaneously and thereby decrease the resources and level of expertise needed by each community. Resources that were previously spent on large crews, large equipment and large amounts of time can now be redirected to one person bands or local community groups.

The question of priorities remains and will continue to remain. There needs to be a compelling reason to use human and financial resources to document a project as opposed to working on the task immediately at hand. Some organizations have considered this a question of short-term priorities versus long-term priorities and conclude that investing the time and resources to document their work now will improve their ability to continue the work in the future. Some organizations feel a sense of responsibility toward the rest of the field and are compelled to document useful and progressive innovations that may improve the likelihood of success for similar development agencies.

Others conclude that their first objective is to be effective in protecting the environment, creating clean drinking water supplies, or generating economic opportunity. Resources spent documenting their work are not perceived as influencing the effectiveness of that work. Projects are or are not effective. Their effectiveness or lack thereof, is or is not documented. There is no causal relationship between the two. Therefore, video documentation is not a priority for these organizations. While I contend that in all liklihood there will never be a uniform answer to this question of whether to spend resources on video documentation, I would also suggest that there doesn't need to be.

The Main Message

The main message in all of this is that video documentation of development projects creates an opportunity for tremendous benefits at significant risk. Both benefits and risks are present at all stages of the process.

In the preproduction phase, development agencies have a rare opportunity to hone and focus their missions and message, both for themselves and for a more public audience. Some agencies have also used the preproduction phase or preparation for shooting as a motivating factor to increase productivity and involvement in the project. The risk for both broadcast and nonbroadcast productions is that that message will be created in a vacuum and will not reflect the reality of the people engaged in the process. Eliminating participants from the preproduction process has the potential to result in the short-term problem of sabotaging the project by those who do not feel it is representative of their work, and the long-term problem of decreasing morale and commitment to continuing the work.

The production or shooting phase of video documentation is the most visible part of the process. Development agencies have used this opportunity to bring additional attention to their work within their own communities and to mobilize support from local groups that may not have been as aware of the project. The shooting phase is also an opportunity to publicly recognize the work of dedicated participants and committed leaders. The same high level of visibility that makes the production phase an opportunity for recognition and mobilization also brings it to the attention of those who would disagree with the choice to engage in video documentation at all. The production phase is when the greatest amount of vocal dissention is likely to occur.

The broadcast/screening phase offers the benefit of reaching audiences beyond the immediate community that has the potential to increase funding, credibility, and recognition of the work. The same attributes that make the screenings beneficial also make them risky. Audiences will tend to rely exclusively on the documentation for information so whatever is presented is considered the undeniable truth about the organization. Development officers are cautioned to consider providing supplemental materials at screenings so that audience members have a more comprehensive perspective of the development work.

The key to maximizing benefits and decreasing the risk lies in the same core principles that have guided successful development work. I believe that community and/or participant involvement in all stages of the process ensure greater validity, authenticity, and value of the completed documentation. The way to achieve all those attributes is to be willing to be inefficient. Those development officers who would engage in video documentation of development projects are wise to anticipate debate and dissention.

One means of diffusing some of the power struggles that may accompany video documentation is to do the work using a number of different videographers and a number of different nonbroadcast cameras over a longer period of time. This allows for a greater depth of perspective and completeness of story, while still engaging project participants in the process.

My Conclusion

The traditionalists would have us believe that in order to be valuable, one group of people can only do video documentation in one single fashion. They would argue that only the experts must stand

at the helm directing full and complete coverage of every step in
the progression of a project.

In my work with development agencies, I have come to see video
documentation as a tool. It is a means to tell a story, to share an
experience, to provide insight, to reveal passion, to transport someone to another place—emotionally, spiritually, and intellectually. It
is a way to share the work of social change. I firmly believe that this
tool, used to its best advantage, can itself create social change. I
believe that this tool belongs to anyone who has a story to tell.

8

Trapped: Women Take Control of Video Storytelling

✳

K. Sadanandan Nair
and Shirley A. White

The documentary video, **Trapped**, began with a startling title graphic of a tiny Sari-clad woman clinched in the large fist of a man. This is the opening SCRIPT: (Melancholy MUSIC low, under the melodramatic voice of a female narrator. CLOSE-UP of portrait of elderly mother)

"This is my mother ... it is a time for remembering the years gone by.... She had a really tough life..."

(IMAGE of a sad looking little girl, looking down at an oil lamp between her feet) **"Of course the cycle of life goes on ... babies are born every minute."**

(IMAGE of new born baby in blanket ... looking sweet and innocent.) **"Do people know what it is like to be a girl ... a woman in this world?"**

(IMAGE of woman walking to field leaving baby in a sling basket hanging on the side of her thatched hut.) **"Does a mother really need to leave her baby alone ... and go to work in the fields? I remember ... distinctly ... when I was just five years old I had to look after my baby brother while my mother worked in the fields..."**

(IMAGE of young girl comforting crying baby under a blanket tent in the field ... background of women in field.) **"Our crops get so much attention...do our children get as much?"**

(IMAGES of a small child crawling across the paddy of newly planted rice, a woman nursing baby, the silhouette of three young girls in a doorway.) **"Can you imagine the kind of childhood I had? I ... and girls like me? Isn't this the time for play and laughter? Yet we had to wait hours on end watching the empty road waiting for our parents to come home?"**

(IMAGE of young girl combing little girl's hair.) **"I don't remember my mother ever combing my hair. My sister had to do it for her. I don't know if she resented it?"**

(IMAGE of five young women walking down road with heavy loads of hay on their heads.) **"Young girls ... sisters ... mothers and aunts ... what choice did we have except to carry the burdens of virtual slavery? Is this the age for such back breaking work?"**

(IMAGE of young girl herding cattle down the road.) **"From sunrise to sunset we had to tend the cattle ... because ... in the traditional village economy, cattle were more important than girls. Cows and goats were assets, while girls were liabilities."**

(IMAGES of girl tending a herd of goats and walking behind a water buffalo. Girl up in tree cutting branches, in the background a temple.) **"That temple represents God, and God, we are told is merciful. Were we created for this?"**

(IMAGES of small girl helping mother who is cutting weeds with a scythe, she is carrying away the weeds in a big bowl on her

head; women working on a road crew, breaking up rocks with a heavy hammer.)

from the video, **The Trapped**[1]

The powerful words and images that opened this video production were those selected from the perspective of a professional videographer and written by a well known female narrator in Indian cinema. Based on research data that identified women's problems, the video depicted the plight of village women in India. The video pictured them as trapped by dire circumstance, deploring their lifestyle and crying out for rescue and upliftment. The documentary was exceptionally well done and effective for an urban, **not** poverty-stricken audience. While it vividly portrayed the serious problems village women face, was it an accurate picture of how village women perceived themselves? Ultimately, Dr K. Sadanandan Nair, director of the research, for which this video was produced, found that it was not. When women took control of video production, they portrayed quite a different image of their life.

Village women of Hivare and Sonori, Maharashtra, with the assistance of researchers, were given the opportunity to orchestrate video images to tell their own story. We will take you through the process used with the women later in this chapter, but, to show the contrast of their "storytelling," they chose to open their tape with rhythmic drum beats over images of women's daily life—20 quick, one second shots, depicting their daily reality. Their title was simply: *Rural Women's Problems (Gramin Stree Samasya)*. They wished to visually depict the realities—their satisfactions and joys as well as their hard work—and omit narration that judged those realities. They wanted to take control of the interpretation of their lives and tell a story from their own perspective.

An Experiment with Video[2]

The rapid spread of the use of small format video technologies in the 1970s, worldwide, prompted many questions vis-à-vis the power of this new media. How could the grass roots person effectively employ the power of video in his/her own community for development purposes if they wished to do so? How could video be institutionalized as an accessible communication tool for bringing about change in knowledge, attitudes, practice, or for empowerment? How could video expose the status of women, particularly women with multiple resource needs. It was questions such as these that prompted experimentation with small video cameras in the hands of villagers at the University of Pune. Could video, in fact, be a tool for not only defining and exposing problems, but as a way to interpret those problems to those holding power and control of resources?

The research team, of which we were both members, knew that video was a tool that did not depend on traditional literacy for its use, i.e., people being able to read or write to understand and use it. We were convinced that video could be used by villagers who were visually and orally literate, enabling them not only to have access to information, but to "tell their own story" and "have a voice." The research, which began in 1985, was committed to the use of participatory approaches which widened the scope for incorporating indigenous knowledge, not only in local problem-solving but also in development decision-making and policy. It was intended that the dialogical interaction of development "experts" and "beneficiaries" would shed light on how to minimize "top-down" development. Facilitating message development through participatory approaches would have the potential to empower people to push development and social change in directions that they deemed desirable.

We saw video technology as an important piece of the puzzle in development communication. The experimental phase of the broader exploration of communication behaviors and village level resources and systems, was designed within the basic framework of the Nair/White transactional model for development communication.[3] Nine video prototypes were developed, tested and evaluated. The goal was to see how effective videos produced through participatory approaches would compare with traditional media practices.[4]

Gramin Stree Samasya: Rural Women's Problems

Women's issues were a primary concern and focus of our entire research. During the first year of our work, our researchers and videographers gathered visual and qualitative data on women in the rural villages of Maharashtra. They learned much about the personal situations of women, how they related to their families and the part they played in farming. When the baseline study showed that women's role as farmers was marginalized, there was confirmation that the problems of women were critical. Essentially, their every move was dominated by the males of their household. Certainly, it would be useful if women could better communicate their perspectives and build confidence in themselves in the process.

Interestingly, the problems of these village women in India were not unlike those identified in the World Bank's recent report on poverty.[5] This report points out that women living in poverty experience inequality and subordination in nearly every aspect of their lives. Even in India, women are often looked upon as the "inferior" gender. Girls are not valued and are normally left out of from any opportunity for education. If choices of health are to be made, boys are given priority. In most "depressed" countries women are dependent on men for their livelihood, for social significance, and for cultural boundaries. They are expected to be subservient in all matters. Domestic violence is pervasive. Women who manage to acquire material or financial resources are expected to turn them over to their husbands. A woman who does not comply or exhibits noticeable independence is most likely to be "disciplined" by their man. The root of "gender-based" violence is unequal personal power, and social structures which foster norms that keep women socially, economically and politically repressed.

There is an appalling extent of sex trafficking in poverty-ridden countries. Fathers commonly sell their daughters as they would their cattle. At the same time, some poverty-stricken families are not aware that their daughters are becoming a part of the sex trade, rather they feel that they are being given opportunities to earn an income that will benefit their families. This is currently one of the most challenging problems faced by development functionaries.

Sexual abuse is common among poorer, lower status women. In India, their own male family members may rape women. Sex-ploitation and harassment are committed by males in positions of authority—the manager of a road crew, the moneylender, males in the household of a domestic worker or servant, for example. For the most part, these offenses are not reported. The woman is violated and humiliated, but does not report the crime because of

feelings of self-blame, shame, fear, or the feeling that they themselves are to blame for having "motivated" the rape.

Domestic violence is a frequent occurrence for families stricken
by poverty. Sometimes, women believe it is necessary for their man
to beat them when they make mistakes. They believe that beating
is a sign of strong manhood—the man who beats them will then
"make up" and their love will be improved. Situations that provoke
abuse often arise when men take to drinking to solve their problems. In hard times, when a crop is failing, when men are out of
work, or when resources are nil, men are volatile. They don't want
any "back talk" from their wives or their children. They just want to
be left alone. The natural result is more anxiety in the household,
more disagreements, a short supply of patience.

Women are doubly rejected. They are not a valued "voice" in the
household, nor are their points of view heard in public arenas.
Women often keep quiet in the presence of their menfolk. If they do
show up in public forums, they are not expected to speak. If they
do, they are rarely listened to. Their public role is often expected to
be that of an "observer." Decisions regarding community issues are
men's business. Women are expected to accept them and "do the
needful." In one of the early researches in Maharashtran villages,
the researcher wanted women to become a part of identifying what
they considered critical health problems in their village. He was
visiting households videotaping people as they gave their opinions.
The women would not express themselves. Later, as he was wan-
dering around the village, camera in hand, he found the women
congregated at the well. They were having a lively discussion. They
had definite points of view; they had excellent suggestions and
were more than willing to be videotaped.[6]

Women take Control of Video Storytelling

From the experiences of the research team while gathering baseline data from 23 different villages in Maharashtra, we knew that
women were experiencing myriad problems similar to the ones just
discussed. We had seen these problems and found images to support them as we produced a pilot video, *Hivare: A Village in
Maharashtra*. Two other researches conducted by Arnst (1989) and

Patel (1990) had also given us some insights into the women's responses to video technology. Both researchers had successfully trained women in the use of video to articulate community problems and issues. In both action projects, women were given an opportunity to define and substantiate their viewpoints on matters of concern in the village, via video. The logical next step was to test and validate our understandings by factoring women into the video prototype development and testing, as a part of the video experiment. The stage was set to produce the three video prototypes on women's problems for use in the research. Two of the prototypes were the documentary and the participatory approach.

The concept of "participatory video" was emerging, as well as the process it required. The documentary tape, to be produced by our media team, led by our professional videographer, seemed the right place to start with the productions. Earlier in our study we had isolated the status of village women as a major issue. The team then began work on *The Trapped*. They had a good start, with a large collection of excellent images of village women going about their daily activities, which had been captured while making the *Hivare* video. Content for this documentary was planned on the basis of information gathered from literature on rural women and the knowledge gained from the baseline survey of 24 villages conducted during the first year of the research project.[7] The story line was defined and a script developed. It was to follow a classic documentary style, heavily dependent on narration to interpret images.

This video documentary presented some general but important issues *we* perceived about rural women—the misery of their back-breaking work, lack of educational opportunities for girl children, alcohol abuse by men, the dowry and associated socio-economic problems. That documentary followed the communication specialist-based message design closely, i.e., informing, highlighting events, sensationalizing, and emotionalizing issues with the intention of capturing the attention of an audience. After the "Video Rough Draft" was complete, *The Trapped* was previewed by the entire research team, together with several women from a randomly selected village. Interaction and discussions with these women led to a consensus that the themes were appropriate for the prototype videos we were developing on women's issues. They confirmed the authenticity of those issues defined by the research.

At this stage we were not at all clear as to how a "participatory process" might procede to develop that prototype. In a sense, we had started "where we were," with a communication specialist-based message design philosophy in making *The Trapped*. As the researchers reflected on the review of the documentary with the women and listened to their suggestions, they agreed that it would be feasible to involve the village women in producing a video, soliciting their own perspectives on their problems. Additionally, on the basis of their input, several edits were made on the video they reviewed. Now our goal was to move toward the participatory model of message production.

It was at this point that the "catalyst communicator" concept began to take form.[8] The major role for the researchers, acting as development communicators, would be to catalyze thinking and action among the women as partners in the process of producing a video. It was because of the feedback from women who had seen the documentary, the researchers thought that in a participatory production women could not only identify and explain their own problems but also come up with their own solutions. Our participatory production would involve women at every step of the way including having the women themselves handle the cameras.

For the participatory video process we needed enthusiastic village women, excited about cooperating and who had time to do it. The women needed to feel comfortable enough in their groups to engage in open dialog with researchers and among themselves as well. The language and visual imagination of village women would make the production more *authentic* to other village women. The researchers thought that the participatory communication process would ensure that authenticity. In order to meet these conditions, our researchers would need to visit the villages and interact with the women before selecting villages for the participatory production.

The First Step of the Participation Process

Getting to know the community through home visits, informal group discussions, meetings with community and group leaders, and participation in day-to-day group activities, was where we started. A media specialist and two women researchers paid visits to prospective villages to select a site for the production of the participatory video. Their first visit was to Jakongoan, a village in Ahmadnagar district, about 90 kilometers north of Pune city. Prior to their visit to the village, the team had enlisted the help of a medical practitioner/social worker who had been involved in village development activities for a long time.

The research team talked to women gathered around the village well, visited homes, and established a rapport with them through participation in their activities. The social worker helped the team organize meetings of the village women in the hall next to her dispensary. The researchers engaged themselves in informal group discussions and talked about the possibility of participation in the production of a *videotape* to depict their problems. Although the women showed enthusiasm, they were preoccupied with the important task of weeding the fields and had no time. The team returned to Pune and shared their insights with the entire research group. They then identified a second village to contact.

A week later, the research team visited the next village selected, Punthamba, in Ahmadnagar district some 80 kilometers beyond Jakongoan. Punthamba had a delayed agricultural season and therefore, the women were relatively free to participate. The team enlisted the help of Asha Kendra, a radical grass roots level NGO which had been active in the village for over a decade. Asha Kendra organized meetings of the village women. The idea of producing a participatory video was eagerly accepted by a group of women who had already been conscientized by the NGO. These women quickly decided on a plan for production without consulting other women in the village. This overenthusiasm signaled potential problems of exclusion of other women there. So, the research team again returned to Pune to reflect on their experience and to brainstorm with the entire research team. After considerable discussion they concurred that the overenthusiasm of some women, was likely to negate the principle of participatory processes. So, they sent a message to the village that they did not find it feasible to continue further.

The research team then gained entry into three more villages in Pune district—Lonikhand, Hivare and Sonori. Each of these villages was located within a 50 kilometers radius around Pune city. At Lonikhand, a village midwife helped the team establish contact with the village women. The researchers called on the village sarpanch, head of the village council, and other power holders to enlist their cooperation even though they would not be involved in the group process that might have been jeopardized by their presence. Next, the researchers visited Hivare and Sonori, the two villages that were associated with the earlier video documentary, *The Trapped* and had cooperated with Patel and Arnst in earlier studies. Over the next few weeks, the two female researchers made frequent visits to these three villages, lived with the people for a few days so they might establish purposeful relationships, particularly with the groups of village women. After carefully considering all options, Hivare and Sonori were selected for experimental work.

The Second Step in the Participation Process

In Hivare, the researchers catalyzed several group meetings of women organized by the Mahila Mandal, a voluntary group of village women. Through many discussion sessions on random issues, the women slowly began to focus on their own problems. In each visit, the researchers brought the data gathered on problems of rural women from previous visits to other villages back to the women's group for validation and to establish authenticity. This process of sharing information and reflections of the group reinforced confidence and trust. The Hivare women discussed various issues and problems, not only from their own perspective, but also from the perspective of the women in other villages.

At the end of the second group meeting, the researchers suggested that they could facilitate production of a video message if they would like to share their problems with their sisters in neighboring villages. The suggestion was supported enthusiastically by two women, while others were indifferent. Laxmi Bai, who did most of the talking, directed a pointed question to members of the group: "Haven't you heard our friends from Pune telling us about how our sisters from other villages feel about their problems? We cannot go to them and tell them our views, because we have to work. Already our husbands are angry with us for spending so much time here. Why can't we try to make a cinema and show them in nearby villages? Moreover, it will be fun."[9]

She went on persuading the group members to get involved in the production of the video so that they could share their experiences with the women of the neighboring villages. Some women were still not convinced, but some were. So the research team went back to Pune to continue to brainstorm on what course of action to take next. The women were asked to continue their discussions as well. They were not asked to make a decision but were asked to meet with the researchers for further discussion of the issues. The process in Sonori was similar. Upon the second visit of the researchers, women in both villages agreed to be a part of the participatory video experience.

Researchers were now prepared to initiate the video production process. They mapped out their plan taking into consideration the wishes expressed by the women. In a sense this was a sharing–articulation–reflection–verifying–modifying–rethinking process. The goal now became one of facilitating a dialog among the women in order for them to define and reflect on their own problems in group sessions. Interaction, observation, and reflection about the problems of other women in the village, who were not in the group, followed their discussions.

The researchers found themselves in a constant state of reflection as the women went about their activities. The brainstorming sessions of the research team centered around how to enable people to realize the need for investigation of community problems by themselves on their own. The expectation of the researchers was that such a process would lead to consciousness building, critical awareness and social action. The researchers constructed a *Trigger Tape* to catalyze this process, using visual sequences from *video-taped* images of rural women shot throughout earlier days of the research. Some images were selected from *The Trapped* and *Hivare: A Village in Maharashtra* documentaries. The purpose of the trigger tape was to generate a discussion in the participating groups. The tape did not contain any commentary or music, only a random collection of images and scenes depicting problems as perceived by the media team.

The women in Hivare and Sonori were shown the *Trigger Tape* in subsequent meetings. Before viewing the tape, the women were told that the images they would see presented an outsider's point of view on the problems of village women. As they watched, they would identify which images were not accurate in portrayal of those problems. They were asked to share the way they viewed their own problems. One woman, Savita Bai, a middle-aged mother of two girls and a boy, pointed out that we were wrong to imagine that cooking food for the family using firewood was a problem for women. She noted that indeed, those of us who lived in the city were used to smokeless gas burners or electric stoves. She mentioned that village women were only too happy to cook provided they had enough firewood, grains and vegetables. She insightfully explained that the real problem was "shortages" rather than having to cook for the family.

Water problems were another issue of discussion. Ratna Bai, asked us: "Do you know how stupid the government officials can be? They bring drinking water to us in a tanker. Instead of distributing the water to us they pour it into our dry well. Then we just have to pull it out again."[10] Another woman pointed out that the tape did not tell the "whole story" in the way we depicted alcohol abuse by men (an image of a man lying in the gutter with his liquor bottle beside him). She told us that many men create problems for women and children by abusing them *after* they have been drinking. "If they lie down in the gutter it doesn't matter, but when they beat us up it is a problem." Another woman contributed saying that sometimes her children refused to go to school because their friends made fun of them since they were the son or daughter of a drunkard.

In addition to pointing out how our images were not true depictions, they also discussed many other important problems such as the health of their children and how superstitious beliefs lead to serious health problems. They agreed among themselves that the witch doctors in the village caused more problems than they could solve. The women also wanted the issue of dowry to be elaborated in detail in the tape.

Initially, the *Trigger Tape* was shown to the women in its entirety, but later they asked that it be played over and paused so they could talk about each segment. In addition to the discussion, the researchers conducted free flowing interviews that were audio taped and played back to the women whenever asked for. The primary role of the researcher was that of a catalyst to get the women to discuss their own problems. The *Trigger Tape* led not only to discussions of problems, but also to the decision to produce a participatory tape jointly with the researchers. The researchers concurred that the reason the women agreed to do their own tapes was that they thought that the researchers depicted their way of life incorrectly. As such, they realized that the researchers made a lot of mistakes just like they do, and therefore were not superior to them. The women felt they could do it because our tape wasn't all that good. All of them were excited about doing video to have some fun. They wanted to show it to their friends and relatives in other villages.

Commitment to the Participatory Video Process

At this point, the women made a commitment to work with the researchers to produce the video. Out of the groups who participated in the discussion meetings, a small group of five women volunteered to spend more time for the production of the videotape. Shanta Bai emerged as their leader. They decided to collect more information about their problems from other women who were not present in the meetings. They agreed to come up with more ideas for the production of the tape by the next meeting. The researchers agreed to train the women in using the video camera, operation of the VCR and monitor. The five women from Hivare village were interested and willing to learn so the researchers then began training them on how to use the cameras and other equipment.

Training sessions were not prestructured or sequentially planned. Instead, the video trainer was prepared to work with the women individually or in groups as and when the women had time. The researchers made themselves available in the village and the women came to the researcher when they could manage and learned to use the camera. The researchers tailored the training to suit the members of each group and let them set the pace of learning. After the group gained basic competencies, a camera was left in the village. The women were then asked to document whatever they felt was important about the issues they had been discussing. When the researchers returned, the women had shot about an hour of footage documenting drinking, old women and the creche (infant-tending center), general shots of women and their problems, and agriculture activities.

During this visit of the researchers, the village women gathered together and the images on their tape were viewed. Their reactions were documented. Their video catalyzed further discussion. In succeeding village visits, the women and researchers jointly pieced together the problems faced by rural women through group discussions, meetings and data collection. Collective analysis of issues went on simultaneously with video training, off and on for a six-week period. These meetings helped not only to raise issues, but also to find solutions to problems through collective action.

The following problems were analyzed and solutions generated in these meetings:

The Problem of Education of Girl Children in the Village

It was generally felt that the girls were unable to go to school because they were required to look after their younger siblings, while their parents were away at work. They also had to help their mother cook and clean, and assist with feeding the animals, tending them, driving them through fields, etc. The idea of a night school for the girls was put forward by one of the women. This was discussed and rejected as they would not like their young girls to be out in the night. An old woman, Leela Bai, suggested that she could help look after the infants since she had nothing else to do. The idea was picked up, further discussed, and the women arrived at a decision to establish a creche (care center) for infants. The old men and women of the village would take care of the infants so the young girls could go to school. This was accepted as a good solution.

The Problem of Fuel for Cooking

The women decided this problem could be solved by adopting biogas plants. They knew about such plants from a recently established plant in the village and felt that cow dung, which is an important source of manure, not be wasted for cooking, since it was needed on the fields. Biogas plants would help resolve both problems.

The Problem of Children's Health

The women decided that they needed to make a strong case for the improved health of their families, and subsequently highlight the shortcomings of the belief that the witch doctor could cure their illnesses. The women wanted to stop people from going to the witch doctors, and go to the primary health centers instead. They pointed out that they had to make people understand why that would be better somehow.

The Problem of Drinking

All the women were agitated over this issue. They decided that the only solution was to get together and stop the sale of liquor in the village. They decided that they would all go to the liquor shop, sit in front of it in the evenings, and try to dissuade, even force people not to buy liquor. Eventually, after 3–4 months and after the tape was completed, the women were actually able to get the shop closed down temporarily, through joint action. They sat in front of the shop and would not let people go inside. This movement spread to the nearby villages. This also led to a minor crisis when the village men and shop owners blamed the researchers for this action.

The Problem of Dowry

This issue was discussed at length. Women felt helpless because of the associated social pressures, because it was a norm and a well established custom. They suggested that young girls not marry anyone who asked for dowry. If this decision were implemented, they reasoned, no man would get a wife, and the evil practice would then disappear naturally. This would, however, take courage since all families wanted their daughters to marry.

Production of the Video Message

Researchers took back with them the videotapes shot by the women, and also the audio taped discussions. From this collection of images, they made *Trigger Tape 2* that was a longer version of women's problems. In this tape they incorporated all the view-points of the women and their solutions to their problems. *Trigger Tape 2* was then shown to the same group of village women. Again, they suggested modifications and with assistance from the technical team, shot several new sequences. This process went on for about a week, with the researchers—Punima Prabhu, Nitan Birmal, Shalini Moses and Reva Malhotra—and Shivaji Navarath, the cameraperson. The women then discussed editing and what they wanted done. Three village women sat with the video editor to make decisions on editing.

Finally, the 15-minute edited version was completed with their choice of music, style of presentation, selection of images—all decided by the women, with technical assistance. The women were quite assertive in this process and at times reached fiery consensus. Their tape had special characteristics that reflected the indigenous thinking of the women. The women decided that the first three minutes of the tape should be only images with music because they were depicting normal activities. They thought that the images would be understood by other village women and needed no explanation. In depicting the problems faced by the young girls they asked them directly what they wanted and those specific sequences had been shot at their request. Additionally, they included images of village women talking and giving their own viewpoints.

Several unrealistic image sequences were rejected, for example, pounding of rice and grains. They reasoned that very few village women had to do this anymore because there was a mill in the village. So they included images of women using the mill facility. While editing, they were not satisfied with the length of the marriage scene. They asked the video editor to have the tape pause so the women could better see the bridegroom on his horse. They wanted to dwell on certain images. They suggested this "stop image" approach when they wanted a longer shot. They were also not happy with close-ups and zooms, feeling that they distorted the scene. So, many of these were eliminated from their image selections. They did not like much of the music used in the original videos they had seen, so they requested that new music like that from their own rural instruments be used to accompany their images.

After they completed their video production, steps were taken to pretest it in the village. Women from the village assembled and their reactions were documented on video. The women producers were excited about this showing and the audience showed happy, enthusiastic responses. A long animated, discussion followed. They were pleased to see each other on tape. The researchers questioned the women after they viewed the tape, and from the feedback noted that their comprehension levels were high. They observed that everyone in the larger group joined in the discussions in some way or the other. A few suggestions were made by the pretest group about minor changes in the tape. These changes were subsequently made by the video editor. This final edited version was then ready for testing with other villages.

After this pretest, the video was shown in five other neighboring villages where they knew many of the people. The responses were essentially the same, with women responding enthusiastically and positively. Since this was so, researchers deemed the presentation of women's problems on the video to be an authentic representation. These experimental showings were carefully documented using video. We now had a testable prototype for our research.

Women in Control

If you view the *Trapped* and *Rural Women's Problems* tapes sequentially, the contrast of perceptions of the producers leaps out at you. Village women respect themselves and their sisters. Beneath the outward appearances of their "hard life and abusive life space" they have a bond of dignity. They do not want to be perceived as downtrodden and they value the daily aspects of their lives, even though difficult at times. This pride shows through in the participatory tape they produced.

The *Trapped* was a "poor me" story, while *Rural Women's Problems* was an "I am Me" story. When women could tell their own story, they carefully portrayed the reality of their daily life, without pity or apology. They declared themselves as people who clearly recognized their problems and had ideas as to how to solve them.

And with this small group of involved women came transformation. The brief experience they had with the researchers allowed them a "voice" and a forum for expression that they could define in their own terms. Though not a long-term involvement, they were transformed. They had formed alliances and gained confidence that their points of view were valuable. They had a videotape that proved this. There is little doubt that the video did empower the women for a short duration. The researchers were careful not to create long-term expectations, but new expectations were certainly formed. They did feel proud of the tape and of the contribution they made to the University of Pune research. They felt valued because they had been given full rein to tell their own story in their own way.

At the time of this research, there were budding efforts in India to make video a tool for the "oppressed" to document their situations. CENDIT, SEWA, the Kheda project were getting underway. Our research was a systematic effort to document the processes entailed in genuine participation and be able to make definitive statements about the potentials of participatory video as an essential tool for development, but focusing on the outcomes of the "process" as well as the "product." What we learned from this particular experience in the research process was that women were in a position to be a force for defining, articulating and communicating the issues of their villages. When they are in control of their own "storytelling," they paint a different picture. There is no doubt about this. They believe that they *can* be a force for solutions and courses of action that will lead to an increased level of "well-being" rather than "ill-being" for their families and their village. *And, they can be.*

Notes

1. *The Trapped* was a documentary Video produced by videographer Prem Wadia, as a part of the Development Communication Research Project at the University of Pune, Pune, India. (In Marathi language the title was *He Chaka Thambawayala Hawe*, literally translated as "This Should Be Stopped!") The research was directed by K. Sadanandan Nair, Professor of Anthropology and Development Communication. Shirley A. White, Professor of Communication, Cornell University, was Chief Cooperating Scientist representing the U. S. Department of Agriculture Office of International Cooperation and Development. This chapter is based on one aspect of the experimental phase of the project that tested approaches to message development utilizing video technology.

2. The research base for this chapter is taken from experiences during the Experimental Phase of a six year action research project in Maharashtra, India. The research evaluated prototypes as alternative uses of video technology. A comprehensive, theoretic framework was developed to guide the development of video prototypes, which were tested in rural village settings. Briefly, this framework was a message typology of treatment and function, i.e., documentary, folk, and participatory tapes aimed to persuade, motivate and stimulate.

3. See Nair and White, 1993, Chapter 3. The Transactional model emphasizes the dialectical and interactive nature of both the communication process and the participation process. The major components of the model—source, message, channel, receiver—take on new dimensions as they are continuously shaped by these processes. *Organizational change, socio-cultural change, common goals and conflicting interest* are key concepts of the model. *Teamwork and team-building, consensual decision-making, and enablement* are concepts operating within the participatory communication process (p. 53).

4. Bandewar (1990). Conceptual framework, methodology and preliminary findings of the Experimental Phase of the Development Communication Research Poject.

5. Narayan, et.al. (2000)

6. Patel, (1990).

7. DCRP Annual Report, 1987.

8. See Nair and White (1999) for an elaboration of the catalyst communicator concept.

9. Translated from field notes of the DCRP research team.

10. Translated from field notes of the DCRP research team.

References and Select Bibliography

Arnst, R. (1989). *Participatory Development, Communication, Research and Video: A Discussion and Exploratory Study.* Unpublished MPS Project Report, Department of Communication. Ithaca: Cornell University.

Bandewar, S. (1990). *Message Strategies for Development Support Communication: An Experiment.* DCRP Research Report. Pune: University of Pune

Nair, K.S. (1987). *DCRP Annual Report.* Pune: University of Pune.

——— (1994). *Participatory Video for Rural Development: A Methodology for Dialogic Message Design.* Unpublished manuscript. Rome: DSC Branch, FAO.

Nair, K.S. and S.A. White (1993). *Perspectives on Development Communication.* New Delhi: Sage Publications.

——— (1999). 'The Catalyst Communicator: Facilitation without Fear,' in S.A. White, (ed.), *The Art of Facilitating Participation—Releasing the Power of Grassroots Communication.* New Delhi: Sage Publications.

Narayan, D., R. Chambers, M.K. Shah and P. Petesch (2000). *Voices of the Poor Crying Out for Change.* New York: Oxford University Press.

Patel, P. (1990). *Operationalizing a Participatory Message Development Model: An Exploratory Study Using Video in a Development Context.* Unpublished MPS Project Report, Department of Communication. Ithaca: Cornell University.

White, Shirley A., K. Sadanandan Nair and J. Ascroft (eds.) (1994). *Participatory Communication: Working for Change and Development.* New Delhi: Sage Publications.

White, S.A. and P.K. Patel (1994). 'Participatory Message Making with Video: Revelations from Studies in India and the USA,' in S.A. White, K.S. Nair and J. Ascroft (eds.), *Participatory Communication: Working for Change and Development,* pp. 359–86. New Delhi: Sage Publications.

White, S.A. (ed.) (1999). *The Art of Facilitating Participation: Releasing the Power of Grassroots Communication.* New Delhi: Sage Publications.

9

Magic Roots: Children Explore Participatory Video

*

*Ricardo Gómez**

In 1990 we started working in the province of Ocaña (Colombia, South America) with a group of children aged 9–12, using participatory video as a means of strengthening group interaction and self and social awareness. As a result of the experience over 20 short stories and documentaries were produced on tape by the children, a book presenting their version of local history and tradition was published, and a short documentary presenting the project was produced. Probably the most outstanding outcome of the project was the increased sense of self-esteem gained by the children—their capacity to work collectively as a group, their willingness to train groups of younger children in their communities on the participatory use of video, and sharing their experiences by participating in children's media events in other regions of the country. After the six-year experiment, the 15 initial

* in cooperation with Benjamín Casadiego, Claudia Martínez and Luis Fernando Barón

*participants have engaged in an unending phase of the project:
the expansion of their learning experience.*

"Today is our 11th birthday, we started eleven years ago," says a
young voice from the other end of the table. It is February 17,
2001, and the original *Magic Roots* group members have met in
Bogotá to have a dinner together. This group meets every time they
have vacations—evidence of the strong commitment to the process
they have shared for over a decade. This time, they plan to record
an audiocassette so new members of the group can listen to them
back in Ocaña. The story they will narrate marks a most important
reference point in their lives—a date that many of them will never
forget even though they are far away from home and busy with
their university studies. They left their home to go to university five
years ago. In Ocaña, a new generation of young people is joining in
to participate in the *Raíces Mágicas* experience. They are picking up
the thread of history that "flies like a kite."

The Raíces Mágicas Experience

Raíces Mágicas or *Magic Roots*, is a children's media workshop we
initiated in 1990 in Ocaña, a small city in Northeastern Colombia,
in which, we had planned to use a "participatory" approach from
the beginning. We held the strong conviction that no single formula
could ensure the success of facilitating this kind of approach. Our
intent was to focus attention on local possibilities, needs, and
resources. Coupled with innovation, creativity and a constant dedication to learn from our mistakes, we believed we had the tools to
facilitate participatory processes.

Earlier, in 1989, a local cultural institute that promoted activities
with children and adults in the region organized a literature workshop for children aged 8–11. Some of the kids who attended that
workshop began to form part of a children's oral history research
project, which over time became the core of the *Raíces Mágicas*
group. After an initial workshop a local children's newspaper containing their stories was photocopied every month for local distribution. This eventually resulted in the publication of a single

history book, *The Stories of our Grandparents*, which narrated the history and culture of Ocaña from the children's perspective.

Simultaneously the cultural institute received a video camera as a donation. It was a small home video camera: an insignificant, inexpensive, unsophisticated camcorder. The members of the group now thought they would be able to produce their version of the region's history on video. They would have access to the world of television and mass media. This did not happen. However, what they did achieve was far more important than the mass media success they dreamed of. Between 1991 and 1996, hundreds of stories were written and more than 30 short videos produced by the children in the *Raíces Mágicas* group. Each production exercise was a new challenge—documenting their history, their reality and their imagination. They sometimes produced local news programs, while at other times they made documentaries or reconstructed historical or mythological stories from the region. They used video to exchange visual letters with other children on the continent, and to tape and observe themselves describing their own lives and dreams.

However, more important than the book or the videos themselves, these activities gave the group the certainty that projects could be carried out by working as a team. It also became clear that even though the formal history or the pervasive violence in the region would not be changed by the workshop's activities, *Raíces Mágicas* was having a definite impact on the children's sense of belonging to their collective roots, and on their individual perceptions of themselves. Some of the participants wrote:

The most beautiful thing of this workshop is not to forget the special experiences we share when we are together. All the cool things that happen and that we then remember happily, good or bad. Through them we've learned to be more united. We've learned to laugh and to cry, to dream and to remember and hang out together, understanding each other, helping each other, and agreeing always, even though we sometimes fight. To know and understand we're a group, and that there are or were rivalries between us, that's all normal, and we've learned to overcome them.

Video for Fun and Self-expression

Using video, the children could extend the outreach and scope of their initial literary adventure, this time observing the world through the viewfinder of the camcorder. They were confronted with a new form of production through which to narrate their stories, and new requirements that emphasized teamwork and cooperation. Before the introduction of video, the children had already developed a strong sense of collective action and of planned tasks, and had learned the importance of listening to others.

What we learned working with them was that video was not the product. It was only a pretext, an excuse for something else—a flashy disguise. By using video, we had to reach a consensus about what to do, how and where to do it, and about who would perform each particular task. We had to learn to be individually accountable to the group, and to be collectively responsible for our tasks. We had to reinforce the children's sense of pluralism and tolerance, and to sharpen our tools for collaboration and friendship. We had to learn the basics of participation and democracy. But first and foremost, by working together to make videos, we experienced an excellent opportunity to have lots of fun.

Parents and teachers, on the other hand, expressed their satisfaction in seeing the children gaining in responsibility and group facilitation skills. One schoolteacher, who had two of the *Raíces Mágicas* participants in her class, said that they had become more responsible and displayed more initiative to do things than their classmates; they were better able to plan their tasks and carry them through. Another teacher said he was happily surprised to see that the group members in his class were good students, motivated to learn history and geography, and that they wanted to help others improve as well.

At the same time, this exercise in media production brought about an awareness in the children about how media is constructed. The process-centered approach used in the *Raíces Mágicas* experience helped de-mystify media, allowing the children to develop an informed critical perspective on media by strengthening their audiovisual awareness. Audiovisual literacy has resulted in an increased capacity for critical analysis of media messages, allowing the children to question and minimize the appearance of absolute truth of the local radio, TV and press. In other words, by participating in the process of making their own entertainment and news programs, they learned the basics of visual language, which allows them to have a critical perspective of the mainstream media they are exposed to. They have learned that what is shown on soap operas or the evening news is not necessarily the only valid way to explain the world around them.

This critical awareness has frequently permeated into their families and classrooms, as they are able to explain how messages are constructed and certain choices have to be made to satisfy both form and content requirements. One parent proudly mentioned being surprised by his child, who one night concluded that the kind of camera movements and editing tricks used in a particular news broadcast could easily deceive the viewer.

A product-centered approach to children's media, on the other hand, could possibly reinforce the fetish some have about media technology—preparation of those children who were a part of the workshops to be uncritical cogs in the wheel of media production. By centering on process the *Raíces Mágicas* children learned the basics of media syntax, at the same time focusing on having fun, being organized and a part of a team effort. The use of video and ensuring collective experience have not only enabled self-expression, but has also contributed to the gradual shaping of their identities. The experience not only impacted their individual identity, but their collective regional, national and world identity:

♦ being part of and belonging to the world,
♦ being different and at the same time related to their group mates,
♦ knowing their history and learning about other countries where other languages are spoken and other cultural values shape living,
♦ constructing a sense of citizenship in their particular society, and in our whole planet, and
♦ living a life with high regard for tolerance, multiplicity, difference and pluralism.

Living in a society that has grown increasingly intolerant and violent, based on the notion of extermination of the other, it has been difficult to support a working dynamic based on mutual respect.

We have supported the expression of disagreement through dialog, and the recognition of the importance of feelings, ideas and dreams. It now becomes evident that it is possible to strengthen a group that operates on these ethical principles, basic to the construction of democracy.

Facilitating the Group Process: A Cartography of Dreams

The group facilitator was a key component of the project. He not only had to prepare all the materials, contact the elder to be interviewed the following week, and make sure all worked out well, but he also had to become friends with each one of the children. He visited their homes and shared their dreams and homework, met their parents and discussed the extent of their involvement, revised and assisted each participant's accounts and descriptions, and prepared all the materials for each session. To increase the parents' participation, special history and literature workshops were designed, in which both parents and children participated. All work was done outside regular work and study hours, and nobody was ever paid to do any particular activity, including, for a long time, the facilitator himself.

It is no easy task to maintain the attention of a group of children for a four-month extra-academic program. All too frequently, such programs designed for children follow a logic of intellectual pursuit which is designed for adults, and thus loses the seductive appeal needed to engage young active minds and help gather their enthusiasm. Nevertheless, the *Raíces Mágicas* group, seduced the children from the very beginning, and made them responsible of their own advancement.

The adventure of learning was placed in the participants' hands, with concrete short and medium-term goals, and with assistance provided whenever needed. The children had to prepare weekly stories and interviews, and produce a monthly newspaper with their collection of stories and findings. Later, they had to prepare feasible production schedules, research their topics, and produce videotapes, while continuing to write, learn about other countries, and keep up with their regular schoolwork and other activities.

When treated as autonomous, capable, creative individuals, the children learned to give their best.

In their process of learning, there have been no preestablished good or bad interpretations, only a battery of instruments to enable them reinvent their world and their relationships with others and with themselves. Multiple realities converge, as perceived by each one of the participants. Each one is constructing his or her own map, each one becoming a cartographer and voyager with the benefit of previous and simultaneous experiences, but with autonomous judgment.

A *map of dreams* is a good metaphor, as it not only points out to the existence of other places and peoples, but it suggests horizons, pathways. The group process, thus, became a map that indicated its own way, and each of the children was assisted by the facilitator–cartographer in interpreting their own cues to define their courses, their needs, their paths. There was no single way out of the maze, but multiple ways into the mystery of growing into life; they all had to be discovered, and the teamwork only made the task richer.

The introduction of video to the group was used as an additional instrument to strengthen the group and its participatory action orientation. The institute had had previous experiences of typical authoritarian video directors producing their own pieces with the collaboration of community members, and we were weary of repeating the pyramidal structure of classical crews into the interactions of the group of children. However, care taken in presenting video production as a collective exercise, and the participatory experience gained by the children in the previous activities of the workshop, made it possible to assume the new medium as a tool for teamwork and consensus building. Had the group been inexperienced in collective decision-making and action, or had video been introduced as a technology requiring high degrees of individual specialization, the whole purpose of building consensus and group dialog might have been defeated. But as it was, the challenge of creating stories on video put to test the children's participation skills, and helped deepen their collective information gathering, discussion, decision-making, and action skills.

Video not only became a new tool for self-expression, but a new window to the world as well. With the support of a video lending library in the capital city, a variety of video festivals were organized, featuring alternative and independent video productions from all over the country, from other countries in Latin America, and from the rest of the world. In this way, the children gained access to images from other regions on the map, fueling their interest in the study of other people, places and cultures, and providing them with examples of narratives and audiovisual constructions different from the dominant mass models they had grown used to.

Growing Up

Progress with the initial core group of *Raíces Mágicas* began to attract the attention of other local children and institutions, and we began to consider whether the experience should be expanded. In a few months, four new children's participatory video groups had been formed, and they slowly began to prepare their own stories and to tape some of them on video. One of the participants describes this experience:

As time went by we started to see the changes in our personalities, as well as in our physical appearances. This made us think more maturely and do things better. This was when we started teaching the younger kids all that we've been learning. That was the most beautiful part of all. We remembered our life in the Workshop, when we were like them. We played together and that made it even more fun. They were responding well, because they wanted to learn more and be like us.

A more detailed follow-up on this experience is needed, to assess the quality of the processes the children have been engaged in. Even though the participants speak positively of the experience, it is our feeling that they may be a bit overwhelmed by it. It is very possible that the results of their effort would end up being a mechanical reproduction of what they perceived to be of interest in their learning process, and not an attentive listening and responding to the needs of the children they are now teaching.

Over time, being part of the experience of the group's growing up, from childhood into adolescence, has been most valuable. Their written and taped stories are evidence of the shift in their ways of thinking, in the definition of what interests them, what attracts them, what turns them on. Their increased awareness of their intimate attractions made touching one another different; physical changes and sexuality became an issue of concern. The transformation from their infantile skin into the fragrance of youth, made them regard their initial stories and videos as too childish. While at first they were interested in documenting the history and social reality surrounding them, they became more attracted as they grew older to observing and developing their own feelings and thoughts. Their earlier stories about working children, or about the traditions of the neighboring village seemed less relevant now: they had a growing interest in exploring their experiences of physical attraction, of falling in love, of questioning and negotiating parental authority. Their roles in the group changed, and their sense of priorities and worldview changed with them.

New challenges were met, as word of the group's progress spread, and they received an invitation to travel to the department's headquarters, Cúcuta, to share their experience with another group initiating a similar experience. They lived an adventure away from their homes, visiting the city, staying in a hotel, tasting new foods in a new place, and learned from what others were trying to do with an inspiration akin to theirs. A few months later the group was invited to Barranquilla, a large port city on the Caribbean, which has one of the oldest children's radio projects in Colombia. The children were to meet with them to share experiences, and help them initiate a youth video workshop. This trip was an indescribably rich experience for all the participants, and opened a new realm of experiences to be shared and exchanged.

New Challenges

By 1996 the participants of the *Raíces Mágicas* experience were all adolescents, attending local high schools and slowly getting ready for adulthood. They were an experienced group showing its work, sharing its path with other groups. A series of exchanges were initiated, confronting their experience with that of other children and youth groups working with literature, journalism and media. Their objectives were compared with those of others, and their strengths and weaknesses put to the test.

At this point, their resolve to continue to facilitate the learning experience of new groups of younger children after them is still strong. We, however, feared that they might not be prepared to confront the multiple tasks ahead of them, and that the institute might not have more resources to commit to the expansion of the experience in due form.

The diffusion of the videos produced by the children, the youngsters, was not a priority of the workshop. For technical and contextual reasons, they were shown to small audiences at a time. Their worth surfaced only when the participants talked about the experiences beyond the screen. On the other hand, the expansion of the workshop's experience to include other groups was only a by-product of the process, and we came to think it would be less important than its timely conclusion.

These were the challenges the group faced after six years when they came together, with nervousness and with sweaty hands to begin an oral history exercise. We knew we would also continue to learn with them, sharing their hope that the other children would continue to join this learning adventure.

The Thread of History: *Raíces Mágicas*, 11 years later

At the end of the year 2000, *Raíces Mágicas* received a long awaited copy of a video that was recorded in 1996 by the cinema department of the National University and the Ministry of Education: "*Miro que soy Mirddo*" ("*I See They're Watching Me*"). It turned out to be a totally boring hour-long documentary that tried to tell our story and offer it as an example for schools all over. How could a school follow a methodology so crudely presented and lacking in creativity and expect it to be adopted as an innovative method of education? The ministry had not followed any of our suggestions. The result: a useless video that nobody would ever want to see, nor would they be willing to invest in the proposed methodology. We were disappointed and felt betrayed, to say the least. The video itself represented the communication chasm that exists between government agencies and the people. But the video was useful in that it triggered reflections about the group and its aspirations.

The Dreams of a Video School

1996: A transition year—a time of crisis. The group was opening other frontiers that made them remember their origins and practices and enabled them to "rise again like a kite." In 1996 the boom of local community television was consolidated in Colombia and the first channel was launched via cable in Ocaña. It is strange that in that year when the people in the region started seeing themselves in newscasts and cultural programs, the *Raíces Mágicas* group no longer had cameras and were not engaged in any large video projects. The experience that had started in 1990 was concluded as far as their audiovisual activities were concerned.

Since then we have seen huge changes on the local scene. The neighborhood television marked the beginning of a daily broadcast devoted to provincial news, to opinion programs on local matters, familiar faces, the unsuspected knowledge held by neighbors. Great anonymous heroes emerged from the darkness to shine before us every night. At the same time, television started searching for its own identity in local matters, and began to copy big national productions. It became a coarse twin of the great media power that intervened in our electoral process, deciding for the community and choosing the faces to be photographed. The stations sought advice from consultants outside who had no idea of the region paying at least three times more than they would people internally who understood what could be done within the region. For the *Raíces Mágicas* group there was nothing to do because others were now doing precisely what the group learned *not to do* during the last five years.

1997: A difficult year for the group—complex, without a compass. The group started a project for the region: a video school, thinking of the many community television sets that were beginning to appear in all the municipalities. The strategy of the school was to teach theoretical and practical courses on audiovisual language. The curriculum would include workshops on social and cultural studies that would help to give a framework to these local producers in the very place where they are working, so as to strengthen them in their activities. We thought that the video school would be assisted by the cinema department of the National University, but after many drafts the project died: the University had no financial means to participate in this program. We sought funding from the Ministry of Communications in view of the general television act, but they couldn't provide funding either.

This year's group is coordinating studies throughout the northeast region of Colombia, investigating the legal framework for television, its productions and the community view of these activities. Several members of the group attended meetings in various Colombian cities, meetings in which videos were shown and people asked how the group was organized. The people were delighted by this method of self-expression, the confidence with which things are said, and the emphasis that is placed on the importance of working in a team.

Since 1996 we were all working on a project, a book that systematizes and documents the *Raíces Mágicas* experience. It was published at the end of 1997 with the title, *Raíces Mágicas: A Participatory Video Production.* The methodology for working with children, developed with children was now available for others to try. The book brought together the history of the group, its beginnings, its oral traditions, and its work in video and its everyday philosophy. The launching of this book in December 1997 marked the end of this process, even though the group members found it difficult to believe that they had finished their task. The Valledupar group attended the launching; this was the last remnant of our activities in video.

How Can We Recover What We Have Learned and Lost?

1998–99: Stop. Return to our origins. We were searching for some context within which to continue our learning. We reflected on our past to map a future. The original group was born of the oral literature tradition—making trips to villages with notebook in hand, ready to listen to the people. However, since the advent of the video camera, we were thinking differently about the body. Experiences with yoga have been conducted, and for years we have thought of food as a reference point for the body and spirituality.

Ricardo and Claudia had scribbled notes along the way that connected these thoughts. These were the ideas that finally illuminated a way to recover our work, which the video camera seemed to have hidden. We concluded that we had to return to our origins, begin from a fresh perspective: that of the body that lives in the region and in the city.

We started a workshop on food and self-care. We worked intensely for six months traveling to villages, talking to people about their food habits; we created strategies for changing nutrition habits; we recovered recipes and stories told in the kitchen. A new emphasis was given to the education of the senses, the body. We were understanding food from oral traditions, from anthropology and literature. We were returning to the use of the notebook and the pencil.

That year we also published the results of the national diagnostic study of community television on which the group worked. The book is called *Smoke Signals: Community Television in Colombia*. In the evaluation of this document the need to train the people in charge of these productions became quite clear. The experience of *Raíces Mágicas* was offered as a model for training, an example to be emulated, but the suggestion was not heard.

It is now 1999, heading to the year 2000. The picture of the country is developed: we are at war. Before, it was a hidden war; now it is seen in all its grandeur. How can we think about education as a means to reconstruct the social tissue of a nation at war? The situation in Colombia left many educational programs without any future. The drug trafficking money, the crisis in the countryside, poverty, and the economic crisis all require change. What can we tell these young people? How can we plan strategies for the future? Can small-scale strategies like *Raíces Mágicas* be useful?

1999 is a very important year in this transition that has been lived by the group: from the recovery of oral tradition, paper and pencil, to the entry of technologies, though not abrupt, but bringing with them inevitable and huge changes. From paper and the typewriter, we merged into the computer and the Internet. The computer speeds up the work and makes it systematic; it makes it visible. Utilizing this tool, we finished *Experiences of the Raíces Mágicas Workshop in the Kitchen,* a book that places the group within its local history and marks the end of the "crisis."

The *Raíces Mágicas,* as a workshop experience, is now stable but has transformed into a different experience for children. The group is no longer a base group with a board composed of family men and women regularly holding general evaluation meetings, and with funds for activities. Now, it is formed for a specific experience, at the end of which the group disintegrates to permit the entry of other young people. The latest book is used in schools to teach about the body and nutrition, and is used to provide readings and other cultural views on peoples eating habits and the future. It also presents a very vital approach to ecology. The book has generated interesting teaching practices in the school: it can be used to plan workshops and sections of it can be reproduced for greater flexibility. The book is displayed at the national book fairs, and a US organization working with Latin American children bought 50 copies because they saw the book as providing an opportunity to work on a vital subject. Maybe this time our example will work for other groups; that possibility fills us with hope. Ironically, it is the print media, rather than video, that has enabled us to pass along the significance of this continuing learning experience.

The Challenge of New Technologies

What *can* new technologies do to strengthen the experiences within the group? With the support of the International Research and Development Centre (IDRC), which has its headquarters in Ottawa, Canada, the group participated in a program for using the Internet in Latin America and the Caribbean. This small project put the *Raíces Mágicas* group in the middle of some great processes concerning the use of the Internet, important questions on the meaning of education for the region. The group was given a computer to systematize the experience, to make visible its strengths and its weaknesses, and to speed up the drafting of documents.

New technologies were blending smoothly into the *Raíces Mágicas* scenario. We know that in the beginning there was the Word and writing and that, in order to operate the new technologies, we needed to learn more refined skills than those used for turning on the TV or the radio. However, in the same way that one learns to handle or use an audiovisual language and to focus on an action, we were going to learn to use these tools. This experience harkens back to the teachings of the past. We were looking for old stories, no longer exclusively from elderly people but from people living in the city and the participants themselves who came to share their experiences in the city. We printed a newspaper and we created a web page where we provided instructions for the workshop; we prepared questionnaires; and we proposed lectures and forums. The web page in its turn offered training for schools in the use of the Internet, but the group found that the tool was very little used or rather misused in education and the web page was seldom consulted in the region, even though abroad there was some appropriation of its materials.

It is difficult to balance the wishes of a group that proposes ideas and working methods from inside the educational system, proposing changes for small projects in such an isolated manner that they scarcely relate to the philosophy that guided the group from the very beginning. We can ask ourselves, as many activists and thinkers do, what the Internet can do to improve the quality of life. We have seen that the Internet can facilitate the creation of spaces for dialog, reflection, reading, research, and writing. It is an ideal tool for entering into communication with people and groups, and that is a good thing, since it favors a diversity of opinions and helps in reaching a consensus. Through the Internet one can have an effective means of communication that is less expensive than any other. We can send and receive information at the same time. However, in order for this to happen in a way in which experiences are not turned into a great supermarket of failed illusions, there must exist a big project around the network, and this is what we are trying to create now.

2000–01 brought silences, reflections, communication with other groups, radio, photography, new languages. Fear. We can no longer travel to the villages in trucks as we used to do without the risk of being attacked. There are changes in technology and practices within the group; the country too is changing. Violence seems to be taking possession of every human act, and it is no longer possible to travel to meet with people without giving rise to suspicion. Attacks against people and institutions are now common. Death is the daily diet of a country guided by the means of communication that show violence as a way of life. These circumstances reinforce the work of the group.

The great banners of learning now are to listen to others and to our own bodies, and to meet together to reach a consensus on decisions, however small they may be. When we published *La historia que nos contaron los abuelos* in 1993, we tried to make these stories accessible to the children and adults of the region, all those who didn't know how to read the staid language of historians. Now, however, this language has been revised in a time of war, a language that the media has emptied of content, where one is not invited to discuss but only to shoot.

The group is now facing these challenges, having learned many important lessons from their work with the Internet. They know now that they must participate in the great questions of the region from the cultural point of view, and creatively. The Internet by itself doesn't play any role in the development of a community or in the development of individual skills. Our new effort is to develop a new process, one that interfaces Internet with community radio.

The Years to Come

The crystal ball of the future is the one we have built, not with witches' potions but with our work. From there we can think about the future; we can imagine it. We can say that we have survived our crisis in the midst of adverse circumstances where culture is not indicative of development. In retrospect what saved us was our clinging to our great dreams; the creative revision of our memories. In our dark moments we resorted to what we had been and it was from there that we recovered the "thread of the kite" that seemed to have escaped from us. In all our texts, videos and artistic creations, we tried to imagine creatively, region and a country in crisis from another scenario: from dialog, from creativity, and from the vision of other teachings in the world that tell us we are not alone. We tried to agree on how to construct or deconstruct our legacy: a constant revision of personal and community memory in order to find ways that will lead us back to a place where we want future generations to live.

The challenges are within reach, but they are not simple; the schools must change, internally, not externally, and we have to work under conditions of violence. We face the challenge of creating a new language suited to the current circumstances. The country and the region are facing other harder challenges, and we are touched by these. Government institutions have lost their credibility, and budgets are insufficient to support the few cultural institutions that encourage such activities as those of *Raíces Mágicas*.

Thus, the future of *Raíces Mágicas* is woven from the initial challenges that where mapped 11 years ago without much conceptual clarity, but as an organization strengthened by new technologies and the new communication links that we have been building with other groups in different parts of the world. The group has to take the responsibility to lead and promote through meetings, experiences and dialog. This is its great mission, and this is what the group has not forgotten.

These are some reflections from the dinner table on February 17, 2001 in Bogotá. "Today is our 11th birthday, we started eleven years ago"—truly, a meaningful celebration of the past and the future.   •

Books from Raíces Mágicas:

♦ *La historia que nos contaron los abuelos*, 1993. Fundacion para el progreso de la Humanidad, Bellas Artes: Ocaña, Colombia.
♦ *Raíces Mágicas: hacia una pegadgogia del trabajo participatvo en video con ninos*, 1998. CINEP: Bogotá; Bellas Artes: Ocaña, Colombia.
♦ *Un toque de Laurel: Raíces Mágicas en la cocina*, 2000. Minga and Bella Artes: Ocaña, Colombia.

Part 3

Video That Empowers

10

Arab Women Speak Out: Self-Empowerment Via Video

❋

Carol Underwood and Bushra Jabre

> *19-year-old Samia and her mother own a busy vegetable stall in the central market located in the Egyptian town of Beni Sueif. Though reputed to be shy and reserved, it was Samia who convinced her mother that they should join a group of women with rotating credit so that they could start a small business. Samia's entrepreneurship has brought her much more than money. She has gained confidence in her own abilities and has won the admiration of her father as well as recognition from her community. Recently, she was able to improve the everyday living conditions of her family when she paid to have electricity and water connections extended to her family's home.*

Samia's resolve to change her circumstances sprang from her participation in the women's empowerment training program, *Arab Women Speak Out*, which centers around video portrayals of women who have achieved their goals by overcoming social, economic or political obstacles. In this setting, Samia not only learned how to network and secure social support for both social and economic improvement but was also motivated by the real-life examples of the women in the videos to take action. As she put it: "The women in the video did very simple things that any woman can do. I followed their examples." More than 60,000 women like Samia have participated in the *Arab Women Speak Out* project since it was launched in the winter of 1999.

Project Development and Theoretical Framework

The catalyst for this project was the recognition that media images can influence beliefs and inspire—or stifle—action, as each of us seeks role models to assist us in the process of formulating who we are and how we should or could act in our respective environments. Women in the Arab world are active participants in day-to-day practices and struggles that create opportunities and improve the conditions under which they live. But, women in the developing world in general and the Arab world in particular are often presented as powerless, and passively subordinate to men. Such images of disempowerment are both self-perpetuating and inaccurate. Unfortunately, there are few accurate portrayals of Arab women in the media today. Yet, having worked for several decades at the community level throughout the region, we knew or had heard of many women who, despite many obstacles, were able to effect positive changes within their families and communities. We felt that these women deserved to be recognized and, more importantly, could serve as role models to encourage other women to take action and change their situations.

Therefore, we turned to the social learning theory, originally developed by Albert Bandura in the 1970s and 1980s, to guide the development of the program. Bandura maintained that individuals learn new behaviors by identifying their own strengths when they see those capabilities modeled by others. According to this theory, learning a new behavior is a cognitive process. That is to say, behavioral change involves thinking about the behavior and involves:

♦ Attention to a behavior being modeled by another person.
♦ Retention or remembering the behavior observed.

♦ Reproduction or copying of the new behavior.
♦ Reinforcement or receiving positive results from the new behavior and after testifying on behalf of the behavior or modeling it, seeing the behavior adopted by others.

Compelling role models draw the attention of the intended audience by conversing or acting in memorable ways, thereby giving audience members reasons to emulate them. In an effort to counter negative stereotypes and give women positive, realistic role models whose actions they may choose to duplicate, the *Arab Women Speak Out* (AWSO) project was born. It features the stories of women who are actors in their own right, rather than objects of other peoples' decisions or of others' representations. Given this theory, viewers of the video profiles should be better informed, more knowledgeable, have higher levels of self-efficacy and, therefore, more likely to undertake changes than nonviewers of the videos.

The video profiles would have more of an impact if they were discussed within a group setting, we reasoned, than if viewed individually. Therefore, even though video portrayals of compelling role models were central to the development of the AWSO project, we recognized the need to provide women with the chance to discuss the video profiles and draw lessons from those discussions. We therefore turned to the participatory development theory to inform the process.

Participatory approaches to development are ultimately indebted to the Brazilian educator Paulo Freire (1970), who argued that as men [and women][1] "develop their power to perceive critically the way they exist in the world with which and in which they find themselves; they come to see the world not as a static reality, but as a reality in process, in transformation" (pp. 70–71). The goal of the conscientisation process is to encourage men and women to analyze their circumstances critically, come to understand that the world is subject to change, and ultimately feel empowered to rise to the challenge of changing the world in which they live.

Freire's approach entails "problem-posing education," which encourages and coaxes the emergence of critical consciousness through facilitator-lead group discussions. Since the *Arab Women Speak Out* project adopted that approach, training materials were designed to

facilitate discussions to give women a venue where they could analyze, critically and collectively, the social, economic, political, and
cultural conditions that enhance or diminish their ability to act.
Used in conjunction with the documentary videos, the training
manual provided the framework through which women at the local
level discussed their needs, concerns and opportunities with their
peers. Impact evaluation was planned as part of the project to
assess what difference, if any, participation makes for women at
the community level. We hypothesized that women who viewed
and discussed the video with their fellow participants would be
more likely to act in ways demonstrated by the women in the video
profiles than would nonparticipants or nonviewers of the video.

Participatory Development: Identification of Role Models for the Video Profiles

Conceived by the Johns Hopkins Center for Communication Programs, *Arab Women Speak Out*, was developed in association with
CAWTAR, the Center for Arab Women Research and Training.
Social scientists from each of the five countries that would be represented in the video profiles—Egypt, Lebanon, Palestine, Tunisia
and Yemen—were selected and asked to identify women according
to the agreed upon criteria. A guiding principle of the project was
to profile women who could provide realistic role models for other
women in the region, in line with Bandura's principle that "the
impact of modeling on beliefs of personal efficacy is strongly influenced by perceived similarity to the models" (Bandura 1986: 3).
Studies of elite women can be instructive; however, they are unlikely role models for village and urban women of limited means
who constitute the majority of women in most societies. Therefore,
the women profiled in *Arab Women Speak Out* come primarily from
modest backgrounds. They are women with whom many others
can identify—women whose concerns and priorities are broadly
shared at the grass root level by their societies and whose strategies
for change are compelling and instructive. They have contributed
to the expansion and redefinition of women's familial and public
roles.

Discussions with the social researchers in the Arab region helped us identify the criteria that would guide the selection of women. Specifically, those women were selected, who:

♦ are engaged in social, economic or political change,
♦ are known and admired in their communities,
♦ come from modest backgrounds,
♦ have had limited access to formal education, and
♦ are credible role models for other women.

Given the importance of the family in the Arab world, most of the selected women were married, had children, were of reproductive age and enjoyed mutually supportive relationships with their husbands.

The social researchers were asked to work with local field officers to identify and submit short descriptions to Johns Hopkins University (JHU)/The Center for Communication Programs (CCP) of potential role models. A meeting was held at CAWTAR in Tunisia to review the cases and select women for the project. From the 120 women nominated as role models, 30 women who represented a wide range of social, political and economic activities and who came from diverse backgrounds were selected. Case studies of the 30 women were published in *Arab Women Speak Out: Profiles of Self-Empowerment*.

Ten of the 30 women were profiled in the videos. In their own words, two women from each of the five countries described their life stories and how they were able to change their situations. Their husbands and children also commented on their achievements, from their perspectives. Arab women video/film producers, who worked closely with the social researchers, produced the 10 videos, of 20-minutes each.

The case studies as well as the videos provided the raw material for the development of the training manual. The case studies were analyzed for common factors to guide development of the training modules. A strong sense of self-worth and self-respect, good decision-making and negotiating skills, and solid social support (particularly from the father or the husband) were among the basic features that were shared by the selected women. Training modules were thus designed to enable women acquire these skills through group exercises that guided and encouraged critical analysis of situations and roles. Discussion guides were developed to accompany each video profile and were designed to enable viewers to focus on various aspects of the lives of the profiled women and draw lessons from them. The *Tool for Critical Analysis of Images of Women in the Media* was developed to help participants recognize, and reject, stereotypical images of Arab women, including the objectification of women as commonly seen in imported, and, increasingly in local, programs and advertisements, and was integrated into the training manual.

The AWSO package includes:

♦ Case study publications: Profiles of self-empowerment.
♦ Ten 20-minute videos: Portraits of self-empowerment.
♦ A training manual that comprises eight modules.
♦ A 60-minute composite video that includes highlights from the 10 video portraits.
♦ A Tool for the Critical Analysis of Images of Women in the media.
♦ A 15-minute advocacy video.

The primary purpose of the AWSO project is to share these individuals' stories with other women throughout the Arab region, as well as with development workers, community leaders, policymakers and donors. These life stories have been used to inform training, communication and advocacy and have proven particularly effective in facilitating:

♦ Dissemination of information about those factors which the women feel enabled them to participate in social and economic development.
♦ Dissemination of information about the effective roles women can play within their families and communities.
♦ Promotion of indigenous and innovative approaches to involve women in development programs.
♦ Awareness among policymakers of the pivotal role women play in their communities.

Participatory Training and Project Implementation

The successful introduction and continuation of the AWSO project required a strategy that would focus on building partnerships in the region. Given the complexity of introducing and disseminating the multifaceted package that would require ongoing backup support for trainers, we sought reliable partners who could integrate these activities into their action plans, adapt the project to local contexts, and undertake process and impact evaluations. Of the many agencies identified in the region as potential partners, 25 agencies from 10 Arab countries were interested in integrating the project into their ongoing community interventions. These agencies were already working for the advancement of women's education, social, economic or political activities at the grass roots level and had demonstrated their capacity to conduct training activities with men and women. Representatives from each agency signed a no cost Memorandum of Understanding with JHU/CCP stating that they would support, conduct, monitor and evaluate the *Arab Women Speak Out* training in their own countries.

JHU/CCP provided technical assistance to each organization during the initial phase of the project, and continues to provide technical assistance with respect to impact evaluation as needed. JHU/CCP also provides copies of the videos and print materials upon request. Project implementation was left to the individual agencies and organizations. The process through which the project has been and continues to be implemented demonstrates its participatory nature, which was designed so that it could be fully integrated into ongoing programs in the region, whether by nongovernmental organizations (NGOs), governmental agencies or international agencies.

In December 1998, 25 partner agencies sent their representatives to a regional training session where they were trained as master trainers. Upon their return to their countries they developed strategies and action plans for women's empowerment within local communities and local contexts. The project was integrated into various fields: women's health, education, social action, microenterprise, family planning, legal aid, agricultural production, and combating domestic violence, among others. Master trainers then trained national and local trainers and facilitators to implement the field activities and devised systems for monitoring and evaluation. By the summer of 2001 some 60,000 women in six countries—Egypt, Jordan, Lebanon, Palestine, Tunisia and Yemen—had participated in the AWSO training, all organized by local agencies or agencies working at the community level.

The facilitator-led workshops enable groups of 20 women from similar classes and backgrounds to join together to rethink gender roles, explore new ideas, and acquire negotiating skills. They also discuss the importance of women's participation in social, economic and political life, and benefit from the social support that accompanies expanded networks of like-minded women, and men, in their communities. The central purpose of the training is to enable conscientisation to unfold by providing an atmosphere in which participants can critically evaluate their circumstances and, within that context, decide upon the next steps they will take.

The workshop facilitator's role is not to prescribe action, but to enable action, thus meeting Kiiti and Nielsen's (1999) distinction between a facilitator and an advocate. They state: "An advocate is often driven by an external agenda while the facilitator seeks to understand and help people determine their own agenda." The facilitator organizes the training sessions at a community center, a health clinic or even in the homes of participating women. The duration of the training does not exceed 20 hours. It is up to the facilitator to arrange the training schedule to suit each group.

The training manual is comprised of learning exercises designed to help women strengthen their self-esteem and self-confidence, develop their negotiating, networking and decision-making skills, identify sources of information and support, gain access to available resources, participate in public life, communicate with authority figures and safeguard their own health. Following the training, one woman stated: "the training helped me gain confidence in myself, now I can give my opinion and my husband listens to me. My husband's family wanted to take away the land, so I planted it and stood up to them." Another participant said:

> It changed my life completely, I used to be very negative and did not do anything to help my husband. Now I have opened a store with the money I saved from the household budget and

help him out. He respects me and we share responsibilities inside and outside the house.

The Process Evaluation: From Exploration to Efficacy

At the end of each training workshop, facilitators and participants alike were asked to reflect on the group discussions and give their feedback on the videos, training and media-monitoring tool. The facilitator was instructed to interview those participants who were not literate and to give self-administered forms to those who could complete their own forms. The short questionnaire included closed- and open-ended questions about the usefulness of the training and the project materials—the videos, media monitoring tool and manual.

Findings from the Facilitators' Workshops

Participants in the facilitators' workshops rated the video very favorably with respect to its ability to provide meaningful role models. The central themes of the *Arab Women Speak Out* project were readily grasped by the participants: self-esteem, decision-making, negotiating skills, the importance of networking and social support, and learning about new life options that convey new approaches (see Table 10.1).

Responses to the open-ended statements echo these findings. Participants' visions regarding their abilities were strengthened and broadened by viewing and discussing the video. Many facilitators gave multiple responses to these questions. In particular, they learned that they were capable of making decisions and left the workshop with renewed determination to work in concert with like-minded others. They also seemed determined to express their own opinions and to try to build a sense of awareness and self-confidence among others in their communities. A third of the facilitators noted that they had learned that their responsibilities are not limited to the family. However, since there was no baseline study, we do not know what percentage of facilitators already understood

Table 10.1

Facilitators' Mean Scores in Response to a List of Statements about
the Video (Scale: 0–10)*

Statement	Mean Score (n = 50)
The video didn't give me much insight into ways to improve my life	1.9
I have faced some of the same dilemmas	7.1
The women's husbands are like the men in my community	8.0
The women portrayed in the video are similar to women I know	8.2
The video helped me see things differently	8.2
I learned about new options and how to pursue them	8.9
I think the women in the video can serve as compelling role models for women in my community	9.0
I learned that teaming up with others helps everyone	9.3
I learned effective ways to negotiate with others	9.4

* A score of 10 indicates complete agreement with the statement.

this fact. Some 27 percent mentioned that they learned that they have the same level of responsibilities as men do. In the words of another participant: "I learned that women everywhere have hidden abilities and, if given the chance, their capabilities will take them to higher places, just like any man with similar abilities."

Participants were asked what specific skills or strategies they had learned from the videos and during the course of the workshop that they would incorporate into their own lives. Again, some of the same themes appear: communication and negotiating skills; the importance of developing interdependence within the family as well as with like-minded community members; enhanced awareness of women's rights and empowerment. However, the most consistent theme—and one that runs throughout the responses gathered for this analysis—is a strong sense of newly-acquired self-efficacy and community efficacy. The women who participated in these workshops developed a more lucid vision of their actual and potential roles within the family as well as in the society around them. As one facilitator put it: "I used to think that women's responsibilities ended with caring for her husband and children, but now I understand that women ... can enter into any field, including politics, which I thought was only for men."

Findings from Community Level Workshops

To date local workshops have been held in Egypt, Jordan, Lebanon, Tunisia, Palestine and Yemen. Grass roots workshops are planned throughout the year in the aforementioned countries.

Process evaluation forms received from 38 workshops in Egypt (representing approximately 750 women) and seven workshops in Jordan (140 participants) were analyzed and constitute the findings reported in the following sections. (The open-ended responses are restricted to the Egyptian participants.) Participants rated the video very favorably with respect to its ability to convey the central components of the *Arab Women Speak Out* project (see Table 10.2). In particular, local participants felt the video gave them important insights into negotiation skills and the importance of networking and social support.

Responses to the open-ended statements mirror these findings. The major way in which the video changed their vision of women's abilities was that they came to understand that women are capable decision makers. They also came to recognize that they are able to

Table 10.2
Grassroots Participants' Evaluation of the Video
(n = 750; Scale: 0–10)*

Statement	Total Mean
The video didn't give me much insight into ways to improve my life	3.4
I have faced some of the same dilemmas	8.2
The women's husbands are like the men in my community	8.2
The women portrayed in the video are similar to women I know	9.0
The video helped me see things differently	8.6
I learned about new options and how to pursue them	8.2
I think the women in the video can serve as compelling role models for women in my community	–
I learned that teaming up with others helps everyone	9.6
I learned effective ways to negotiate with others	9.1

* A score of 10 indicates complete agreement with the statement.

find solutions to problems. About one-fifth of the women discovered that they are capable of making important contributions to society. As one woman said: "I realized that women are not merely reproductive engines but important and successful agents of social and economical change."

Many women came away from the workshop with a resolve to take a more proactive role in their families and communities. More than one-third of the participants said they would apply their expanded understanding of women's roles and responsibilities to their own lives. In particular, decision-making and negotiation skills, the importance of working with others, and a stronger sense of self-trust were reinforced by the video and the ensuing group discussions.

Importantly, more than half of the respondents said that they had developed critical thinking skills and, rather than acting quickly in response to an event in their lives, they would first analyze it from all angles. The women clearly came away with a dramatically enhanced sense of efficacy with respect to their own strengths, abilities, and potential contributions to the world around them. Yet, the question remains: "Were they able to act upon their convictions?"

Impact Evaluation: From Efficacy to Empowerment

Process evaluation can document changes in self-efficacy—the belief or conviction that one can carry out a particular act. Impact evaluation, when properly designed, measures changes over time not only in convictions and self-understanding but also in the ability to act.

The impact evaluation survey was fielded in March and April 2001 using a "posttest–only" control group design. The population from which the sample of participants was chosen was restricted to individuals trained before June 2000, thus allowing participants enough time to make changes in their lives. A total of 220 participants were randomly selected for face-to-face interviews (141 Egyptians, 63 Jordanians and 16 Yemeni women).[2] As a baseline study was not conducted, it was necessary to have a control group for comparison purposes. Since AWSO training workshops are ongoing, a comparison group was randomly drawn from the community women—all of whom had been invited to participate in the program immediately before their training commenced. The control group comprised 101 women (72 Egyptians, 20 Jordanians and 9 Yemenis). The experimental and control groups were equivalent with respect to nationality, age distribution, educational attainment, marital status, number of children and work status.

Multivariate analysis, conducted while holding age, educational attainment and country of origin constant, found that 35 percent of participants compared with 17 percent of non-participants started their own businesses. Moreover, 50 percent of participants versus 30 percent of nonparticipants took part in community activities designed to improve social, political and economic conditions. The data analysis controlled for background characteristics and found the higher rates of civil and economic participation, among those who took part in AWSO workshops and those who had not yet begun their training, to be statistically significant.

Life histories of 12 participants, together with a series of open-ended questions posed to all survey respondents provide further evidence of the empowering effect of video. The women presented in the videos became important role models as participants began to rethink and restructure their lives. In the words of a participant named Hanan: "AWSO videos reflect reality, TV portrays fantasy. All women should see the video and learn how they can change their situations. I started a dairy business after seeing what Samia and Atteiyat were doing." Another participant added: "All simple people should see this video as it touches their lives and realities. I learned a lot, we women allow others to dominate us, but once we know our rights and responsibilities, then we can ask the men to stand by us."

One participant noted:

> I used to quarrel with my husband all the time and leave the house. Now I am working on my relationship with him based on what I learned in the program. I have enrolled in literacy class to make up for what I have always missed, and to initiate a new project to earn a living and raise my kids better.

Rather than storming out of the house, as one would expect in a social drama, this woman chose to follow the lead of the women in the videos, who negotiate and discuss their differences with their husbands as they search for a mutually agreeable resolution.

The video presented alternative options women may have even as it gave them the strength to stand by their decisions. As Amal noted, "The video gives ideas that any women can apply immediately. I learned how to win [my husband] over. Now he asks for my opinion. I decided not to circumcise my daughter."

Advocacy Seminars: From the Community Level to the National Level

While community-level implementation is paramount, support from key players at the national level, including governmental, bilateral, international and non-governmental organizations, is vital for sustainability. For this reason, National Advocacy Seminars were organized in Egypt and Yemen to highlight the approach and methodology used in AWSO, which aims to change stereotypes of women in the Arab region. It also aims to sensitize development agencies to the real needs of women by providing for a forum in which they can express their own needs and concerns.

Decision makers at the highest levels, including prime ministers and ministers of planning, health and social development, as well as donor and development agencies attended these seminars. The invited guests watched short segments of the videos selected to highlight some of the barriers women face that could be overcome by policy changes. Several AWSO participants related their own experiences regarding the training and the impact it had on their lives. Naima, who is 14 years of age and from the Upper Egyptian town of Souhag, had been denied the opportunity to attend school. She told the audience that the training had given her new direction, so she enrolled herself in a literacy class and, shortly thereafter, decided to continue her education by enrolling in a regular elementary school. She explained that she does not mind being older than the other students because she has a single focus: to attain her high school diploma and go on to college.

The national seminars made an immediate impact on several governmental as well as nongovernmental programs. For example, in Yemen a representative of the Ministry of Education pledged to make every effort to incorporate AWSO into the literacy program, while a senior staff member from the Ministry of Social Affairs suggested that AWSO should be integrated into the small loans program administered by the ministry under their Poverty Program, which attempts to reach the most disadvantaged women. A representative from the Deutsche Gesellschaft für Technische Zusammenarbeit (GTZ) hopes to integrate AWSO into projects GTZ is currently funding in Yemen in the fields of agriculture, education, health, community development and small business. In Egypt, both the Minister of Health and Population (MOHP) and the first Undersecretary of Population expressed their full support for incorporating AWSO into the 700 Women's Clubs that are associated with the MOHP. This has since been implemented.

Conclusion

Qualitative as well as quantitative findings demonstrate that the *Arab Women Speak Out* project has been successful in responding to women's needs and concerns across the region by providing a venue in which they can explore new options and opportunities. For activists, NGO members, and program planners who would seek to replicate the *Arab Women Speak Out* project, some of the most important conclusions, which could also serve as recommendations for other programs, include:

◆ Media images help women examine alternatives, reassess their self-images, reevaluate their own capabilities, and inspire them to emulate the women portrayed in the videos.

◆ Facilitated group discussions allow women to assess the extent to which the information conveyed and the skills taught are applicable to their everyday lives, thus making the training more realistic and the goals they set more likely to be achieved.

◆ Bringing the media to local communities is very cost effective and can have a tremendous impact on the lives of the people.

◆ Visual images are vital for the initiation of public discourse on gender constructs, which must be introduced in a culturally sensitive manner.

♦ From conceptualization to implementation and impact evaluation, individuals and groups from the intended audience must be actively involved, guiding the process whenever possible.

♦ While local partnerships are imperative for the continuity of activities, it is also essential to gain support at the highest levels feasible to enhance the likelihood that the program will be expanded and sustained.

♦ Building the capacity of local NGOs in implementing, monitoring and evaluating is crucial for the sustainability of interventions and should be built into all development programs seeking social change. The success of field activities not only benefit the communities, but also enhance the efficacy of the agencies and help them grow.

The *Arab Women Speak Out* project gives women a venue where they can—and have consistently chosen to—reclaim their voices. Viewing the videos and participating in group discussions about the issues raised have allowed women to make dramatic changes in their lives. Those changes may seem incremental from the outside, but shifts at the margins can ultimately bring about broader social change, consonant with the vision of those who will live with the unintended as well as intended consequences of social change.[3]

Notes

1. Freire uses the term "men" generically to refer to men and women; we will add women as needed.
2. One Yemeni, 11 Egyptian, six Jordanian facilitators conducted the interviews and were given guidelines to direct the random selection of participants.
3. *For further information*: The case study publication and the training manual are available in Arabic as well as in English. Individuals affiliated with private, public and non-governmental organizations are invited to contact us should they seek to implement this project or to discuss development of a similar project for other regions of the world. Information about this project can be found online at, *www.jhuccp.org*, by contacting Ms. Bushra Jabre *(bushra@aol.com)*, Dr. Carol Underwood *(cunderwood@jhuccp.org)*, or by writing to us at The Center for

Communication Programs, The Johns Hopkins University, 111 Market Place, Suite 310, Baltimore, Maryland 21202, USA.

References

Bandura, A. (1986). *Social Foundations of Thought and Action: A Social Cognitive Theory.* Englewood Cliffs: Prentice-Hall. [A seminal work on the role of cognition in individual action.]

Freire, P. (1970). *Pedagogy of the Oppressed.* New York: Herder and Herder. [A classic in participatory approaches to social change.]

Kiiti, N. and E. Nielsen (1999). 'The Advocate and the Facilitator: What's the Difference?,' in S. White (ed.), *The Art of Facilitating Participation: Releasing the Power of Grassroots Communication.* New Delhi: Sage Publications.

11

Guatemalan Mayan Women and Participatory Visual Media

————— ✻ —————

Padma Guidi

*The Centro de Mujeres Comunicadoras Mayas: NUTZIJ has be-
come a permanent access center for the Internet, multimedia,
video production, and education for indigenous women in the
Departamento of Sololá, the highlands of Guatemala. It was
founded in the winter of 1997 as a social action project. Its board
of directors is comprised entirely of local indigenous women,
with technical advice from Padma Guidi from the United States.
This Center has trained more than 100 women in the past three
years in technical and communications skills, working with the
women to develop curriculums and workshops for their communities. This chapter is an account of the Center's purposes, participatory processes and potentials from Padma's perspective, based
on observation and research.*[1]

In Guatemala, as in many developing countries, there are modern
services in the cities, which slowly dwindle as the area becomes

more rural. Some *pueblos* have battery-operated radios, but most often, the first services a *pueblo* will receive will be electricity. Toilets and running water can come long afterwards. Since the region is so mountainous, the advent of television has been slow and laborious, and is centralized in larger *pueblos* where a local cable company can make a reasonable profit providing such a service. Telephones are very scarce in rural areas, which have relied on the government for expansion. Sadly, it once again proves that the high percentage of poor in the highlands are not considered a body of consumers, but merely a severely underpaid labor pool.

The level of technology available in the village can be illustrated by the following example. A woman in Guatemala, barefoot or in plastic shoes, carries food to the market, or water from the lake, on her head. She might have a baby or a toddler strapped to her body as well. She might have just finished the laundry, standing for several hours in freezing water at dawn to scrub her family's clothes on a rock. Her health is poor, and health care unavailable. If she has two *quetzales* she can buy rice for her family, and if she has two more, she can buy her baby a Pepsi. The Pepsi is what "development" has brought the people, along with the need for extensive dental care and a taste for other cheap sweets.

A Center with a Purpose

The work of the CMCM NUTZIJ is focused on the empowerment of nonliterate indigenous women and bridges the "oral" and the "technical." It brings rural and private voices to a global forum through auto-reflective methodologies for using multimedia, the Internet and video. Using an agenda of "technical empowerment" as an approach to development paradigms enables all participants to experience analytical depths concerning issues addressed, many of which are subliminally introduced. By becoming technically aware and competent, women can now communicate via oral and visual means, bypassing the need for traditional literacy, i.e., being able to read and write.

Upon my arrival in Guatemala to provide technical advice to the Center, my goal was to accommodate any form of access and participation that was desirable to the women. I began by entertaining the interest of anyone and everyone who stopped by the Center. Eventually, several small groups of women were able to commit themselves to the center regularly over a long period of time and form the nucleus of the organization as it is now, more than three years later. The women are all nonliterate or first generation literates, and maintain an identity with their oral tradition, speaking the language and wearing the "*traje*" of their *pueblo*. The technical learning at the Center instigated a quantum leap from nonlinear oral tradition to nonlinear digital empowerment. I facilitated the technical learning, and the women participating were choosing the activities and understanding the process. This approach is rooted in a simple idea that puts "machines" in the hands of women and allows them to create a learning environment on their own.

A major influence on the decision to be in Guatemala was the enthusiastic response of women coming to take advantage of the offer. I was constantly thanked for the opportunity to experiment with hi-tech equipment otherwise unavailable.

Theory Base for this Approach

Snowden's *Fogo Process*, developed in the late '60s and '70s provided a significant part of the theory base for this approach. I introduced the use of video as "dialog" as a problem-solving mechanism (Snowden, 1984). Participants in video workshops, for example, all have "hands on" experience with the camera. "Dialog" or "process" video encourages ongoing interaction in the learning experience, creating an analytical distance and objectivity in the participants and opens up new options for personal expression, addressing issues and solution to problems.

The nature of visual technology is self-reflective: we look at our environment and ourselves. The nature of the research I pursued was also reflexive, the process itself resulting in instantaneous reactions of women participants, both conceptual and physical.

♦ What happens when the women start watching themselves in the viewfinder and on the television screen?

♦ What happens with their communication skills, starting with their contact with me and their interest in the availability of the equipment?

♦ What will they choose to do with the medium: will they make local media or global media, will they choose political topics or cultural topics?

♦ If they've had very little prior contact with popular media and haven't been programmed for a lifetime to frame things in a common visual picture as we who have seen television since childhood tend to do, will they frame things differently, give media a fresh visual perspective?

♦ Will edited videos follow other patterns, reflect another sense of time or sequence, create new effects, and be used in novel ways?

From the start, I asked the participants to tell me what they wanted to learn and we defined our processes as a group. Each workshop took a different form, based on the interests of the participants. As far as possible, I gave them video production tools and asked them to pass those tools on to new volunteers in their own way, helping them organize basic curriculums for the practices they found most useful.

I believe we humans are naturally curious about ourselves, which leads us to look into each other's motivations: for reflections, for clues to the universe, for solutions to sociological difficulties, and for emotional and physical support. In a culture where the silence of women is so predominant and powerful, an interpretation of them by outsiders is not likely to be accurate or of much value. As people and as a culture, their impression of themselves will show us much more about them than we can surmise on our own. For these reasons, the surrender, or handing over of the process is vital to the project.

Women can transform the personal into political. After an initial workshop in camera use, women can take a camera home and practice. In the camera's eye, captured on tape, is the evolution of the choices the woman makes, what she sees, what she thinks is important in her life. It is a record of her voice, her choices, and her perspectives on her own life. She is researching herself and creating her own documentation. We can also analyze some of her influences through the choices she makes: what she shoots, what she frames. Some women choose to tape festivals or church events, some create interviews for each other, mimicking things they have seen or that are part of their public life. Even without televisions in all the homes, people are aware that letting one's image be re-corded is a public event. Ultimately they are making a political statement of who they are and what they stand for.

What is immediately obvious is that the community has a strong identity and way of interacting within itself. Acts of communicating outside the community are thought out and formally presented. Groups of women, usually living in the same *pueblo* or sharing a professional interest (i.e., all teaching at the same school), form groups in which they decide among themselves what they would like to do next with the medium.

Teaching vs Conscientization

The paradigm I have to confront and contradict at every turn is what Freire described as the "banking method" of education, which has a colonial stranglehold on all of Guatemala. "In the banking concept of education, knowledge is a gift bestowed by those who consider themselves knowledgeable upon those whom they con-sider to know nothing" (Freire, 1970, p. 53). Even the universities, boasting the cream of the country's academic crop are taught by rote and respect the hierarchical bureaucracy. Other than in experi-mental foreign schools for expatriates, there are no short cuts per-missible or "active" learning theories exercised in any Guatemalan schools.

For example, when I give an assignment as part of a class in com-puters, and a woman has not worked with me before, she will not take even one step until she checks on my approval for each time she touches or moves the mouse. She shows absolute fear of giving me a wrong answer. Her hand is sweaty and, she can appear physi-cally and mentally paralyzed. This stage can usually be overcome quickly. In a few sessions a person can become convinced that they won't break the machine, which is their first thought and fear (Video interview with Dolores Ramirez Sojuel in *Abriendo Voces*, 1999).

It is natural to feel somewhat intimidated by video technology at first. Women in particular often feel this way initially. Almost all newer cameras now have automatic procedures such as auto focusing, automatic white balance and automatic light setting to make the equipment more user friendly (Protz, 1989, p. 46).

Proving to a woman that she can handle the mouse, or the buttons on the camera, are the first "liberations" with a power of their own. It helps overcome such a big misconception about one's ability to learn—pushing buttons on machines is not difficult. She catches on that she's been "had." What follows is the reasoning that if she can push buttons, then *just maybe*, she is capable of anything. Thus the power of putting technology in women's communities really doesn't depend on a complex methodology, simply access to the technology. Self-esteem is automatic.

The video camera has another significant impact. Not only is it easy to use, but it projects images of ourselves and our neighbors on a television set, where nonindigenous people have never been seen before. Suddenly it has a sociological context, and participants have a place in the picture, they are no longer invisible. When the women make the video in their own *pueblo* themselves, with their own family and friends, they present themselves in a context relevant to their lives. This has empowering positive self-imagery and is a credible documentation of her life for herself, and her community, to be shared with outside researchers and viewers. They have become "*conscientizada*," roughly meaning as "enlightened" vis-à-vis their own significance to their family and others.

When involved in a PVP (participatory video production, my parenthesis) a poor woman takes the camera for the first time and focuses it on one of her women friends, on her house, or on her *barrio*. At that moment, a qualitative shift in her self-perception occurs. The viewfinder, acting as mediation between her and her world, creates an artificial distance. From this distance, women are able to look at themselves and their world in detail: from the way their faces and bodies move to the aesthetic characteristics of their environment. A metaphor of somebody looking in a mirror for the first time could illustrate this phenomenon (Riaño, 1994, p. 164).

Through that mediating and distancing process a self-analysis and analysis of one's place in the world results, stimulating insights, options and choices.

The information, which results from the actual video documentation, can be viewed and analyzed in various ways, the most important being the effect on the producers themselves and their growing self-awareness. With visual mediums, contact stimulates reflectivity of perspective and a desire to create with the tool. After having access to cameras and editing procedures, and watching more productions from other cultures and countries, the producer develops a familiarity with the tool, part of which is a perspective about herself in a greater world, her individual importance, and the strengths of her contribution. What she chooses to impart to the world after that initial familiarity with the medium is established becomes her own thesis on what she cares to share.

An Analysis of Women's "Space"

For most rural women there are no clocks; hours and even days are not exact, and travel is difficult. It was handy to be able to offer a kitchen and a bed, friendly common hospitality, a sense of security and personal interest; our *Centro* provided a practical "space" for the women, an environment for transformation.

> The women need to believe that there is a strong personal interest in them in order for them to open up and share their personal lives and worries. People do not open up as readily if they feel that there is a schedule or agenda that has to be kept (Protz, p. 31).

Because of the supportiveness of the *Centro* and the personal nature of my research approach, I learned about the people in a very feminine way, through gossip and personal histories, and by making individual alliances. I encouraged each individual to use the computers and the cameras and invite friends and interested acquaintances to small introductory groups. From these initial encounters and from visiting various ongoing development projects in the area, the nucleus of the group was formed and evolved.

Putting the control of communication into the hands of women has fringe benefits, one of which is that the focus of the interests and activities of women is mainly nonviolent and apolitical. Political factions turn communication into "journalism" and attempt to use it to sway a larger public into sympathy with its violent cause. Women with cameras from our *Centro* almost never choose to address these issues.

The Centro de Mujeres Comunicadoras Mayas opened its doors to any type of discussion, as long as it was done with cameras to create a reflexive environment and to include the voices of those who don't read or write. I tried pushing buttons by bringing up political issues or asking for war stories and got silence in return. Little by little, I heard the stories, always in confidence. The wounds go deep, and the result is raw fear. Most women just don't want to talk about it.

Topics that women feel comfortable communicating about are plentiful. It is a thrill for a woman to take a camera to her home and community; she is often the first person in her *pueblo* to have access to one. The whole town is happy for her to record cultural or church events. She is encouraged to frequent a center where she can learn about computers and the Internet. Her technical advancement is not perceived as a political position or threat.

"Women's politics" in Guatemala center on local construction of cooperatives, the commercialization of handicrafts and the education and health care for children. They seek "development" on this level, to better their economic stance and make a better life for future generations.

> ...regardless of their origin or culture, women are taught to manage prescribed resources from the time they are children, whether it is so much food for so many mouths, so much space for so many to sleep, so many potatoes from so many fields, or so much money from selling in the market place or the husband's pay cheque. This tradition is invaluable preparation for women as they move into playing their part in sustainable development (Dankelman & Davidson, 1988, p. 162–63).

The laws that changed with the signing of peace have made some of this much easier; indigenous languages and 'traje' (traditional woven and embroidered clothes) are now finally accepted in public schools and this alone has afforded many new opportunities. Illiterate people however do not turn out to vote and most often lose their options to better their situation through legal means.

By placing our examination at the grassroots level and by identifying the various dimensions of women as community, social, and public communicators, a more holistic picture emerges. Issues of women's representation and access to communication resources are linked with their social roles and their participation in the exercise of community democracy and transformation (Riaño, 1994, p. xv–xvi).

Meanwhile, alongside the heavy handed partisan political movements, Guatemala makes use of private international funding to implement individual programs that create services, for example saving acres of rain forest or installing a local ambulance. Women with some training can use videos to learn and educate others through local cooperatives, dealing with topics like health care or environmental issues, often because the funding comes from a private and nonpartisan source.

Through the Internet, a connection is created with a global perspective and the possibility of conducting business in a global economy. Education of women seems benign and nonrevolutionary to the partisan politicians, so the information slips in almost unnoticed, creating a whole new database and many new opportunities within the communities themselves. By creating a space for alternative values, participatory methodology challenges the traditional paradigms of both research and media. Academic research, for example, formerly insisted on quantitative and objective analysis and documentation from the standpoint of an unimplicated observer. Participation with video and digital imagery is immediately a subjective experience, creating documentation on its own, which can be accessed for later analysis if necessary, but stands as a material document of the participants' truth. It also invites multiplicity of truths, a nonlinear and very human reality. Participatory technology threatens the whole economy of media in that the focus is on the production process and the relevance of the message it conveys, rather than how well it "sells." The ultimate use of the material documentation in participatory methodology is the effect of the communication process on the participants themselves—success is not based on ticket sales.

Stages of Empowerment

According to the methodology that evolved from this study at CMCM NUTZIJ, familiarity with the equipment (as described in the previous section) is the *first stage* of technical empowerment. It reaches the largest number of people in various forms, often through workshops oriented around an issue of interest, providing an immediate reflexivity and group analysis. This kind of experimental and often brief contact with media access is the bare beginning to a true participatory experience.

In order to hand over the service to community access, local facilitators, or "*comunicadoras*," are needed. These are local women who are interested in working with more advanced analytical skills, researching and interviewing, and thinking in visual sequences to present ideas. This next *stage* of empowerment also includes technical skills of lighting, sound recording, script writing and editing. The use of the Internet is encouraged: reading articles and taking part in e-mail news lists, finding sources for useful information, and using international contacts for commercialization or education.

In the *final stage*, the work is taken to the public; videos are shown and discussed by participants and other community members. The ultimate is achieved when the *Centro* is co-opted by the community and acts as a public service, the "*comunicadoras*" motivated to create projects to interest and benefit the community. The equipment and methodology is known to a majority of local people. The videos themselves are a resource available to organizations and individuals, the property of the access center. CMCM NUTZIJ, and other communication centers like it, encourage locally created media and bridge it with global information services.

The screening of a video and the relationship of the audience to the video and to the production are the important factors in a truly participatory process. It is at this stage that there is the maximum danger of public confusion with the message of the medium; most people, agencies and educational services, therefore, equate video with what they know: entertainment television, and commercial and political propaganda.

"One-way media" has taught people to be watchers, not participators in the media message. The worldwide media hierarchy has well established and capitalized economically on this passive role. However, the Internet has made media more participatory and interactive, giving the individual more control over content and possibilities. The combination of video and the Internet brings an immediate interactivity and possibility of discussion between people, formerly worlds apart.

Guatemala is particularly reactive to media projects because of its political relationship with media, which makes it extremely important that people be well informed about the participatory process. We are often confused with an activist, antigovernmental movement called "popular communications" that is sometimes aligned with "indigenous autonomy." There is nothing further from the truth. The women may develop political preferences as they increase their contact with the outside world, but here in Sololá they have not yet chosen a political theme for any of their productions. A worse assumption in my opinion, and one too close for comfort, would be to be thought of as a journalist—thereby a spy, eligible for torture and death. Ecological issues are still a major point in spite of the "peace" in Guatemala. Subject to persuasion of a violent nature the government has an armed military force in constant vigil, especially in the Petén where use of rainforests is most controversial.

Development agencies, both governmental and international, see us as a production studio and would hire us to create educational material, but again, strictly from a top-down viewpoint, i.e., what we can teach the poor in order to help them. We have been invited to bring cameras into various forums, but most often with a product-oriented goal in the minds of the coordinators. There are rewards to these types of productions as well. Since men most often lead formal group events, especially in the case of agriculture and land use, having women work as video technicians changes the power structure of the group, profiling women in a role that is as important, or more important than the men in the activity. From a position of professional respect, it's far easier to insert a woman's voice. To create a more participatory space, CMCM NUTZIJ organized workshops and a video about these workshops with small groups of indigenous women. It showed images of their intimate interaction with the cameras that they expected would transmit a concept for interactive video use with more varied groups when locally distributed in the future (Video: *Taller en Dos Sesiones,* 2000).

Process Video

The *process video methodology* that has been developed often results in different types of "video productions." But, the most important outcome is that of the interaction of individuals and their own personal growth that comes about during the process of production. The results of their learning are evident in the video-tapes produced, but the greatest value of their learning is the growing experience that has taken place during the process.

In order to bring this experience to the greater community, I worked with two women, our president, Fermina Chiyal, and a volunteer field coordinator, Juliana Julajuj Hom. We developed a specific workshop for organizations and cooperatives who already had organized groups and wanted to use video cameras to focus awareness on a certain issue or process of their own. Some of these issues could be organizational, such as choosing key actors and maximizing resources; others thematic, such as education or environment, commercialization for artisans, self-esteem and gender roles. The women who designed this workshop had prior experience working with their communities, specifically with women's groups, and acted as the facilitators, speaking in their own language. They adapted the activity to the group, using only small 8mm cameras, a monitor, and a playback of edited material.

Using interactive and participatory approaches to media sometimes creates more work for the facilitator/technician, especially if there is editing planned between workshop sessions. However, the myth that video is expensive proves untrue under these circumstances: when we are not creating a documentary for commercial television, but using video as what I call *Process* video.

Participatory videos are simple to make, inexpensive, and reach smaller audiences. Participatory video need not be of the highest quality. In many cases, the immediate feedback is the most important use of the recording (Stuart, 1989a, p. 10).

Description of a Process Video Workshop

"One way is to use it within a village to show individuals or groups what they already know. Used this way, video becomes a mirror."

Snowden

First Day: The local facilitator, a young indigenous woman, meets with the group, camera in hand, and runs down a list of topics to discuss in the local language. Smaller groups are better because more people will talk. All the facilitator has to do is monitor the time spent on each topic and shoot the video, which does not have to have high technical quality; it is basically disposable. The workshop probably seems a little like a party, and people could be encouraged to voice whatever is on their minds. Since no outsiders are present, the people feel comfortable adopting their normal roles with each other, showing the major actors and the dynamics between them. Formats vary, depending on the group, the topic, and the desired result.

In the office, the facilitators observe and make choices as to what is relevant to stimulate the follow up discussion. These are editorial decisions on the part of the "comunicadoras," young women leaders in the community, and based on their understandings of the process and the expressed needs of the specific group. It could be as simple as grouping sequences according to the topic, cutting out dead parts, condensing and seaming the content together, in preparation for playback at the next session.

Second Day: The same groups replay the video and spontaneous discussion takes place. Then, the CMCM facilitator shows the video again, stops it at a proscribed place in the tape, and records the discussion. At this point, participants are redefining their own positions, understanding better how they relate to each other and to the issues being discussed.

♦ The discussion can start with asking people to express their general feelings and thoughts about what they have seen.

♦ The discussion should focus on the relevance of the video for the community. If people disagree with the video's treatment of the subject matter the facilitator should attempt to clearly isolate concerns and work to encourage consensus. Once the participants have fully discussed their feelings and ideas, the facilitator can direct the group toward discussing visions for change. Again, dyads or small groups would be useful for this purpose.

At this point they can be asked to formulate a presentation of the issues, which again can be videotaped rather quickly at the end of the second day. Each person who wants a copy of this presentation should be able to place their request for me and receive it.

This presentation, along with other data gleaned from watching the long version of the tape, will fulfill all the needs of any research requiring documentation. Local women can translate and interpret the activity for institutional or archival use. When suggestions are made to the community later, they are based on information volunteered and witnessed on a tape that remains the property of the community, created by the community, and a source of pride and motivation.

Evaluating Videos

In interviews asking the women to comment on their experiences with the video cameras, I received a variety of responses, including many noncommittal statements such as, "I like doing it," or "it was fun." On the other hand, women who visited regularly over a long period of time, cultivated an active interest in media use, became fluent in its language, and incorporated it into their lives. For many, contact with the Center stimulated their interest in higher education. At present, two of the center's graduates, Ana Isabel Coc Mendoza and Santa Patricia Guarcax Sicajau, are communication majors at a local university.

Obviously, each production would be individual, and participation would have a variety of definitions. Most important to any media awareness training was to make each woman feel like she owned the video, the process and the actual tape; that she was in control. Coming up with an actual "video" in the end was always less important than the exchange of information during the process of employing the visual format: the camera, the playback, and the subsequent reactions. Incorporating multimedia and Internet communication gave video clips an international forum, resulting in further communication opportunities for participants.

The "'Process Video" methodology places less importance on the actual tape than on the process of developing it. In workshops created to playback the tape and generate discussion and further development of an issue, the tape itself will become archival. To indigenous Guatemalans, concerned now more than ever with "human rights," it is very important that they are part of every decision on how the actual videos are used, who sees them and in what context.

Archival footage is useful to organizations and cooperatives, and to the pueblo and the region, furthering local understanding of the workings of its own society and economy. It is a resource for future productions, for when an organization chooses to use local footage in presentations for fund-raising, local promotions or educational materials. This type of production values content as opposed to the technical quality of the video, and is interesting to a small, specialized audience, mostly local.

Interactive video incorporated directly to Internet interactive multimedia, is a less expensive and more immediate format in which to further effective communication from rural communities to international forums. Used efficiently, it can create a database for projects and individual research, both locally and for the global community.

A Conclusion

If women can take control of a communications center in the same way they take control of the kitchen when they are "tortillando" (making tortillas) or their part of the bay when they are washing clothes, they can incorporate some of their own ways and styles into popular media as it explodes into interactivity. It can bring diversity to the world and pride to the community. The solution to communications access is through the visionaries, the leaders of the community, who can ascertain a trend and have the nerve to take action on decision. When any one of these women starts growing into this role, her peers automatically follow her; and when one of these visionaries is talented, advancing rapidly in communications, she can become internationally active overnight, due to Internet access.

Champions can be identified by looking toward those agencies and staff members who already evidence a predisposition to information sharing, dialogue and people's participation. Once identified, they must be encouraged, provided with recognition and be given access to technical and human resource support (Richardson, 1991, p. 17).

This presents a whole new set of complications, moral, spiritual and physical. When we talk about the results of a communications development project, this perhaps is one of the most tangible. Women make the choice to come out of their communities; often they change their lifestyles. Each one makes her own separate way, her own decisions. She has more information. She can use more modern tools. She sees a wider horizon. She incorporates a communications strategy into whatever life choices she will make.

The result is her process, and it doesn't stop with the end of a video. It doesn't stop when she gets married and has five children. It goes on happening, because it is a process of her growing awareness and continued access to a growing communications technology.

The technology infuses the culture, becomes a defining part of the culture—as it happens in the north, so it will be in the south, soon. All cities have their malls, the same shops, the same products, the same fashions; even language is shared through media. Making the effort to ensure access for all populations makes way for diversity and plurality in expression, values and choices for all.

Note

1. The Centro de Mujeres Comunicadoras Mayas started as an experiment; the people place their interest in it, and it survives. We are seeing that it can generate more self-sustainability, and that the *pueblos* are beginning to think of ways to benefit from technology on their own, with their own purposes in mind. Already we are only one small contribution to a global technological movement that is unavoidable, linking ancient forms of communicating with the future. CMCM NUTZIJ functions as a telecenter, providing information and access to Internet and its resources. (On line) (http://www.interconnection.org/cmcm) Its activities continue to expand local interest in and understanding of its usefulness in accessing educational opportunities, news and information on a global to local level, and a direct international market for the local products, agricultural or artisania. (On line) (http://www.interconnection.org/cmcm/coop2.html).

References and Select Bibliography

Dankleman, I. and J. Davidson (1988). *Women and Environment in The Third World*. London: Earthscan Publications.

Freire, P. (1970). *Pedagogy of the Oppressed*. (1st Ed.) New York: Continuum Books.

Protz, M. (1989). *Seeing and Showing Ourselves: A Guide to Using Small Format Videotape as a Participatory Tool for Development*. New Delhi: Iona Enterprises.

——— (1991). 'Distinguishing Between "Alternative" and "Participatory" Models of Video Production,' *Video, The Changing World*. New York: Black Rose Books.

Riaño, P. (1994). *Women In Grassroots Communication Furthering Social Change*. Thousand Oaks: Sage Publications.

Richardson, D. (1991). *Steps to an Effective Participatory Video Project: From Introducing the Project to Evaluation*. Guelph, OT: University of Guelph.

——— (1992a). *Video Globally—Video Locally*. Guelph, OT: Video Arts Centre.

——— (1992b). 'Participatory Video Projects,' presented at the Canadian Sociology and Anthropology Association, Annual Meeting: Prince Edward Island, 1992.

Snowden, D. (1984). *Eyes See; Ears Hear*. (Supplement to a film under the same title.) St. Johns, NF: Memorial University of Newfoundland.

Snowden, D., L. Kusegak, and P. MacLeod (1983). *The Kaminuriak Herd Film/ Videotape Project, A Case Study*. St. Johns, NF: Memorial University of Newfoundland.

Stuart, S. (1986). *The Village Video Network: Video as a Tool for Local Development and South-to-South Exchange*. New York: Martha Stuart Communications.

——— (1989a). 'Access to Media: Placing Video in the Hands of the People,' *Media Development*, Vol. 36(4), pp. 42–45.

———— (1989b). 'Training and Organizing For Change in India: Video as a Tool of the Self Employed Women's Association,' *Media Development*, Vol. 36(4), pp. 40–43.

———— (1990). 'Video as a Tool in Training and Organizing: Experiences of Video SEWA,' *Development Journal of Society for International Development*, Vol. 2., New Delhi: SID.

CMCM NUTZIJ Video Productions

1998

Comunicacion, Una Esperanza Maya. A collaboration with the women of the Centro de Mujeres Comunicadoras Mayas, an explanation of activities and objectives.

1999

Abriendo Voces. Elena Aguilar Reynoso and Alice Marcia Ennals, on the use of communications in development. 13 min.

PSA for AMSCLAE. 'Autoridad para el Manejo Sustentable de la Cuenca del Lago Atitlan y su Entorno', Santa Patricia Guarcax Sicajau, Claudia Jovita Gonzalez Julajuj and Ana Isabel Coc Mendoza, on the awareness of water use and supply. 40 sec.

PSA for AMSCLAE. 'Autoridad para el Manejo Sustentable de la Cuenca del Lago Atitlan y su Entorno', Santa Patricia Guarcax Sicajau, Claudia Jovita Gonzalez Julajuj and Ana Isabel Coc Mendozas, on the awareness of garbage disposal. 40 sec.

La Educacion como una Luz. Fermina Chiyal and Michele Doncaster, on the education of women in rural Guatemala. 12 min.

La Mujer Guatemalteca y su Mundo Natural. Elena Aguilar and Evelyn Knight, on health, spirituality and traditional medicine. 9 min.

Un Dia en La Vida. Emiliana Aguilar Reynoso and Raquel Clift, an intercultural work. 10 min.

2000

Taller en Dos Sesiones (Workshop in Two Sessions). Fermina Chiyal, Julianan Julajuj, and Padma Guidi, on Process Video, presentation of the methlodogy of video self-evaluation.

Investigacion del Internet. Carmel Vaisman and Sandra Xoquic, on the problems of access and local uses of Internet in Sololá, Guatemala.

El Rescate del Lago Atitlan (Rescuing Lake Atitlan). Produced for AMSCLAE, 'Autoridad para el Manejo Sustentable de la Cuenca del Lago Atitlan y su Entorno', in 3 languages: Spanish, Kaqchikel, and Tsutuhil, to show their environmental work and gain local support.

2001

LOGROS NUTZIJ. Medley of clips from the workshops and events at the Centro NUTZIJ from January to July, 2001.

12

The Struggle to "Empower": A Woman Behind the Camera

———————— ✳ ————————

Sabeena Gadihoke

This chapter discusses strategies for the democratization of video practice from the point of view of a camerawoman and trainer concerned with extending the access of this technology to others. It presents an experiential account of the author's concerns about the meanings created by the camera, focusing specifically on the representation of underprivileged women in the "Third World."

In India, film and video have been elite and expensive mediums of communication. In seeking to democratize these practices, practitioners of "participatory" methodologies have emphasized extending the reach of these technologies to people at the grass roots, assisting them to create their own messages.[1] From the early 1980s, there have been a number of endeavors with community video in different parts of the country.[2] However, many of these have remained isolated initiatives; it will take some time before the underprivileged can truly "tell their own stories." While acknowledging the sentiments of egalitarianism in the goals of "participatory video," this essay would seek to strike certain notes of caution in its actual practice. It would also argue that it is equally crucial for video practitioners who make films about underprivileged to critically examine their own practice.

Empowerment as Goal-oriented Visual Media

In a third world country like India, there has been no lack of "issues" to make films about. Unfortunately the "cause" has often tended to overshadow "form." "What" was said was given far more importance than "how" it was said. Most early documentaries on "development" issues, especially those made by the state sponsored Films Division, were marked by dull and shoddy production values.[3] The advent of television, and later video, brought some changes. Electronic formats were more accessible since they were smaller, lightweight, portable and easier to handle. Video was also less expensive and more importantly, less "visible." It became easier to have access to situations with the camcorder that were not possible earlier, giving rise to a new genre of activist films made on both low and high end formats. This genre was somewhat appropriated by the mainstream in the early 1990s through television news and news magazine programs.

The next major landmark in media in India was the advent of satellite broadcasting and cable networks that displaced the earlier monopoly of the state over television. While these channels have promoted a certain diversity of programming, they are driven by a market which encourages software only if it has "entertainment value."[4] This has marginalized the fund-starved documentary movement further. More recently, technological developments such as inexpensive Digital Video (DV) cameras and computer-based editing seem to have revived some independent filmmaking; this is a trend to watch out for in the future. While the DV revolution may have brought down the cost of production so some filmmakers can now afford their own equipment, the issue of the funding of these video/films still remains unresolved.

Major sources of funding for "development" and "empowerment" oriented videos during the 1990s were non-government organizations (NGOs), government ministries and international aid agencies.[5] Made on a wide variety of subjects from land movements, grass roots struggles and other empowerment initiatives, to rights of women and other underprivileged groups such as the *dalits*, workers and peasants, these videos would broadly be considered as part of "alternative media."[6] This chapter presents an experiential account of the author's experiences as a teacher and as a cameraperson working within this genre of films. It specifically focuses on the need for the democratization of video practice from the point of view of extending the access of this technology to others, as well as the need for an engagement of the image and representation with the issues.

Access and Control for Women

Media technologies are still highly expensive and inaccessible to most living in India. Most of these technologies including video are developed in the first world and for first world climatic conditions. Until a few years ago, a lot of film and video equipment was heavy, bulky and cumbersome, limiting video access to particular groups of users. Of all the processes of film and video practice, the camera has been given primacy, probably because of its power to look and scrutinize. It is also a skill that has excluded women the most. This exclusion is not merely an issue of numbers, but has to do with the deeper structures of power within this field of specialization that culturally codes this activity as predominantly "male."[7]

Like any other discipline, science and technology are grounded in social systems. Technologies do not evolve in a vacuum but as products of societal needs which are often determined in ways that are not as impartial and objective as they are made out to be. Once we understand this, then it becomes easier to see why women were excluded from using the camera. While it was obviously not a deliberate "conspiracy" to keep women out, they were never seen as potential users of the camera.

However, the culture of technology goes beyond light or heavy cameras. This culture encompasses a wide world of skill and

technique, knowledge systems, practices, language and experience. All of these must be negotiated by women. Preconceptions
about gendered roles in the world of technology are reflected in
both the learning environment as well as the workplace.[8] The camera is also considered a male domain because it is "out there" in the
physical environment. It evokes notions of physical strength, of a
particular body type and a work atmosphere from which many
women feel excluded. It is interesting that this gendered segregation of skills also intersects with economics. Camera work is one of
the highest paid technical jobs in the industry.

Teachers and facilitators, irrespective of their gender, are not
outside of culture and many preconceived notions about gender
roles are often reinforced while teaching technology. For example,
women are often encouraged to become editors because it is considered more "suitable" for them. Then there are also the power
dimensions of "knowing" or having technical knowledge. A lot of
technical knowledge is often picked up by men through informal
networks such as male bonding with other technical staff, while
most women get excluded from these channels. Since technical
knowledge bestows a certain power, to be ill-informed is a sign of
weakness, so a culture of silence develops where those who know
less are afraid to ask questions while those who have knowledge
are possessive and further mystify it.

If we believe technology or representation to be inherently
"male," then things do appear to be bleak for women. However, if
we believe that these categories are "cultured" and constructed,
then the potential for change does exist. Women can and do negotiate; they actively resist and subvert structures of power within the
world of technology as they do in any other sphere. The Digital
Video revolution has altered the media scenario in diverse ways,
making cameras both user-friendly and inexpensive. More women
now are operating the camera and mainstream television compa-
nies are at least open to employing women on their payroll as
camerapersons.[9] Trainers and facilitators of media technologies
can aid this process by being aware of some of these issues, by
demystifying this technology, and by making it accessible to those
who have been excluded from its use and benefits. These concerns
are especially significant when conducting training or in participatory ventures involving technology. It is very important to see that
underprivileged women and other maginalized groups get access

to the technology and that already existing structures of power, such as that of the upper castes or the (predominantly male) panchayat in the village, are not reinforced.

The Image and Representation

Do women look at images differently just because they are women? Obviously not, because perspectives do not change overnight by the mere fact of new users operating the camera. Women are not an undifferentiated, homogenous mass of people. There are differences among them and between them; ways of looking are ultimately contingent upon ones own politics and beliefs. Along with control over the technology of video/filmmaking, there is a need for a more critical engagement with images and their construction. This is a major critique of many participatory video ventures where the technology is often treated as a mere tool to be used for "empowerment," without any deeper introspection about the medium and its aesthetics. Video faces this danger more than other means of visual communication because of its user-friendliness and seemingly instantaneous ability to replicate "reality." This often results in the assumption that learning how to operate the technology is enough.

Images are not innocent, existing outside culture and politics. Use of technology must be accompanied by a critical engagement with form. For too long, alternative media has focussed on "issues" and reduced questions of representation to simplistic associations of angles and shot sizes or the number of "talking heads." There has been little challenge to predictable and internalized visual representations. What is needed is a greater diversity of images and ways to present ideas. There is also a need for a deeper engagement with the subjects of our films. Many "development" videos, while professing to empathize with their protagonists, are patronizing in tone and distant from them visually. How do we involve them in the process of representation? Can we work at strategies with which to tell stories that are not our own, with dignity and respect? There are no easy answers to these dilemmas and no perfect solutions to these issues. Yet, they must be debated and discussed so that we question ourselves and our practices constantly.

Some of these questions are highlighted in the recent shooting of a documentary on the Durbar Mahila Samanwaya Committee (DMSC) or the Durbar Committee for the Coordination of Women, a collective of sex workers in Kolkata (Calcutta).[10] Among overlapping categories of working class, lower caste and minority identities, sex workers are a particularly stigmatized group as the state does not provide them with any rights under the law. In representing the complete "other" of the "respectable" woman, they also relinquish all rights to bodily integrity and security by civil society. With a membership of over 50,000 women, men and transgendered sex workers across West Bengal, DMSC opposes trafficking and has set up self-regulatory boards to check it.[11]

DMSC however recognizes the right to consensual sex work and the need to secure both a legal status for the profession and fight the social stigma attached to it. Their long-term political goals are to fight for decriminalization of adult prostitution along with social and political benefits for the sex workers that are available to all citizens of the country.

What are some of the challenges of representation that our film faces? *Tales of the Night Fairies* traces the political mobilisation of five sex workers within the organization who have opted to stay in the profession by choice. In documenting their story of self-empowerment, the film also attempts to discuss the issue of social stigma that both the sex workers and the larger society within which they are embedded, have internalized. Another objective of the documentary is to complicate the understanding of "victims" and "agents." Visibility has not been an issue for the sex worker before as s/he has been represented in popular cinema and a few documentaries. However, these narratives of the vamp or the courtesan have predictable trajectories: the "fallen" woman or the "victim" of exploitation are in the ultimate analysis "punished" for their "immorality" or are "rescued" and "rehabilitated." These discourses and other questions of self-representation have been debated within DMSC and the film is seen as part of this advocacy.

In keeping with some of these objectives, the documentary seeks to challenge the conventional segregation of spaces such as "respectable" neighborhoods and "red light" areas. It does not limit the sex workers to their brothels and instead shoots them in public spaces of Kolkata (Calcutta). The camera follows them to the parks and *maidans*, terraces, the metro, fishmarkets, upmarket streets and the stadiums of Kolkata (Calcutta). Familiar narratives of "rescue and rehabilitation" or of "clandestine and illegal" acts are consciously avoided. For instance, there is no hidden footage of sex workers soliciting clients. The film also seeks to challenge preconceived notions of how sex workers "look." One of the central protagonists in the film, Sadhana Mukherji narrates an incident when she tried to convince a group of sex workers to use condoms with their clients. They did not believe she was a sex worker herself. Sadhana had to convince them of her identity while adding (to us): "After all, sex work is not written on our bodies."

Since sex work was not an experience shared by the filmmaker or cameraperson, it was important that the film give adequate voice to the protagonists. There was a need for "talking heads" which allowed the subjects to express their concerns, while retaining interest and attention. The question of locations was an important one too. Brothels were to be avoided as the camera would put other sex workers at risk by identifying them. Yet there was a need to shoot interviews in spaces where the protagonists would feel at ease. As a consequence, the film has both *verite* sequences and constructed sets where the women were interviewed by transforming their everyday spaces. Many of them "dressed" for the camera and were framed with lights, patterns and coordinated colors. Their "real" issues were highlighted through the language of both "realism" as well as performance. The film also planned to use certain fictive elements in the reconstruction of memory.

Representing Reality

In its efforts to represent the voices of the underprivileged, the alternative video movement in India has relied largely on a certain language of "realism." This tradition has often emphasized a search for "truth" and "authenticity." There are some problems with this approach. It assumes that there is one truth or reality available for depiction. It also assumes a certain notion of "authenticity," often presenting the subjects of the camera as if they were in a time warp: primitive, unspoiled (as opposed to corrupted and adulterated) and a-historical. There has been little deviation for instance from presenting rural India as a spectacle, or from presenting this experience in cliches of poverty, disaster or exoticism. No doubt the rural is all of these and much more; representation must encompass this heterogeneity. We need to come to terms with the fact that the "real" within documentary is also constructed and that the placement and selectivity of the camera alters "reality."

In our efforts to present our characters as "empowered" we also run the risk of representing them as unidimensional and devoid of all conflict and contradiction. In trying to narrate "success stories" we often gloss over inadequacies, problems and weaknesses. We faced this dilemma in the shooting of the video on the sex workers. The formation of the union saw many ups and downs. The protagonists themselves had contradictions. How does one present these complexities without weakening the central theme of their empowerment?

We also often simplify the "real" to mean the "visible." In doing so, we marginalize whatever cannot be seen or depicted through the camera. In an interesting essay on some of the videos made by the Kayapo Indians, Rachel Moore gives the example of institutionalized Kayapo practices of violence against women as an example of some of these hidden from the camera "realities" that are often ignored or not articulated at all.[12]

> Meanwhile, if media exposure comes to mean cultural survival, if ethnographic film continues to maintain that what you see represents the significant rather than the selected, regardless of who has the camera, a less horrific, but still crude hierarchy emerges separating visible people and practices from those that defy visual representation (p. 135).

Apart from the representation of what has been articulated as the "real" there is a world that exists outside of what the camera cannot see, that encapsulates feeling, subjectivity and the unconscious. Can there be more evocative styles of representation that can hint at some of this? Can we for example, include the worlds of fantasy, memory, dreams, nostalgia and loss in our representation of "reality?"[13]

Finally, can there be more experimentation with form that leads us away from videos that "tell" us what to think and instead "allow" us to think? This has been a major critique of alternative media and its representation of reality. Shohini Ghosh responds to this issue by discussing the divide between alternative media and the main-stream.[14] She notes that mainstream media has been considered "bad" because it was popular. Instead of examining why audiences liked popular cinema for example, alternative media has moved away from the audience and marginalized itself further. However, in critiquing mainstream media, it has been unable to offer audiences anything different.[15] As Ghosh puts it, our media practice has lacked "pleasure, fun, desire, variety or irreverence in both style and content." Without becoming clones of the mainstream, can we recuperate some of these elements?

Sharing Power: Can Power be Shared?

Filmmaking is an extremely hierarchical process. Inspite of the entry of small format video, film technology remains expensive and inaccessible to most in India. A problem to be grappled with con-stantly is the power relationships that our films have with their subjects. Most of them are rural, lower class and lower caste, often women who have absolutely no link or connection with the film-maker. How can they be represented with dignity, respect and most importantly, with their consent? This is a complex issue, which is also embedded in questions of representation.

However, we must remember that power is not monolithic and there are gaps and fissures through which agency creeps in. Our subjects are more media literate than we think. People learn very quickly about what the media can do and how they can use it to their advantage. This is apparent on shoots where protagonists pick up what locations are good for the camera or how they should move, or "perform" for the camera very fast. In another essay on the Kayapo experiences with video, Monica Frota points to the Metuktire appropriation of their "popular" image as aggressive and bellicose.[16] Here, she describes how when news teams went to their villages, this tribe would often "enact" this behavior because they understood very quickly that this was what would give them visi-bility. As Sanjay Kak points out:

Secured by convention to reality, many documentaries simply don't survive the search for real anchors to hold ideas down.

Real people and things have their own agendas and their own spaces, and they cannot easily be conjured into performing within the domain of a film idea. (It is possible, but that takes real skill.)[17]

This knowledge often comes not from "making" images but from "viewing" images as an audience, an activity that is often ignored within discussions on representation. It is important to not see the image as created only by those who operate the technology; long before video and even television people have engaged with their own representation in popular cinema for example. We have to bring this "active" audience back to our scheme of things as film-makers and facilitators. Instead of seeing ordinary people only as victims of the media, we have to learn to recognize and respect their right to control and negotiate media messages. Representation is a contested terrain between the filmmaker, subject and audience.

In the ultimate analysis however, while the hierarchies of power between a filmmaker and her/his subjects can be narrowed through mediation, it can never be an equal situation because of the director's final control over representation.[18] Even a first person narrative ultimately represents the subjectivity of the filmmaker who selects, edits and crafts the film or video. One way of dealing with this (and this may not be the "only" or the "right" way) is to engage with the process of filmmaking: to delineate "our" narrative from "their" narrative, to foreground subjectivity, to be aware of the process of filming as "constructed" and to be reflexive about ones own positioning vis-à-vis one's subject. This issue cannot be easily resolved—at least till the time that they can "tell" their own stories.

Stories They Tell

Having made certain points about the hierarchies inherent in our own media practices, there is also a need for caution in over-celebrating the stories that "they tell" themselves. As Donna Haraway points out, that "the view from below is not an innocent one."[19] The "grass roots" is not devoid of power and hierarchy and even when the camera is taken over, the terms of image construction very often remain unaltered. Moore points to some of these problems in videos made by the Kayapo Indians themselves where the camera shoots men in dynamic movement while women are relatively immobile. She asks: "Are these conventions learned from television and anthropologists, or do they reflect the general state of affairs there as well?" Discussing the often naive belief among anthropologists that power relationships get magically transformed at the grass roots, she says:

> This argument assumes that indigenous Video-makers are immune from "hierarchical power structures" and ignores the possibility that image making itself carries its own hazards. Who gets the video camera and how they get it here is a simpler matter than the envy ridden struggle for control of the image and its interpretation that characterize Euro-American film production. Without the barriers of power and finance, of structures of thought and representation which so scuttle our own other worldly ventures, indigenous video performs a theoretical feat for us by taking up the mechanical tools of representation (p. 128).[20]

The other more problematic assumption in most "empowerment projects" through video activism is that grass roots people lack empowerment or voice prior to the introduction of the video, and that video would magically "give voice to the voiceless." As Moore points out, this voice is often just a desire for "reason" and "coherence" as a convenient way of communication for those who believe that empowerment must be directed and driven in particular ways. In other words, it is often our own inability to communicate in any other terms other than our own which leads us to assume that our means of communication are the best for them as well. Part of this problem has to do with the somewhat idealized role that video is assumed to play in the process of empowerment. As Burnett (1995) notes:

> Empowerment begins with the assumption that something is missing either in the community or in people's lives. The intervention of the videomakers, accompanied by the use of the medium on the part of "ordinary" people, supposedly leads to shifts in identity and further claims of self determination ... these claims must be examined very carefully if we are to avoid idealizing video and its effects (p. 229).

Ultimately we must not forget that any venture with participatory video has to be accompanied by other political action. There has to be a deeper socio-political engagement with a community that goes beyond making images. Video or film can only be a facilitator in a larger process that involves other agents.

Conclusion

This essay does not deny the role of video for empowerment: it only questions its perceived impact and problematizes the need for a critical engagement with relationships of power inherent in this process. The role that video can play in the process of empowerment is often oversimplified to merely teaching people how to use the technology. This approach suffers from a lack of critical thinking about images and how they work. It is time that media practitioners and trainers relook their forms of visual expression. In doing this, we have to critically engage ourselves with a diverse range of images, both "alternative" as well as "mainstream." We must also engage in more serious introspection about the various hierarchies present in our own practice and teaching and be aware of these before we even begin to take on the responsibility of "teaching" participation to others. We must develop ways of telling stories of others with the empathy and dignity that they deserve. There are no mathematical formulas to arrive at "participation": the only way is by having a discursive engagement with technology, our subjects and the process of representation.

Notes

1. See White, et al., (1994) and Servaes, et al. (1996).
2. Some of these early projects include the Kheda project conducted in the village of Pij by ISRO from 1975–85 and one aspect of the Development Communication Research Project at the University of Pune in Maharashtra (a participatory video project conducted by Pradeep Patel and Shirley A. White, Cornell Cooperative Extension, Department of Communication, Cornell University in Sonori village, Maharashtra and Washington County, New York in 1987–89). The SEWA video

network in Ahmedabad has probably been the most enduring of these endeavors. Video SEWA was initiated as an outcome of a workshop conducted by Village Video Network, New York in 1984. It teaches nonliterate, self-employed women in Ahmedabad the skills of video, who are then encouraged to make films about their own issues. There have been other smaller video workshops by non-government organizations like Prerna in villages of Badarpur in Delhi during 1991–92. In 1996, a project with community radio was initiated by the Deccan Development Society in Hyderabad. More recently Jan Darshan or the ISCN project opened a community audiovisual training unit in Raipur, Madhya Pradesh (1999).

3. "Development" is being defined here in the sense of an older paradigm of modernity which places faith primarily in economic development. In post-Independence India, this discourse included five year plans, industrial development, the Green Revolution in agriculture and the building of "sites" of development such as canals, ships, big dams and atomic reactors. These were the subjects of early FD films.

4. See 'The Current Crisis and Distant Dreams: Independent Filmmaking in India,' Paper presented by Shohini Ghosh at Dhaka, 1997.

5. This has actually worked to the detriment of the independent documentary movement in India as these funders often dictated the style and format of the films they commissioned.

6. Commissioned by NGOs, these films were not necessarily telecast and are therefore distinct from mainstream television programming.

7. See Paper: "Women's Relationship with Technology in the Media: Some Reflections" in Tankha (ed.), 1995.

8. Gendered coding of language often exists within technical language: Machines are called hardware, there are "hard" sciences vs "soft" sciences and it is always the camera "man" and the light "boy." This "male" world is also depicted in advertisements and other visual representations of technology where women are largely marked by their absence.

9. It will take some time before older patterns change. Most of the women who work in the mainstream television industry are still greatly outnumbered by their male colleagues and many would testify to the same forms of exclusion that have been described here. Those who work in the alternative media often work in spaces that are coded along gendered lines. For instance women camerapersons are more often than not asked to work on projects that are on women.

10. DMSC was set up in July 1995 by a group of sex workers from Sonagachi to focus attention on their own issues and identity. Sonagachi is one of the many brothel areas in the city of Calcutta. The film *Raat Porider Kotha* (Tales of the Night Fairies) currently under production is directed by Shohini Ghosh and is being shot by the author. The insights on the film in this chapter are part of discussions between us about the shooting in Calcutta during December 2000 and March 2001.

11. Like other professional bodies within the medical profession, these boards stipulate some minimum standards for joining the sex industry of which age of the sex worker and their consent are two main principles. (From the DMSC website)

12. See Moore, 1994.
13. In the film, *Three Women and a Camera*, (Directed by Sabeena Gadihoke, 1998) photographer Dayanita Singh discusses her earlier work with sex workers in 1993. In attempting to express some of their issues, she considers doing "posed" photographs with them where they would perform for her camera. She therefore contemplates expressing their "realities" through a form that moves away from "realism." This strategy has also been deployed by Dayanita in her subsequent photographic work on the upper middle class family in India.
14. Ghosh, 1997.
15. This is especially true of many media training workshops for activists and grass roots workers that glorify the "alternative" even if it is didactic, boring and technically shoddy. Experiments with participatory methodologies are often quick to oversimplify the long-term results of their interventions. The following is an extract from a report on a project teaching video to a group of adolescent girls: "The single most significant outcome was the negative reaction to the hours of mindless programming that was being churned out by Doordarshan (National Television) and cable television. When we heard that the girls had shifted their attention from the prime time entertainment programs to the documentary slot on National Television, we took this as hard evidence of the maturing of a critical and aware mind." (This series of workshops were conducted by Prerna, an NGO in six villages in Badarpur, Delhi between October 1991 and December 1992. Extract from Aggarwal and Sarkar, 1995. My personal experience as a resource person at various feminist media training workshops in 1992–93 was that while a lot of time was spent trashing images of women in popular cinema and television shows, not enough attention was given to a much needed critique of "new wave cinema" and its depiction of women. Inevitably the "night sessions" at these workshops were composed mostly of popular cinema and songs!
16. See Frota, 1996. A note of caution: We must remember that a popular representation may not be the most desired representation.
17. "Playing with Flux—Constructing an Argument in Documentary Films" by Sanjay Kak in *Double Take: Looking at the Documentary*. Ed. Raqs Media Collective. Foundation for Universal Responsibility & Public Service Broadcasting Trust, 2000.
18. I also refer here to the access that a subject from the same class as the filmmaker would have to the final product in terms of influencing decisions about representation. Even if this were not overt, it would still be a pressure on the filmmaker that is almost absent in the case of subjects from less privileged backgrounds.
19. See Haraway, 1991.
20. Moore, 1994.

References and Select Bibliography

Agrawal, S. and S. Sarkar (1995). 'Seeking to Reinterpret Education: An Open Journey through Video', in Thankha (ed.), *Communication and Democracy:Ensuring Plurality*. Penang: Southbound.

Burnett, R. (1995). *Cultures of Vision*. Layfayette: Indiana University Press.

Frota, M. (1996). 'Taking Aim: The Video Technology of Cultural Resistance,' in E.M. Renov and E. Suderburg (eds.), *Resolutions: Contemporary Video Practices*. Minneapolis: University of Minnesota Press.

Ghosh, S. (1997). 'The Current Crisis and Distant Dreams: Independent Filmmaking in India'. Unpublished paper presented at the Goethe Institute, Dhaka, Bangladesh, February 5.

Haraway, D. (1991). 'Situated Knowledge's: The Science Question in Feminism and the Privilege of Partial Perspective,' in R. Simians (ed.), *Cyborgs and Women: The Reinvention of Nature*. New York: Routledge.

Moore, R. (1994). 'Marketing Asterity,' in Taylor (ed.), *Visualising Theory: Selected Essays from V.A.R. 1990–1994*. New York: Routledge.

Raqs Media Collective (eds) 2000. *Double Take: Looking at the Documentary*. Foundation for Universal Responsibility of His Holiness the Dalai Lama & Public Service Broadcasting Trust, New Delhi, India.

Servaes, J. (1989). *One World, Multiple Cultures: A New Paradigm on Communication for Development*. Leuven: Acco/Amersfoort.

Servaes, J. and T.L. Jacobson and S.A. White (1996). *Participatory Communication for Social Change*. New Delhi: Sage Publications.

Tankha, B. (1995). *Communications and Democracy: Ensuring Plurality*. Penang: Southbound.

Taylor, L. (ed.) (1994). *Visualizing Theory: Selected Essays from V.A.R., 1990–1994*. New York: Routledge.

White, S.A., K.S. Nair and J. Ascroft (eds) (1994). *Participatory Communication: Working for Change and Development*. New Delhi: Sage Publications.

13

Voice, Visibility, and Transparency: Participatory Video as an Empowerment Tool for Colombian Domestic Workers

Mary Jo Dudley

Yesterday, I couldn't seem to get things done quickly enough despite my rushing all day from the moment I jumped out of bed at 5:30 A.M. After dinner I had put the children to bed with just enough time left to finish the ironing and to hang the last few towels on the clothesline before I would need to go to bed. To get home in time for Sunday lunch with my children, I would need to leave the house by 6:00 A.M. There just never seems to be enough time to get everything done. I had prepared all my employers' meals for Sunday, my only day off. I hung the last freshly ironed shirt in Mr. B's closet, and set the breakfast table before I fell into my bed exhausted. I was just starting to think about what I could cook the next day for my own children when I heard the door open. Mr. and Mrs. B had been at a concert and had stopped for drinks before coming home. I heard the indignation in her voice as she told her friend Berta "you just can't get good help these days—look at how filthy this house is!" I was hoping that if I didn't make a sound she would let me sleep.

Margarita. Get up this instant! I need you to serve us some food right away. We have guests.

I threw on my uniform, and dragged a comb through my hair. I didn't have any extra ingredients in the house since she kept me on such a tight budget, but maybe I could stretch that last can of tuna for a few of those fancy sandwiches she likes...

Oh Margarita, can't you even cook us something decent. These sandwiches look like something the street children eat. This isn't anything that respectable people like us should eat. You domestic workers are more trouble than help. Why is it so difficult to get good help these days?

Excerpts from an interview with Margarita

Based on a participatory video project, this chapter illustrates how Colombian domestic workers used video to explore their personal stories, and subsequently to challenge public stereotypes. Mary Jo conducted and documented the project through a participatory research process.

Domestic Workers in Colombia

Domestic service continues to be a major source of employment for women throughout Latin America and the Caribbean. Historically, domestic work has been defined as that work which is culturally assigned to women as part of their principal social role, that is, caring for and serving "family" members. Domestic service may include myriad tasks such as house cleaning, child care, food preparation, clothes laundering, gardening, house security, and tutoring. In some industrialized areas, these services may be displaced by labor saving devices (washing machines), offered by state sponsored programs (child care programs), or purchased outside the home (laundry services). However, most of these tasks continue to be carried out by women, primarily without payment. It is only when these tasks are carried out for a family that is not her own, that this work becomes "salaried domestic work."

Payment for domestic services does not assure fair remuneration, nor does it eliminate the fact that it is undervalued socially. The existence of salaried domestic workers[1] is due in part to the exploitation of marginalized sectors of society—women, children, the uneducated, and those from rural origins, who are most vulnerable to the pressures of the market and therefore to the whims of their employers. Consequently, domestic workers are frequently mistreated and many are unaware of their legal rights. This began to change during the 1980s as domestic workers throughout Latin America began to organize themselves in the hope of gaining recognition for their contributions to the economy and the society at large, and to advocate improved working conditions and benefits. As a result of these efforts, laws were enacted in some countries to improve wages and to provide some basic protections for domestic workers. One country that reexamined its legal protections for domestic workers was Colombia.

In Cali, Colombian domestic workers learned about their legal rights through a series of free workshops offered by a group of lawyers and social workers from the Center for Assistance to Mothers and Children (CAMC). The weekly workshops provided information on two broad topics: domestic workers' legal rights and women's health and sexuality. During the legal rights workshops the participants discussed their many challenges (legal, social, economic) and how they could address unfair treatment, insufficient wages, and the lack of full employment benefits. Some of the women chose to form their own organization—UTRAHOGAR (Domestic Workers Union)—to advocate domestic workers rights. This loosely organized group of approximately 60 domestic workers decided that through UTRAHOGAR they would find ways to publicly denounce illegal and unfair employment practices. They wanted to challenge negative stereotypes about domestic workers by raising public awareness about the important role domestic workers play in the daily functioning of the Colombian household. To accomplish this they planned to develop media pieces that could be broadcast through Colombian radio and television.

Designing a Participatory Video Project

In my initial correspondence with UTRAHOGAR, they expressed their interest in learning how to make a video to give greater visibility to their situation. They were particularly interested in video because the medium could allow women with low levels of literacy to communicate their ideas to a broad public audience while documenting their own histories. Moreover, video could provide a format for advocating improvements in their lives. Since our interests coincided, they invited me to bring my equipment to Colombia to train them in the basic technical aspects of video production.[2] Together we planned to produce a video to present their concerns to a television audience.

Examining Media Stereotypes

During my first meeting with UTRAHOGAR, I listened intently as the women talked about the potential focus of the video project. One of the project goals was to understand how media creates stereotypes as a first step to constructing a new positive public image for domestic workers. They began by discussing two television programs that portrayed domestic workers as both stupid and evil. In one popular soap opera, the domestic worker character spent all her time trying on her female employer's clothing and makeup, while plotting to steal the woman's husband. In another soap opera, one of the central characters was an illiterate, unintelligent maid from the countryside who never washed herself or her clothes. While the characters in both soap operas were fictional, the women noted that these images fed into well established stereotypes of domestic workers as being dirty, illiterate, stupid, and dishonest women who were not to be trusted with one's home or husband. Consequently, rather than being presented as one who assists her employer with the smooth functioning of her household, the domestic worker was depicted as her female employer's greatest potential threat. These stereotypes were demeaning and created further distance and mistrust between domestic workers and their employers.

They were also critical of nonfiction television productions on domestic workers. A few months earlier, a well-meaning group of feminists video producers had made a documentary highlighting the injustices suffered by domestic workers. Although several UTRAHOGAR members were interviewed for the documentary, they were disappointed with the final edited version since it distorted their reality by portraying them simply as helpless victims.

Since one of the group's goals was to improve relations between domestic workers and their employers, the group decided to begin by addressing inaccuracies in the media. The UTRAHOGAR members agreed that rather than rely on the good intentions of others, they would design a video to present their own stories from a position of strength rather than simply through a plea for compassion. They were committed to developing a piece that would challenge negative stereotypes by highlighting the many positive roles domestic workers play within a typical Colombian household—as cook, counselor, laundress, caretaker, nurse, and tutor to mention a few. They were also excited about the potential for using video and radio spots to contact other domestic workers.

As the discussion ensued, the group identified five main objectives for the video project:

♦ to illustrate the important role domestic workers play in the Colombian household,
♦ to challenge negative inaccuracies perpetuated in the media,
♦ to advocate for better working conditions and benefits,
♦ to reach isolated domestic workers, and
♦ to give public visibility to illegal and unfair employment practices.

Exploring Personal Histories

In order to address these goals, our initial activities focused on familiarizing the women in the group with the video equipment. We began with some basic workshops on camera use and video production. Each interested domestic worker was assisted in videotaping some of the regular activities of the group during their Sunday meetings. At first, some women were intimidated by the equipment and worried that they would damage it. This fear quickly passed as they became more familiar with the equipment. We also set up a meeting of the women with the staff from a local television station to discuss long-term plans for those who wished to increase their technical knowledge. The initial workshops set the stage for ongoing training in the use of the camera.

One of the more difficult tasks began as the group discussed how we would gather information to construct a message. The group agreed that the first step of this process should center on using the video to explore the personal histories of the members of UTRA-HOGAR. They agreed that although they had been meeting regularly, they really didn't know much about the individuals in the group. We approached this task initially as a "storytelling" exercise. Each woman had a story of interest for the group. We agreed that I would continue to guide those who were interested in videotaping, and begin to interview the women using the list of questions drawn up by the group. These questions focused on the domestic workers' personal backgrounds; how they arrived in Cali; how they found employment; how much they earn and how they spend it; the tasks that are included in their daily routines; the number of hours they work; the treatment they receive, including the kind of food they are given, and when and where they eat; their relationships with their employers and their employers' children; incidence of physical, emotional, and sexual abuse; their rooms and uniforms; how often they are allowed time off; the kind of worker protections they receive; their participation in UTRAHOGAR; their relationships with their own families, husbands, and children; and what they envision for the future.

We agreed that in viewing what we were videotaping, we would continue to think about some of the larger questions related to the goals of the project. These were questions like: Who's voices should the video reflect? To whom should the message be directed? What should the central focus of the video be?

Some excerpts from the initial interviews captured the shared sense of isolation, discrimination and hardship experienced by domestic workers:

♦ This work is hard, for example, one has to get up at 6:00 A.M. In my case it's 6:00 A.M., but in the case of some other workers, they have to get up at 5:30 A.M. to get the kids off to school, because instead of the mother doing it, the domestic worker gets the kids off to school. In terms of food—sometimes the domestic worker eats food left over from that served at the table. If there isn't any left, she doesn't eat.

Q: Why?
Because the employer thinks that their employees don't have the right to eat the same things they eat. Their food should be separate. The domestic worker's food should be one thing and the employers food should be something else.

Q: Why?
Because if she is just an employee she shouldn't eat the same things as they do, because their food is fine food. I had an experience where they told us to make a thin soup, to freeze it, and then to take some out to defrost when we were supposed to eat. There were two of us working there and we couldn't eat what the family ate.

♦ The person who gives the orders is the employer. They are the bosses and one has to accept what they tell you to do as if you were a slave.

♦ I had to learn about my new conditions, in a new place with new people. I had to learn a new job, and eat new foods. One can feel bad about that and begin to have another kind of life.

Q: How do you feel about your work?
One feels inhibited because you can't just arrive and be yourself…. They want to push you off to one side. You can't sit in their chairs, or anything of that sort, but rather you have to stay far away, separate. Your dishes are separate from theirs, and that's that.

Q: Why are your dishes kept separate?
It must disgust them, right?

♦ My room is always full of boxes, cases, junk, knickknacks, old mattresses, boxes, old tires. All kinds of junk. They put everything there.

As a result of these interviews, the women recognized the different ways in which employers discriminate against domestic workers through subtle mechanisms to maintain them as separate from the employer and their families. They discussed how these practices (separate dishes, crowded sleeping spaces, limited use of family spaces, mandatory uniforms) were used to maintain distance and difference in terms of social class and race. The domestic workers discussed how these practices reinforce negative self-concepts, as well as a sense of powerlessness and economic vulnerability among domestic workers. In a very real sense these practices were perceived as barriers prohibiting the employee from entering the family realm, enclosing them in a limited physical and psychological space. As we discussed these interviews, the members of the group became interested in understanding how employers view domestic workers and we began to organize interviews designed to meet this need.

My role in achieving this goal was clearly outlined. Since some of the women feared reprisals by their employers, they suggested that I approach employers explaining my interest in understanding the role of domestic workers in Colombian society. It was agreed that employers could be interviewed separately or in groups. My task included setting up and videotaping individuals or informal gatherings of small groups of middle class women who employed domestic workers in their homes. I learned that many employers felt more comfortable with gathering a few friends to discuss how domestic service has changed over the past few years. Some of the domestic workers who had open relationships with their employers spoke directly with their employers to see if I could speak with them, as well. Once I had arranged some interviews with some individuals and groups of employers, UTRAHOGAR met to develop a new set of questions to be asked of employers. These questions were very open-ended focusing primarily on the theme of changes over the past few years. What follows is an excerpt from one of the meetings I arranged with a group of employers.

Q: *How has domestic work changed?*

N: I think that domestic work was much easier before because the domestic workers agreed with their employers' and followed their employers' orders. Now all of them want to study.

Z: Today, they are much more advanced. They want to study.

C: Yes, they want to study and prepare themselves. Before they were paid very little. Before, there wasn't any obligation to give them anything. Now we have to give them shoes, uniforms, and all the other things.

N: And social services.

C: Before we didn't give them all that. We paid the girls very little and they would do all the work. They would take care of the kids. They would cook and iron. Now that's not the case. If the girl irons, it's a big deal. If you tell her, "you have to do this," she will say "no, that has to be done on such and such a day." And so as you can see domestic worker has changed very, very much.

N: Before a family would employ the same person for years and years, because she would always adapt to the customs of the family. Today they aren't interested in that.

Z: Also now they want to go to work in factories. They want to earn more money, and now you have to pay the minimum wage so the cost of having a domestic worker has increased a lot.

C: If she wants to study you have to enroll her in some kind of study. You have to give her vacation days and you have to pay her a bonus when she leaves the job. Before we didn't have any of this. They would work and work and they would be happy to be working.

Z: Before they had their time off on Sunday afternoons and now they want time off beginning on Saturday night.

N: Today they are earning very high salaries, imagine that.

C: And you have to give them their vacation or if you don't give them their vacation you have to pay them extra.

N: Once someone was recommended to me and she called me by telephone to find out about a job and she asked, "tell me ma'am, how much do you pay, and how many people are there? And will I have to do this and that." I told her that she would have to come to the house and discuss it because I don't talk about these things over the phone.

Z: And they ask if you have a washing machine, or if you have an electric iron.

N: And what's involved in the work. They want to know how many people there are (in the household), and if there are children. If there are children, forget it.

Z: They don't like to work if there are children involved.

C: Right, if there are children they won't work for you. The first thing they ask is "will I have to make *arepas* (flour tortillas), will I have to do this?" Before they didn't ask that. She would make a basket of *arepas* for the whole day, and she wouldn't say anything.

Z: And "what time do I have to get up, because I'm accustomed to get up at 6:00 A.M." They don't want to get up early, and they have to be able to watch their soap operas. Before they didn't do that. They would just listen to the radio. Now that's not the case.

C: Now you have to give them their own room, and you have to have everything fixed up in their room. They have to have their radio, and in fact they want their own television in their room. Otherwise, they would have to sit down in the living room with the rest of us or in the hall outside to watch television. You have to let them sit out there to watch TV, or if not, they get angry. Nowadays we have to adjust to what they want, to be able to get a little help. If not, you just make it difficult for yourself, because if you make a mistake, you have to do all the work yourself.

Q: If now you have to pay for uniforms, how do people afford it?
C: You have to figure out a way to do it because there is more work to do in the houses now. The family is larger.

N: But Chela, I think it's the other way around. It is easier for the domestic worker to work because there are washing machines, vacuum cleaners, and everything is easier. These things help a lot.

C: But nevertheless you have to pay them the salary that they are asking for. I've never been in agreement with those who decided that we have to pay them the minimum wage, what they give to any other worker. Domestic workers earn more than any other worker.

Z: Yes, because they have their housing provided. They don't spend money on anything, not even on a bar of soap or anything.

N: That's right. That's why it's more expensive.

C: Look at any person that works in an office—from the salary they earn they have to pay their transportation, they have to eat, they have to dress themselves, they have to buy all the things that one may need. The domestic worker has her room, her food, her soap, her Colgate, her clothes, the uniforms, and her shoes provided. So she can spend her salary "cleanly" (without subtracting those other costs). So she takes this salary out of my house and has everything she needs provided without spending one *peso*. If she's not enrolled in social security and she gets sick, you have to take care of these costs too.

Z: Or if she has a toothache, (you have to take her to) the dentist.

C: Right now I have a great "girl." I've had her for one year. She is a very good worker, and she's very serious. I shouldn't be paying her what I'm paying her now, but I'm paying her 12,000 *pesos* (U.S. $26.32) per month. She does all the work. In fact she came to me without any teeth and I sent her to get them fixed. I've given her vacations, and I also pay her money. But I keep her on because she is good. Above all she is honest. Because today one doesn't pay so much for the work that she may do, but rather for her honesty. So one can go out of the house and be sure that things will be calm. But this is just like a big lottery, sister.

Z: Yes it is.

C: I consider myself as a very good employer.

Z: Me too. They stay with me for a long time. But a year ago I went through about 10 of them.

N: In these times I think it is a luxury to have domestic service.

Interestingly enough, the most open employers still held very strong views about the many advantages provided by employers to domestic workers, and the special treatment they received from their employers. The emphasis of many of these interviews was on the fact that live-in domestic workers were very well rewarded for their work through salaries, in addition to the housing and meals provided by the employers. The employers frequently argued that since they were required to provide the workers with food, housing, and uniforms, those expenses should be subtracted from their wages. They also expressed resentments about being legally required to pay their workers social security and give them paid vacation days. Employers also made strong statements highlighting their benevolent attitude toward employees who often did not deserve their financial support, trust, or familiar treatment.

During the Sunday UTRAHOGAR meetings, we would review the taped interviews and discuss how our project was progressing. During these meetings the group would make an initial selection of interview segments that might be included in the final piece. The Sunday discussions were forums for the women to brainstorm about what they wanted their public image and their target audience to be. Interviews with group members were closely scrutinized for phrases that the women thought expressed what many of them felt. The discussions about the target audience evolved around issues related to power. How could the group negotiate for power? Who holds the most power over their futures? What images and words would have the most compelling effect on their audience? How could the group use the video project to foster a dialog between domestic workers and their employers/policymakers/others?

Challenging Public Stereotypes: Taking the Camera to the Street

In viewing the videotapes of the women's personal stories several important themes emerged. There was an overall agreement that domestic work is hard work that is underpaid and undervalued. It also became evident that many of the women interviewed had suffered physical and mental abuse, and most (over 85 percent) of the women had been sexually abused. Many times the women would ask that the camera be turned off while they narrated their most traumatic experiences. Even today in Colombia, some young men are sexually initiated with the family's domestic worker. One woman spoke of being awoken during the night when her employer's cousin knocked down her door to force her to have sexual relations with him. When she hid in her bathroom, he shot a gun through the bathroom door grazing her arm with one of his bullets. Other, similar stories convinced the group that sexual abuse of domestic workers needed to be addressed.

As part of the group activities, the domestic workers would regularly go to public parks to talk with other domestic workers about their organization. After the discussion of the prevalence of sexual abuse of domestic workers, they decided to take the camera to a park and interview people there about the issue. They felt that the presence of the camera would facilitate a frank discussion on the topic. At the same time they chose to not just passively ask questions, but to use the interview format to encourage dialog. What follows are excerpts from one of those interviews.

Q: We are domestic workers. What do you think about our situation? What do you think about the work we do?

Well the work you do is very necessary for a family. Now you are more or less abandoned, since you don't have any economic security or social security. A time could come when you could be laid off without a single *peso* and find yourselves out in the street, so to speak.

Q: What do you think about sexual harassment and violence against domestic workers on the part of their employers?

299 ♦

This depends very much on the worker herself. Sometimes she can be intimidated by her male employer through conversation—so she will go to bed with him, right? Well then that depends on the girl herself. Because I think that if a male employer says something, or does something, if the girl mentions it to his wife, there could be a solution. This indicates something about the character of the woman.

Q: Yes, but many times the worker is obliged to comply or is threatened. The male employer will say, "if you tell this to my wife, I will do whatever I want, I will kill you, or whatever." It's hard to say with the current situation what might happen, so if a person is forced, how can she respond? Is it always her fault or is it also the fault of the male employer?

I think that it reflects a lack of character on the part of the woman, given that a woman is capable, let's say even if she is being forced or intimidated, of not going along with it. She has to learn how to confront these kinds of situations. Let's say that if he tries to threaten her or something, she should try to gather up a little courage to confront her employer.

The interviews in the public parks represented an important turning point for the group. Until that time the camera had been used to document stories of the domestic workers or their employers. The topic of sexual abuse was not among the original interview topics, but because of the overwhelming incidence of sexual abuse among UTRAHOGAR members, the group became interested in finding ways to challenge what appeared to be an implicit acceptance of sexual abuse of domestic workers. The exchange in the park convinced the group that sexual abuse was an issue that could be addressed through a public dialog, using the video camera as a catalyst for engaging strangers in a discussion. The exchange illustrated how a very private issue was successfully introduced into the public realm. Where such a discussion might not take place in a simple face-to-face encounter, when faced with a camera that was running the interviewees responded. Through this public dialog about violence against women, the group gained important insights about how they are perceived by the general public.

They were enraged when one man suggested that the domestic worker go to her female employer for support for if she were to do that, it was highly probable that she would lose her job. The other suggestion—"to gather a little courage to confront her employer"— again ignores the fact that her livelihood depends on keeping her job. They were most upset about the assumption that sexual harassment is a reflection of the "character" of the domestic worker, implying an implicit moral deficiency. After analyzing these interviews the group became interested in going to more public places to interview people to ascertain their view of domestic workers.

As we reviewed more of the tapes, the women became increasingly concerned that the interviews with UTRAHOGAR members were too negative and didn't focus enough on how the women would like to change their situation. Most of the interviews clearly addressed the problems domestic workers encounter in their daily lives, but didn't focus enough on ideas for improving their futures. They also discussed how they could express themselves in a persuasive manner and use images to convince others to treat domestic workers with more respect.

The process for selecting segments for our first version of the video was often difficult. Even so, the women involved expressed their point of view that the video project opened a space for dialog and made the situation of the domestic worker more visible. In one review session the group unanimously selected the words of one member of the group who at 55 years of age had spent 42 years as a domestic worker:

> I also think it's important for us to be united in our struggle— because if we can't be united we won't be able to accomplish anything for improving this situation. As time goes by, this work will not disappear even though they say that this is inferior work. For me all work is important. All work is dignified. It's not the habit that makes the nun. It's not the position that determines the height of the person. One has to be very careful about this.
>
> In a very tall building with 40 or 50 floors there are some big columns. But there is also a little switch to turn on the electricity. This switch is a tiny, small thing, but it's important. If it weren't there you wouldn't be able to turn on the electricity. So it has its own importance. The problem is that our work is important but it isn't appropriately valued, and our employers don't appreciate its true worth. Some don't value our work because of their ignorance, and others because it's not to their

benefit. Because to the extent that they give our work its due importance, and for those of us who are educated, we all know that we have to claim what's rightfully ours. And that's why many employers, not all, don't want us to improve our situation and they don't agree that we should be treated as the people we are.

In many houses the real "lady of the house" is the domestic worker. Everything in the house revolves around her—the ironing, the washing, the meals, the children. In fact in some houses, the mother of the children isn't really involved in bringing them up. The domestic worker bathes them, feeds them, takes them to school, and puts them to bed while their real mother only sees them about once a week. When the child wakes up in the morning, it is the domestic worker who wakes her up, dresses her, feeds her, and takes her to the bus. When he or she comes home from school it is the domestic worker who is there at the door to welcome her. When the child has to go out again, it is the domestic worker who will take her out because her mother is already out on the town somewhere. When the mother arrives home at night, the child is already asleep. Many times we are the ones who have to give the children their goodnight kisses. So we are the real "ladies" of the house. For some women, it's because they work, and that's O.K. For others who don't work, it's because they have their friends, their tennis games, the parties at their clubs, and their little *canasta* games. They don't understand anything about how the house works. Consequently, we have to take care of everything.

So one would think that we deserve to receive some recognition for that. And that is something that has never happened. Many *señoras* don't recognize that. They scold us and if we ask for anything, they tell us that we have no right to demand anything because we are just the servants. And for that reason many domestic workers feel humiliated, they feel bad, and they say that they are embarrassed to admit that they work as domestic workers. That has never happened to me. One time I went to a meeting that was full of doctors and professionals and I was the only domestic worker there, but I have never felt that I was less than anyone else. Working in a family's house I feel as dignified as the wife of the governor or the president, because just as they are people, I am also a person. So I have never felt less than anyone else, and I tell you, I never have had problems. And if any person comes to me with "but ...", I say, no, ma'am. If you are a person with any common sense you will know that we are all human beings. We are all worth something. We all have some importance in this life.

Understanding Power Structures

Throughout the project the group discussion included reflections on how existing power structures can be challenged by first identifying the nature and structure of power. For example, governmental representatives are powerful because they can develop policies and laws. The media professional is powerful because s/he has access to the means for influencing public opinion. The domestic worker is powerful because she can maintain or disrupt the smooth functioning of the household. By understanding the nature of power structures and their pressure points, individuals can develop strategies to influence others. In this case, the domestic workers wanted to challenge stereotypes presented in the media by presenting images that reflect their lives. By presenting their situation in a more realistic light, they hoped to advocate improved wages and labor protections.

Knowledge Gained through this Participatory Video Process

This project allowed us to gain a deeper understanding of the roles, responsibilities and dilemmas faced by domestic workers in Colombia. During the three months of the project, we interviewed most of the 60 members of the group, several of their children, 30 employers, several children of employers, legislators, lawyers, doctors, mechanics, taxi drivers, teachers, and many domestic workers who weren't part of any formal organization. The videotaped interviews provided a great deal of information about how domestic workers view themselves, how they are viewed by their employers, and how they are viewed by Colombian society in general.

Throughout the process of developing a video, the group discussed how they could contest negative stereotypes of domestic workers. Consequently, the group members became empowered in several ways.

Perhaps one of the most tangible results of these efforts was learning about the tools of mass media, in particular the use of video and television scripts to construct a message. Before the interviews began, the group examined how domestic workers are portrayed through audio, print and electronic media. Domestic workers are frequently the central figures in many popular radio and television soap operas, and very often the domestic worker is characterized as a husband stealer, a child thief, a homewrecker, or a morally inferior intruder. While the characters in the soap operas are fictional, the threats (primarily to the female employer) presented through these fictional pieces become very real in the public mind. In interviewing people in public places about the role of domestic workers in Colombian society, the speaker often commented on the "domestic worker" as a general category calling upon examples of both real and imaginary domestic worker exploits. This became clear when one man retold the story of betrayal that had been part of a popular soap opera without changing the names of the characters. While it is difficult to ascertain the veracity of the threat domestic workers place on household harmony, many women in the group argued that the popularity of these stories contributes to the construction of barriers between the domestic worker and her employer.

One of the important areas of group learning was the collective realization that these "stories" are created. Second, the group came to realize that they too were capable of telling their own "stories" and these stories could present a positive view of the domestic worker. Furthermore, the women realized that they were able to create and construct messages using the video format. By integrating video images of real domestic workers involved in their daily tasks, the group was able to highlight the many positive contributions made by domestic workers to Colombian household stability.

A second critical area of learning was through our collective experience in using a participatory methodology. Through the participatory decision-making process, we designed our project in a very open-ended fashion that allowed us to change the direction and focus of the project according to decisions of the group. We tried to view our efforts as part of a "process" of learning, rather than focusing solely on the video product. By the very nature of the process, the expected outcomes were altered several times based on the group learning that often paralleled the production of the video. In a very real sense, the video was merely a tool to facilitate a deeper understanding of perceptions held by domestic workers, employers, and the society at large. These were understandings regarding the importance of domestic work, the challenges faced by employees and employers, and the ways in which conditions for domestic work in Colombia can be changed to meet the needs of women. The women's voices were initially shared with peers, and eventually became one of the group's most important tools for advocating change. Moreover, the video project created a space for the women in the group to tell their own stories, and by doing so, to validate the importance of their voices.

The use of storytelling was important since it highlighted the fact that the domestic workers know a great deal, regardless of their level of formal education. As illustrated in each woman's story the video reinforced their wide range of knowledge that goes beyond traditional definitions linked to literacy. Furthermore, the interviews emphasized the fact that domestic workers are often responsible for assisting their employer's children in their studies. While the video provided a tool for construction of persuasive arguments, it also provided a forum to listen and learn from the experience of other group members, thus reinforcing the collective knowledge of the group.

Another critical area of learning was centered on the process of public dialog and advocacy. Through the use of a video focused on the lives of domestic workers as positive protagonists, the women were able to engage in a public dialog in which they could advocate for increased respect and improved working conditions. As illustrated in the video exchange in the park about sexual abuse of domestic workers, the camera provided a tool for engaging in a conversation that would not have otherwise taken place. This was also true in the case of the interviews with the employers. In interacting with interviewees, the camera was used to demand responses to difficult questions about controversial and/or taboo topics.

For many of the women this represented an important opening for public dialog. The fact that the domestic workers were in control of the camera gave them the confidence to pursue these topics from their personal perspective, and if appropriate, to engage the interviewee in a dialog. These dialoges represented a significant change for many of the women, juxtaposing a newly increased self-confidence with a daily work environment in which they often remained silent and submissive. This change was widely recognized within the group, and several individuals expressed examples of how they were able to use this new confidence to address tensions in the workplace. Through the process of engaging in public dialog with the camera, the women discussed strategies for public advocacy that hadn't been previously explored. Thus, the video related efforts were only a small part of a larger ongoing project of empowerment of domestic workers aimed at advocating their employment needs within the public sphere. After the interviews were completed, the video production became a secondary concern of the group, as they decided to focus on other avenues for public advocacy.

The Ultimate Outcome

The sharing of the women's life experiences through storytelling was an essential element for the process of consciousness raising. Through this process, the women recognized common experiences and responses. These stories contributed to the group's understanding of each person's experience within the context of the society, and to the group process of consciousness raising and eventual empowerment. For example, it was extremely useful to learn that sexual abuse of domestic workers was a common occurrence in Colombian society. This recognition of the influence of societal views depersonalized the abuse and decreased the women's sense of guilt, shame and victimization. In this way the sharing of each person's story made a critical contribution to the process of healing in light of many aspects of societal discrimination. Through storytelling the women were able to analyze their multiple roles and differentiate what was acceptable and unacceptable behavior. This analysis facilitated their ability to recognize and challenge many kinds of abuse and discrimination.

Throughout the process of producing the video the group became aware that this method was in fact transforming them from spectators to active participants in the communication process. At the same time, they talked about how this project had increased their sense of self-worth, and had helped them to gain confidence and self-respect. This example sheds light on how participatory research methodologies can be combined with video production processes to empower local communities to publicly engage in discussions to address social and economic injustices. To conclude, there is great hope that approaches such as these will be promoted to provide forums for people to express themselves, to make their struggles more visible, and to actively pursue positive social change.

Notes

1. The women prefer to be called "domestic workers" rather than "servants" or "maids" since the term refers to their employment status rather than their social identity.

2. After reading about how domestic workers had begun to organize, I contacted Magdalena Leon, a well known feminist scholar and director of ACEP (the Colombian Association of Population Studies) based in Bogota, Colombia to find out how these associations function. With her assistance, I was put in contact with UTRAHOGAR, and was later invited by them to collaborate on a participatory video project.

Part 4

Video Action, Access and Impact

14

Guiding Hands and the Power of the Video Camera: A Story from Kenya

❋

Ndunge Kiiti and *Wilfred Amalemba*

"We are a pictorial culture; we see and we learn!" This statement motivated MAP International[1] to consider experimenting with the visual medium as a strategy to bring the AIDS pandemic into the faith community. For too long, AIDS was a forbidden subject, never to be addressed for it broached issues best left unsaid. These were issues such as proscribed sexual behavior, judgment and curses, disease and death. Was there a way to address these issues without being thrown out of the faith community, without "abusing" the sensibilities of the faithful? The visual medium, and the video camera in particular, proved to be a novel way of slipping this untouchable message into the church, almost unawares. In this chapter, we share with you our experience and what we have learned while using the video camera as a tool for creatively communicating difficult subjects. We begin by placing the venture into perspective—why the video? We

reflect on the production process, give you a look into the broadcasting stage using the video and finally conclude with the lessons learned.

AIDS has continued to grip the African continent. According to UNAIDS,[2] of the 40 million people who are living with HIV worldwide, Africa is home to 28.1 million. AIDS killed an estimated 2.3 million African people in 2001 and over 14 million have already died since the start of the epidemic in Africa. Life expectancy without AIDS in Africa was 62 years; with AIDS it has dropped to 47 years. AIDS is threatening to reverse the milestones made in development.

In Kenya, AIDS has continued to escalate to devastating proportions. Approximately 2.5 million Kenyans are infected with the virus and the majority of them are below the age of 20.[3] An estimated 600 people die every day from HIV/AIDS related causes. The lives of the infected, their families, communities, and the country as a whole have been affected by the epidemic.

Many strategies to slow down the spread of the epidemic have been used—some have worked, while others have failed. Without a cure, prevention through effective communication and education will continue to be key components in slowing the spread of HIV/AIDS. The United Nations[4] stresses that prevention must be the mainstay of our response.

The Need: Why a Video?

"There's no AIDS materials available for us to use in educating our communities!" was a common concern expressed by community leaders to the staff in MAP International's Africa office. "What can we do?" was usually the response of the staff. That question led to weeks of gathering data to better understand the community needs. The leaders were quite clear, "We are a pictorial culture; we see and we learn!" The production of a video complemented by posters was suggested and that was the beginning of a journey into discovering the power of video; and indeed, MAP decided to venture into the process of developing a video targeting community leaders in Africa.

The Making of the Tool

Springs of Life was taped in Kenya, Uganda and Zimbabwe. The goal of the 30-minute video was to sensitize and expose communities to the reality of HIV/AIDS and to highlight the role which communities, particularly the faith-based institutions, could play in meeting the challenge posed by this epidemic. With the subtitle, *A Call Beyond Compassion*, the video has helped demystify and destigmatize AIDS, empowering communities to respond to the challenge.

Showing actual footage of people living with HIV/AIDS and families contending with the impact of the pandemic, the video explored various issues such as the debate of whether AIDS is a curse, the struggle of children orphaned by AIDS, and the challenge of modeling healthy family relationships.

The Process: Growing Pains

The video, however, was not produced without struggle. The process took about one year. None of us on the MAP team had any previous experience in the development of a video, so the process was a learning one. We engaged a director and signed a vague contract without clearly defining roles and responsibilities. Without defined boundaries in terms of power and leadership, tension and misunderstandings began to creep in. The issue of ownership of the process and footage had to be addressed. There were differences in what was important to shoot and what was not. The limitation of resources made us deal with the cost issue; there was a difference between what MAP felt they could spend to get the footage needed for the video, and what the producer thought was necessary to make a quality video. The negotiation and clarification process led to the termination of the contract. Halfway into the project, we began to search for a new director.

We found a new director and having learned from experience, we tried to carefully write and agree on a clear contract. This time our greatest challenge was the distance. The director was in a different African country and that created its own problems. The director had not been involved in the initial stages of writing the script, field-testing and getting feedback from the audience. In addition, she did not have much experience in HIV/AIDS work, especially in rural settings. So, although she was skilled in video productions and expressed great interest and excitement to get involved and learn, the concept was vague in her mind.

Having given the approval to shoot the remaining footage we thought we needed, she used her artistic skills and redesigned the process, rewriting parts of the scripts and focusing her footage on her new idea. This was difficult for us at MAP to understand so we sent a staff person to "supervise." This created its own struggles because our staff had little experience in video production, whereas the director had considerable expertise. This also became costly because frequent communication and travel was required between two African countries. In addition, the "new" script required more footage and that meant additional expenses. We had to address this and move on with the process. We used these battles to grow and to learn as a team.

Yes, it was long and difficult, but as an organization we learned things that we couldn't have found in a book. We probably had to go through the experience to learn what to do the next time we are involved in the process.

Video Production Time Frame

We have laid out a month by month production time frame, so you can grasp the process of producing the video. You can see it took a substantial amount of time to conceive and carry out the project.

January 1993	An AIDS video was identified as an effective tool.
March 1993	Research was done; an outline written. Networks were developed for the production of the video. A proposal was developed and submitted for funding. Permission granted by the Kenya National AIDS Control.

License secured from the Ministry of Information.

April–May 1993   Footage shot in Kenya.

May–June 1993   Footage shot in Uganda.

Jan–Feb 1994   Focused group discussions, for script development with community leaders and media personnel (extensive changes made). Finalization of script.

March 1994   Footage shot in Zimbabwe.

April 1994   Off-line edit completed in Zimbabwe. Focus group discussions for off-line edit critique. Online edit completed. Video shown at the AIDS Consultation in Kampala.

1994–1996   Four 16mm reels of *Springs of Life* shown countrywide through Maturity Audio Visuals, reaching more than 2 million people.

1996   Regional Reach purchases video cassettes for its community television program established in several market places in Central Kenya, Western Kenya and Eastern Kenya.

1997   *Springs of Life* translated into Kiswahili, French and Portuguese and distributed in Tanzania, Kenya and Rwanda (K), Rwanda, Democratic Republic of Congo (former Zaire) and Cote d'Ivoire (F), Mozambique and Angola (P). In all, 500 copies were produced per language, totaling 1,500.

2000   Sign language overdubs added, 500 copies produced.

Using the Video

In Kenya, *Springs of Life* has been broadcast through the national television to a viewership of over 10 million, and twice on Kenya Television Network (KTN—city viewership of 100,000) during World AIDS Day activities in 1997 and 1998. The television audience is very urban-based so to reach the rural population, a medium for mass viewership was sought to enable the video to be shown countrywide. The video was translated into 16mm film and Maturity Audio Visuals (MAV), and a local audiovisual company was contracted to show *Springs of Life*. MAV has four vehicles that travel to four different regions of Kenya, every night of the week, showing films using their mobile cinema unit—Cinema Leo (Cinema Today). Each vehicle was presented with a film and evaluation sheets to collect views and comments from the audience. They also kept a record of the estimated number of people who watched the film. Over 2 million people countrywide watched the film. In addition, more than 500 videocassettes were purchased for showing in communities and institutions.

In 1997, a local marketing firm, Regional Reach placed a request for copies of *Springs of Life* to be distributed to its 'community television' centers located in trading centers in Western, Eastern and Central Kenya. Regional Reach had a social marketing strategy that attempted to utilize market places as learning centers. Through these learning centers the communities would be educated and enlightened on community issues such as AIDS, health and child education.

In the same year, MAP International translated *Springs of Life* into Kiswahili, French and Portuguese to cater to the other countries in its geographical scope of operation. This was also an attempt by MAP International to fill a gap created by the dearth of AIDS education materials in these three regional languages. Tanzania, a country whose lingua franca is Kiswahili would benefit. Also to gain from the Kiswahili overdubs were the Eastern Democratic Republic of Congo, Rwanda, Burundi and Kenya. The French version of the video would be distributed in Central Africa and West Africa. Mozambique and Angola, the only Lusophone countries would benefit from the Portuguese edition. In all, 500 copies per language were produced, totaling 1,500.

In 2000, MAP International partnered with Norwegian Church Aid to dub sign language into the video so as to reach out to people who are audio-challenged. The sign language version of the video was distributed to several schools for the deaf as well as faith-based private voluntary organizations that serve the hearing-impaired.

The Impact

The video opened closed minds and hearts, stirring up discussions on AIDS wherever it was shown. The impact was sometimes expressed in a nonverbal way. Following the film, a viewer commented, "there was total silence as people watched." Another viewer commented on the content, "the film helped us better understand what we have heard since we have seen with our own eyes." One of the strongest scenes in the video is a counselor sharing a drink with a person who has full blown AIDS. During the discussion session, the scene always elicits comments. A recurring question has been, "Can one get infected from sharing a cup with someone who is HIV positive?"

The impact of HIV/AIDS on children has been unimaginable. One of the scenes in the video shows two orphans, whose parents died of AIDS, struggling to maintain the daily chores of a home—fetching water, finding food and even planting and cultivating during the rainy season. For viewers, this is a moving scene because it is natural to imagine children under the protection and guidance of their parents or guardians. As one viewer sympathetically described the scene, "it is saddening to see orphans suffering."

Although it is difficult to quantify the impact of the video, it has clearly made a difference in the battle against the HIV/AIDS. It has created awareness. It has educated. It has convinced people to get involved in addressing the AIDS crisis. Perhaps mellowing the hearts and stances of community leaders is one of the most significant impacts *Springs of Life* has had. One community leader after another has found his attitude and stance challenged after watching the video. Primarily, the belief that AIDS is a curse or judgment from God has been challenged strongly in the video, with the continental leader of evangelical churches (Dr. Tokunboh Adeyemo) strongly rejecting this view. His statement that "... many wrongly believe that AIDS is a curse from God ..." has generated discussions that have resulted in a change of thinking, if not a change of heart. For many community leaders, the role of faith communities in AIDS intervention was vague. However, through *Springs of Life* little doubt has been left as to the Church's contribution. If anything, *Springs of Life* has challenged complacency and apathy. MAP International has received many requests from community leaders for copies of the video to show during various functions. The common refrain has been, "We want to let our community members see for themselves and learn." Evidently, *Springs of Life* has been the first step to discussing AIDS for many faith-based institutions.

The success of *Springs of Life* has been, in part, due to its general public appeal and its extensive coverage of the AIDS topic. It is difficult to talk about AIDS without mentioning sex, yet *Springs of Life* has done just that without causing any embarrassment. This has been one film on AIDS with no forewarning since it does not contain graphic pictures or subjects that may disqualify any age group. It is a "general exhibition" video.

What Did We Learn?

It goes without saying that there were lessons learned through the process of production and broadcasting of *Springs of Life*. To see the kind of impact the video had on the public was significant. Some effects may have been anticipated, but there were a few surprises that came our way. We circulated the video with the goal of stirring up the faith community to involve them proactively in AIDS intervention. We achieved that and more. As the subtitle of the video stated, our aim was to get the faith community to move beyond sympathy, even beyond empathy. We wanted a "role–up–your–sleeves, get–your–hands–dirty" response. The video achieved that by eliminating spiritual and physical blocks—the reasons for noninvolvement, dealing a blow to the AIDS stigma and myths, and suggesting possible avenues of action. The foregoing discussion highlights some of the broadcasting lessons we learned. In addition, to these we also learned technical lessons that would help remove any illusions about the "magic" of video in participatory communication and learning.

Broadcasting Lessons Learned

♦ In the absence of "next door" cases, recorded testimonies and experiences of distant third parties from distant locations give communities courage to "open up" when they would otherwise remain silent and even deny the reality of a tragedy like AIDS in their midst. The characters in *Springs of Life* were distant people whom they could "comfortably" identify with, without getting too close to their comfort zones.

♦ The downside is that for lack of local examples and cases, viewers sometimes leave the "theatre" with a self-righteous attitude. "It doesn't (or hasn't) happened to us. It's those people's problem." Without mediated and facilitated participatory learning, the lesson will be missed and lost to the viewer and the desired impact lost.

♦ Through the power of the visual, concepts that are abstract and vague for the average person come alive. One may lecture on the symptoms of full-blown AIDS, but seeing an actual image powerfully imprints these symptoms in the minds of the viewer.

♦ For a low literacy community, video is a powerful means of education. Many "ruralites" who have little time to attend seminars or read publications find the pull of film irresistible. For most people, watching video is a leisure activity, thus educational videos can be strategically positioned for great impact. *Springs of Life*, being only 30 minutes long, was shown before the start of an entertaining film or during a commercial break.

♦ A visual presentation on a sensitive subject like AIDS breaks the silence characteristic of conservative communities. The video presents several talking points on issues that they would shy away from and elicits unguarded comments or questions. This was observed several times whenever we engaged community leaders in discussing the role of the church in AIDS intervention. Issues on sexuality, condom use, embracing people living with HIV and AIDS were debated upon immediately after watching the video. Without the aid of the video, many community leaders would have remained silent on these issues, giving standard "expected" statements.

♦ In itself, the video is incapable of effecting a profound impact on the viewer. There is a need for a mediated and facilitated discourse, otherwise the video becomes one more film for entertainment. Since deep-seated attitudes, ignorance, myths on HIV and AIDS and stigmatized perceptions were unearthed, it was imperative to respond immediately and promptly. Hence, a mediated, participatory approach was applied.

♦ We learned that the power of the video camera is the human aspect. HIV/AIDS has a human face. The documentation of people's lives through video is a powerful and moving process. The process of visiting poverty-stricken homes, sharing the pain of seeing a loved one dying of AIDS, helping to care and feed the sick, and encouraging and counseling orphans, were all part of the video production process. At certain times, the interviewer, the director and the cameraman stopped the process just to cry with the families. In one vivid scene in Zimbabwe, a woman dying of AIDS cried profusely when the team was leaving because she had been so lonely and that emptiness had been filled for a short while during the shooting. In another scene, the team assisted a family by helping in transporting the body of a mother who had died of AIDS. Undoubtedly, producing a video can be a powerful way to share in and touch people's lives.

♦ Video presents unique challenges in a multilingual community or region. Long before the translation of *Springs of Life* into Kiswahili, the common lamentation was the inability to comprehend the video. How many subtitles or translations should one plan for at the production stage? Without a lingua franca, the venture may be cost-ineffective. One would, either have an interpreter in the "theatre" or find a language common to all. *Springs of Life* targeted the literate, community leader, but ended up being viewed by the general public. Due to great public demand, we were compelled to translate it into the regional languages, incurring unanticipated costs. Even then, we still fell far short of reaching the person in the village for whom international languages are foreign.

Production Lessons Learned

♦ We learned that we must define exactly what we want. Write a clear script before shooting, outline the shots you need and shoot to the script. We can't afford to shoot footage with vague ideas or outline. It is too expensive and makes the editing process complex and difficult.

♦ We learned that it is beneficial to have an advisory group that can help in providing feedback about the overall video process. This could include individuals from the target audience, media experts (with background on video production), and an organizational representative. They should be involved in the video production right at the very beginning in technical, management and process issues. The advantage is that they will probably be more objective and see the gaps that may not be very evident to the video production team. During MAP's intervention process, a technical expert helped explain terms such as U-matic, betacam, quality control, generation changes, sound mixing, and translations. It is important to avoid or clearly define terms that may be ambiguous leading to wrong expectations or legal implications.

♦ We found it was extremely important to solicit feedback, from our intended audience, at different production stages (e.g., at the beginning of the project, after the first draft of the script, after receiving the offline edit). The audience has to be part of the process although their opinions may vary. From our experience, feedback from the intended audience varied depending on social, religious, and educational backgrounds. This was good but a balance has to be maintained. One has to really keep the objective/goal in focus and be able to synthesize what is useful in the process of completing the task. The video was examined for contextual value, language, script and medium among others. If there was too much diversity in the feedback we received, we tended to give more weightage to the comments that were repeatedly mentioned by our audience rather than those suggested by the advisory group for the improvement of the final product. When changes were suggested, we always sought ideas on how they could be integrated into the production process.

♦ We learned the significance of a clear and concise contract. Contracts should be written after discussions with both the client and producer. One must ensure that both parties review ALL the points in the contract before signing the final agreement. In addition, technical terms must be written out and defined so there is mutual understanding of the meanings early in the process. If the definitions are spelt out on a separate sheet or document, they need to always be attached to the contract.

♦ We learned that legal counsel adds ease and clarity to the process. Issues such as authority, ownership and copyright guidelines for equipment or footage must be presented in legal terms in the contract. For example, authority must be defined by roles and responsibilities. This clarification also helps when it comes to outlining the credits. Questions related to the recognition of the producer, director, and copyright ownership, must be answered and defined early in the process. If, at some point, these roles should change, this must be communicated, documented and clearly understood by all parties. No assumptions can be made. One should have a file/attachment with the definitions used.

♦ We learned that video production can be expensive and resources are limited. One must develop a realistic budget and work to maintain it. There needs to be a balance for freedom of expression, getting the message across in an appropriate way and using the available resources appropriately and not overextending.

♦ We learned that the process of video production involves many people. Within an organizational setting, it is important to allow for staff participation. They need to know what is happening and how they can assist. It is also good to involve them in the fieldtesting of the video/tool. In this, case, the video did not belong to a particular department— it was a MAP project and everyone was part of that team. The end product will be a reflection of the organization so everyone, at some point, should be involved. The process can be a positive team building exercise.

Conclusion

It is worth noting that the video camera is a powerful tool in communication. One may say the images speak for themselves. We at MAP International have appreciated the way *Springs of Life* proved to be a key that opened opportunities for us to reach unreachable audiences. Through the video we have "gone where MAP's staff could not venture," we have changed people we have yet to come into physical contact with, we have taught and spoken to multitudes at a cost incomparable to what physical travel would have afforded.

Anyone who ventures into the use of video should be prepared for the unexpected outcome or impact. Due to its popularity, we had to translate *Springs of Life* into several regional languages. Through targeting community leaders the video has been well received by the general public.

Yet, one must be willing to contend with the limitations the video camera presents. These limitations will quickly erase the illusion of the "magic" of the video. Production and technological limitations include determining adequate amount of footage, determining target audience and viewership, production costs and other considerations, which make video a challenging and demanding medium.

To enhance participatory learning, it is imperative that one should not let the video do the talking. The video elicits varying feelings and perceptions hence the need to collate these and synthesize them collectively. Only then will the power of the video be effectively harnessed and exploited.

Notes

1. MAP International is a global health organization. A key focus of MAP's work in Africa is HIV/AIDS prevention and education throughout the continent.
2. United Nations AIDS Program (UNAIDS). AIDS Epidemic Update, Geneva, December, 2001
3. Africa Online Correspondent, June 25, 2001, Nairobi.
4. Declaration of Commitment on HIV/AIDS at the United Nations General Assembly: Special Session on HIV/AIDS, June 25–27, 2001.

15

Facilitating Participatory Video: India's NGOs

David Booker

We must guard against euphoria or complacency. One of our articles of faith has been that there are bound to be problems and difficulties, even failures, in any effort to promote change. Introducing participatory development where it has been absent is liable to meet resistance and many setbacks.

Norman Uphoff

For decades, non-governmental organizations (NGOs) in India have been creating visual materials such as poster boards, slide shows, and leaflets. They have organized street theater troupes, and used video camcorders for education, training, advocacy, conflict resolution, and as a medium of self-expression in community development initiatives. Communication professionals have called for the deliberate inclusion of people's participation—the active involvement of beneficiaries at all levels in the process of such community development initiatives.

Participation is a key element of empowerment-based grass roots development. The process can be effective in creating a role for women in local leadership development, literacy education, community decision-making, democratization of local media sources, and social effect analysis. Yet, despite a nearly universal commitment to the principles of participation, many practitioners have found this calling perversely difficult to fulfill in their use of audiovisual media. This is particularly true in rural areas where exposure to electronic media has been minimal. Some organizations have turned to traditional media to encourage local involvement, while others have found effective ways to use the more technical media *with* villagers.

This chapter highlights some of the obstacles, successes and insights arising from some Indian communication initiatives, primarily those using video. The content is based on interviews of Indian development professionals from a research study I conducted with support from the University of California at Berkeley and Cornell University. I visited 62 development organizations over a year's time, 1994–1995, inquiring into participatory approaches and their efforts to use participatory videos.[1] It is my hope that the examples will be useful in identifying and applying similar tactics in your own local situation.

A Challenging Context

Financial stress, organizational and administrative structures, funding and reporting procedures, and the social problems associated with patronage and outright corruption, complicate attempts to engage local participation in the use of video for development. Lack of previous local exposure to effective organizing, inappropriate video communication skills or negative attitudes of staff are not facilitative. Lack of useful evaluations of previous programs as well as disagreements amongst planners on appropriate approaches can also hinder projects. There are many important questions to ponder about:

♦ Who should initiate message making, the expert/specialist, or the beneficiary?

♦ Should participation include both local knowledge, *and* local attitudes or values?

♦ Should the participants be the primary beneficiaries in projects?

♦ In which situations should the emphasis rest more heavily on the process (participation learning, empowerment, dialog, interaction, relationships, etc.) than on the product (videotapes with a specific use objective)?

This abundance of unanswered questions hint at the persistent conflicts in the intrinsically political process of development planning. Given the obstacles, it may come as no surprise that audiovisual projects using video often fall apart, take longer or cost more that anticipated. Yet, despite such problems, exceptional participatory programs do occur and seem to keep pace with the rapid technological, economic, and social change, which has become Indian's reality.

Global Foundations

Many successful video and theater projects in other countries have provided the foundation for similar Indian experiments. In the early 1970s, field-workers from the Extension Service of Canada's Memorial University, who lived in the communities and shared the lives and aspirations of the people, produced a series of black-and-white film modules on rural poverty on Fogo Island, Newfoundland. A project of the Challenge for Change Programme (CFC) of the National Film Board of Canada, focused on individual people. They chose the events they wanted to show, using people engaged in their daily life on the island as the *subject* rather than the *object*. The conventional documentary form examined social and technological issues directly, while the CFC films presented the issues in the context of the community through group discussions. These then became catalysts for consensus building, increased self-confidence and action, as the result of islanders seeing themselves on screen. The films were also shown to provincial cabinet ministers leading to some important collaborations between government officials and the islanders searching for mutually beneficial solutions to long-standing development problems. These modules and their use in the development process are what have become known as the Fogo Process.[2]

Projects similar to Fogo have been carried out in other parts of the world to engage citizens in action, and for extension and technical education. In Ramghat, Nepal, the local staff of Worldview International Foundation (WIF, an international Norwegian-funded NGO) trained 10 illiterate village women to produce video materials on legal advocacy, traditional medicine, and drinking water systems. The women shared the tapes, as *video letters*, with members of other villages on battery-powered field monitors. In rural Peru, CESPAC (Audiovisual Center for Educational Services, a department of the Peruvian Ministry of Agriculture) initiated a large UNDP/FAO-funded video project to train farmers on a range of agricultural topics through short video courses, and to recover, preserve and reproduce peasant knowledge.[3]

Other projects have used video for cultural preservation. In the 1970s, experiments took place in *VCR narrow casting*, or local television production on several Israeli Kibbutzim, in an attempt to control the cultural input from urban sources and to create an empowering communications atmosphere for Kibbutz residents.[4] In the well known Kayapo Video Project in Brazil, native Amazonian villagers created a large video archive for use in documenting and resolving political conflicts, enhancing local cultural pride, and establishing international media contact for resistance against Brazilian encroachment on land occupied by natives. Video has also been used for training and documentation *within* organizations such as teacher training workshops using video feedback techniques at the Alvan Ikoku College of Education in Nigeria, and in the Training for Rural Development Project in Tanzania. UNICEF staff in Turkey have used camcorders as note-taking tools.[5]

In India: Programs of Many Types

The context of participatory video projects in India begins with two experiments: Kheda and CENDIT. Beginning in 1975, as a part of the Satellite Instructional Technology Experiment, the Kheda Project was a low-power television station transmitting to a number of villages near Ahmedabad, Gujarat. This project is well documented.[6]

The Centre for the Development of Instructional Technology (CENDIT), located in New Delhi, is India's oldest video training and tape dissemination facility, and is a central hub of alternative video and communication research activities. Beginning in the early 1970s, it was the first organization in India to train villagers and development workers in the use of video. As a direct result of CENDIT's work, decentralized alternative media training, production and distribution networks are becoming established, along with a number of videotape resource centers. Following the ac claimed successes of Kheda and CENDIT, participatory video projects in India has adopted many purposes and forms.

In local level projects, video has been used as a mediation tool, for advocacy and to generate local community awareness. VIKALP, a program initiated by CENDIT in Sharanpur District, Uttar Pradesh, and funded initially through a project of the Family Planning Foundation, produced candid video recordings, which were used to initiate discussions and negotiations between rope-making villagers and forest contractors, and later to encourage rope-makers in other villages to organize. CENDIT-trained producers have since often produced interview-based documentaries in local languages on topics of class struggle or worker's rights, to educate and build support in labor groups or peasant's associations.

Similarly, with the training support of Communication for Change (New York), Video SEWA, the communication branch of a successful women's labor union based in Ahmedabad, has produced videotapes of and by its members for use in negotiations and trade disputes.[7]

Initiating Local Action

A common image of participatory video is activists and community development facilitators using videotapes to focus public discussions on community problems and to induce local action. The use of video by Auroville's Village Action Group in its agricultural extension program is an excellent example. Initiated in 1994 with funding from DANIDA, Denmark's national development organization, the video project's goal was to instigate local action toward meaningful community water management in the face of an impending salinity problem through a series of village screenings and organized discussions. Aware that an outsider's view might not be acceptable, the producer recruited a local Tamil co-producer from an Auroville-area village to join him on a fact-finding trip to other severely affected coastal Tamil communities. The video makes use of theatrical drama with some professional actors, live festival street theater scenes, and puppetry in an attempt to present this serious topic in a locally acceptable form. A farmer-to-farmer exchange program accompanied the video-screening phase, in order to help farmers like themselves. Despite the outward appearance of community involvement, the video producer describes it as participation in action only. "The villagers involved were only interested in the prestige of being in the video, and are actually quite disinterested in the topic, and I'm afraid they won't continue to discuss the salinity problem now that the video shooting is done."[8] Such an observation is certainly not uncommon in projects initiated by outsiders to a village, despite good will and honest dedication.

The producer stressed two lessons from his experience:

1. Integrating traditional media forms helps to engage people in participation. In the production process, in viewing, and in discussions, the villagers are most interested and engaged through their own local forms of media, particularly theater, in the video.
2. A topic must be of interest to participants. A producer may be committed to a topic, but may find it difficult to engage the people if that same interest is not shared by the community. Discussing the topic with members of one single segment of a community at a time (such as one caste group, or farmers with wells, etc.) may help, since a community as a whole is rarely homogenous in its interests.

Media for People's Organizations

Advocacy campaigns are often the product of the growth of *people's organizations*, groups in which the initiators, producers, and beneficiaries are all the same people. They are groups working to better their *own* welfare. The 1993 production of *Odhni The Veil: A*

Collective Exploration of Ourselves, Our Bodies, by The Audio-Visual Unit of the Tata Institute of Social Science (TISS) is a good example. The video, based on a series of video recordings of a women's workshop, was produced for the project, *Understanding Sexuality: Ethnographic Study of Poor Women in Bombay,* under a larger program on women and AIDS of the International Council for Research on Women. The intention was to create a video to encourage other groups to organize similar workshops. The women in the group were directly involved in the video's production and distribution processes, and the two producers attempted to create a collective investigation on video, rather than a *we* studying the issues of a *they,* even though the producers did join the group to some degree as outsiders with the intention of producing a video about the group. They equated their outsider status with the very nature of development and with the obvious class differences and differences in content and style of conversation within a mixed group. They note that with informal interaction, these divisions were broken down to some extent and friendship and solidarity began to create a unified group.[9]

The producers of *Odhini* shared two important insights:

1. We begin by recognizing that we are outsiders. It is critical in a participatory media initiative for the producers, communication officers, or project instigators to clarify their role and relation to participants. Many of us develop the image that *real* participatory video must be initiated *only* by the people themselves, yet virtually all organized communication projects are initiated by the producer/trainers who enter a community with the intention of helping others produce a video. It is, perhaps, only realistic that this is so. We must be aware, however, that the very act of a producer's initiation will require that his or her bias or assumptions will be injected into the process. The question of who initiated each idea has become so critical in evaluating participatory programming, because the success of participation only begins when the participants as individuals are engaged in determining needs and setting objectives of the project.

2. A useful product focuses participation and benefits more people. If the videotape resulting from a participatory

project is unfinished, overly rough, inappropriate to other audiences, or simply not shared, the benefits of the process will end with the individuals involved. A Delhi-based documentary video filmmaker, known for his participatory methods, suggested that he needed to do justice to the concerns of the people he was portraying. "If I create a visually interesting production, then their involvement can successfully affect many other people who may view it."

Empowerment and Youth

Perhaps one of the more exciting areas of development in participatory programming is the use of visual media for youth empowerment. Agrawal and Sarkar (1994) report a successful program of media education for teenage girls. Groups of 15 young women in each of the several villages in Badarpur area near Delhi met every day for two weeks with Sharad Agrawal and Satyagit Sarkar, the workshop trainers. The young women received hands-on training in camera work, sound production, research and script-writing, and postproduction editing. The program stressed development of intellectual and conceptual abilities through exercises in a group setting in which expression of feelings was encouraged, along with critical examination of norms and mores.

Justice became a theme in the young women's choices of topics for the videos they produced, including investigations, which seem unusually direct and controversial for the work of adolescent women in a north Indian village. Some created artistic pieces about the joys and hardships of the lives of young women, while others created investigatory documentaries on traumatic situations. Facing significant community opposition and hostility they pursued themes on drunkenness and sexual harassment, indifferent community attitude toward filth and poor water quality, and health risks of a dust-producing, stone-crushing industry.

The acquisition of technical skills and vocabulary, or *technical* empowerment, proved to be the beginning of the potentially more significant *social* development and empowerment of the participants, changing their concepts about their own abilities. Agrawal and Sarkar (1994) report that interviewing strangers, especially men and elders, was the first time the girls saw themselves as possible equals to others.

Two lessons stand out regarding youth empowerment:

1. Children and young adults have tremendous enthusiasm. Given the opportunity, youth will overcome very significant social barriers to participate in development initiatives, especially those that teach new skills.
2. Participation, by itself, is not a useful goal. While field-workers in many grass roots NGOs display a consistent commitment to the concept of people's participation, they often do not distinguish that participation form the ultimate goals of their work. Their objectives and strategies frequently get confused. Participation in development programming is generally engaged for two different reasons. The first is approaching participation as an end in itself, needing recognition as a basic human right, as people need to think, express, belong, and affect decisions relating to their own lives. The second sees participation as the means to an end, an important tool in achieving goals, often for mobilizing support for preexisting plans. Realistic and useful goals combine both, and can answer the question— empowerment to accomplish *what*?

Participatory Approaches

Several suggestions and tactics are emphasized consistently by Indian communication practitioners in the field.

♦ Engage children early in projects; adults will follow. A very consistent theme is the early involvement of children in activities initiated by NGO field staff; it is the children whose curiosity is most easily expressed and who are most willing to try potentially embarrassing actions such as singing songs or appearing in a theater performance. Engaging children in program topics is often a first step toward establishing meaningful dialog with adults in a community.

NGO staff often report a need to work with the men, women, and children of a community as three distinct populations, each with its different appropriate medium of expression and involvement. Men may often prefer the format of informal discussion, and the women may only join in more theatrical forms of participation when in all women's groups. It is important to note that participatory video projects, which engage women may often put those women in conflict with husbands and others who would prefer them to, stay at home away from the public eye.[10]

♦ Provide adequate emotional and physical safeguards for participants. While the eagerness of children to participate in many development projects may evoke optimism, it is important to remember that development is inherently political. Participation in development programs will usually raise conflict. When it does, appropriate protection and conflict-resolution measures are necessary. This may include reality-based fictional media techniques to maintain participant anonymity. Providing *every* participant the opportunity to review their appearances on raw footage in a private playback session before they give consent to showing the video publicly is extremely important but often ignored. When village level initiatives battle against the established local political structures, the local *status quo*, it is not surprising that hesitation toward participation is a major obstacle. Methods must be found to engage people meaningfully while providing adequate protections.

♦ Develop quantitative as well as qualitative descriptions of participation in your media projects for use in the funding process. Successfully maintaining meaningful participation in programs over time often requires a number of accommodations at the organizational level, from adjusted time frame and financial expectations, to special care in evaluation and reporting to donors. The very nature of the funding process can be a serious threat to eliciting community participation in development programming.

Inclusion of plans for community participation is a virtual requirement in project funding proposals of most major donors. Yet, project evaluation procedures of the same donors may ensure that nonparticipatory elements of projects take precedence, because their benefits occur within a shorter timeframe and often are more easily quantified for reporting purposes. The resulting pressure to produce and evaluate rapidly in a stressful work environment is often blamed for the lack of local participation in video and film productions and rightly so.

♦ It is important to make good use of local, traditional media. An increasingly popular trend is the incorporation of traditional media and styles in programming, as producers learn that people tend to respond with more sustained interest and confidence to their local art forms. In educational programming, this has often meant presenting messages in theatrical form, following fictional characters in dance and song.

Both as an expression of local and regional cultural form and as a tool for development communications, street theater and puppet theater have seen a revival. A benefit of such art forms is that they *force* the producer to work directly with local artisans. Also, where print, slide shows, radio and television broadcast, and video all have major financial and technical training considerations, street theater productions require no equipment, little or no costumes, relatively short preparation time, and the possibility of more direct involvement of spectators. Theater may often be an excellent medium for accomplishing specific communication objectives.

Conventional documentary films for wider viewing may also use participatory approaches. The Swedish International Development Agency (SIDA), in a project for the Integrated Child Development Scheme (ICDS), has stationed fieldworkers in villages with video equipment to record, over long periods, social struggles and community actions in the villages. The approach, toward production of documentaries for television, is that of anthropological study, allowing the individual videographers the time to assimilate into the daily life of the village. The use of video for internal training has also become very popular, and some organizations are making attempts to carefully document and evaluate the results. Care, a large International NGO, has experimented at length with the use of video in training field officers. Staff uses videotapes of village meetings to critique facilitation and public speaking techniques. Care has also used video in training community health workers about procedures which cannot easily be demonstrated in the field. Care has become well known in India for its careful evaluations of audiovisual projects based on behavioral criteria.

Traditional Media

Literally thousands of local NGOs around India have made extensive use of traditional media such as puppets, street drama, and traditional song in social change efforts. Small arts organizations have been highly successful: CHITRA is a street theater troupe in a state-funded fine arts school which combines classical acting with activism in the streets of Bangalore on health and safety topics. The group's training focus is creating skilled performance facilitation, which engages the audience in the acting and discussion. Traditional forms, either singly, or incorporated into video and film, have proved extremely valuable in engaging local participation in community development efforts.

Large international development agencies have been involved too. In 1986, the World Wide Fund for Nature (WWF), formerly the World Wildlife Federation, organized the Multimedia Campaign for Environmental Action, a nationwide grass roots action event which, at the local level, involved thousands of villagers in street theater performances. Following extensive research on media-viewing patterns, the United Nations Children's Fund (UNICEF) has pioneered the use of traditional media in broadcast pieces on community health and family planning. International donors have supported traditional media use by their local partner NGOs. Many of Oxfam UK's partners, engaged in reconstruction programs in the wake of India's 1993 Marathwada earthquake, used performance arts in social change efforts. Manvi Haq Abhiyan (The Campaign for Human Rights [CHR]), funded indirectly through the Rural Development Committee (RDC), uses drama and mass demonstrations in its highly successful approach to organizing local action against caste oppression. CHR's drama of the unexpected includes children acting out the situation of the truant schoolteacher, or women walking miles and miles to the *Tehsil* (local government) office to present empty water jugs. Each gives a clear message that is difficult to ignore.

Discussion: Ends and Means

Certainly, a number recommendation can be drawn from the experiences with participatory video in the field. In the beginning one needs to be very clear as to whether production for massmedia is the primary objective or whether local input and local interpersonal communication facilitation is the major goal. As mentioned earlier, participation is generally approached in two ways: as an end in itself, and as a means to an end. It is often, both. An understanding of objectives and *priorities* is essential.

Who's Who?

At this stage we also need to clear up any ambiguity in identifying the intended program participants, and in clarifying who is seeking to engage in the participatory process. It cannot be stressed enough that the fundamental nature of participatory programming is established in this early step, and the programming itself only truly begins when the participants as individuals are engaged in determining needs and setting objectives. Focusing participation in a media-based project on one segment of a community at a time may be critical, whether according to caste, religion, gender, or landholding status. Information sharing does not reach all parts of a community evenly if the *whole* community is engaged. Communities are rarely homogenous.

Reluctance

Many techniques have been used to address initial suspicion and hesitancy on the part of villagers toward programs of development. Previous development initiatives may have bypassed potential input from villagers, leaving them with little or no sense of ownership or benefit from the passing interventions. Having received no financial compensation or credit for previous work with NGO staff, an assumption develops amongst some people that they are not meant to be involved in development, and if they are, it will only be a risk and drain of resources.

Overcoming this skeptical attitude and related formal distancing is often described as the first and primary activity of field staff. Building trust and rapport between program staff and participants may take a great deal of time. Spending that time is a prerequisite to sustainable program implementation. This may involve field staff living in the community to supervise program development and to develop local committees and interest groups to plan and adapt programs to specific local needs. Again, initial hesitancy is often linked with the types of prior exposure an individual has had to educational media. In video-based projects, it may be necessary to first spend time introducing more familiar media such as slides and audio tapes and group discussions about content.

Children

A very consistent theme is the early involvement of children in activities initiated by NGO field staff; it is the children whose curiosity is most easily expressed and who are most willing to try potentially embarrassing actions such as singing songs, role playing or acting in a theater performance. Engaging children in program topics can be a first step toward establishing meaningful dialog with adults in a community.

Often NGO staff members report a need to work with the men, women, and children of a community as three distinct populations, each with different needs and appropriate medium of expression and involvement. Men may often prefer the format of informal discussion, and the women may only join in more theatrical forms of participation when in all women's groups. It is important to note that participatory video projects, which engage women may often put those women in conflict with husbands and others who would prefer for them to stay at home away from the public eye.[11]

Safety

While the eagerness of children to participate in many development projects may evoke optimism, it is important to remember that development is inherently political. Participation in development programs will usually raise conflict. When it does, appropriate protection and conflict resolution measures are necessary. This may include reality-based fictional media techniques to maintain participant anonymity. The Kheda project used such techniques extensively after the tragic murder of several television program interviewees. Providing *every* participant the opportunity to review their appearances on raw footage in a private playback session before they give further consent should not need suggesting, but is often ignored at the emotional peril of participants. When village-level initiatives battle against the established local political structures, the local *status quo*, it is not surprising that hesitation toward participation is a major obstacle. Methods must be found to engage people meaningfully while providing adequate protections.

Protection for the media project staff or the NGO itself may also be necessary. In some cases the trust and protection of the local community is sought through building the credibility of the NGO as an organization for *all the people*, without regard to politics. Any lasting success in a social program must clearly be in the best long-term interest of the community as a whole, or those threatened will find ways to scuttle it. Articulating goals in terms of *win-win* solutions is useful here.

In some cases, a project may seek the support of a larger umbrella organization or party if conflict is inevitable. This is the case with the Campaign for Human Rights (a highly political movement), which gains shelter for its staff and funds under an NGO working on less controversial development issues, such as agricultural modernization, water supply development, and children's education.

We, the Outsiders

Again, it is critical in a participatory media initiative for the producers, communication officers, or project instigators to recognize clearly their identity and role in relation to participants. This will obviously vary, depending on the type of project. Many of us develop the image that *real* participatory video must be initiated *only* by the *people* themselves. Yet, virtually all organized communication projects are initiated by the producer/trainers who enter a community other than their own with the intention of facilitating an opportunity for members to produce a video or learn to create a street theater or other dramatic creation. Perhaps it is only realistic that this is so. We must be aware, however, that the very act of a producer's initiation is likely to mean that his or her bias or assumptions will be injected into the process. It is clearly for this reason that the question as to who initiated an idea has become so critical in evaluating participatory video endeavors.

Administration

Another area of potentially useful inquiry is *organizational* constraints to facilitating participation. Administrative structure and norms around financial accountability affect the willingness of citizens to participate in meaningful ways. In organizations with centralized decision-making structures, and lengthy official procedures, new initiatives created by villagers sometimes lose community enthusiasm during excessive processing time. Appropriate administrative adjustments must be made if community involvement is intended. Financial corruption, is of course, another deterrent to establishing community trust. To their credit, many NGOs have adopted policies of *open* finances, displaying organizational finances publicly in the location of field projects.

Perhaps one form of dishonesty, more dangerous in its subtlety, is *pretense* in the management of many community development efforts—upholding an unrealistic image of intellectual propriety, assigning blame for problems outside the organization, rather than admitting mistakes directly. While public NGO materials such as annual reports are not expected to mention mistakes, *intra*organizational newsletters and reports are an excellent, though underused, opportunity for candid discussion of the successes *and* failed experiments in engaging participation. We cannot learn without evaluating what doesn't work.

I have found that a seemingly minor factor affecting participation is the layout and location of the office itself. Accessibility of field offices significantly affects the ability of villagers to approach staff and volunteers, and may be a major determinant in the success of a program. Those offices placed in the midst of the intended program beneficiaries are often full of local people discussing programming with the field-workers, while those located at a distance are likely to be orderly and empty, with staff that work with paper, not with people.

The list of ways in which an organization's structures and operations effect the nature of participation seems limitless, yet I encourage the reader to begin making such a list for their own organization's specific circumstances.

Funding

Another serious threat to eliciting community participation in development programming is the very nature of the funding process. Inclusion of plans for community participation is a virtual requirement in project funding proposals of most major donors. Yet project evaluation procedures of the same donors may ensure that nonparticipatory elements of projects take precedence, as their benefits arrive on a shorter time frame and are often more easily quantified for reporting. The resulting pressure to produce rapidly in a stressful work environment is often blamed for the lack of local participation in video and film productions. The *project*-focus of the grant-competition process also forces NGOs to structure their work in distinct projects, which are often unrelated to the gradual *process* that builds community participation in development. Often, a certain level of dishonesty vis-à-vis the donors results. In the words of a high-level director in the New Delhi office of a major international NGO, "TV is to please the donors, the real work is *in* the communities."

Many examples have been shared with me indicating that the proposal-writing staff realizes that in order to execute a project in a fashion acceptable to the donor agency, people's participation in the media aspects of the program would have to take a back seat. In this Catch-22 situation few people are willing to tell the donors that given the time pressures and requirements, significant community participation is an unrealistic expectation. Invariably, the communications officer in the NGO will instead write the script for the video or drama project, use it in the funding proposal, and *then* attempt to involve villagers in what has already been planned. The unfortunate situation forces the staff, often committed to empowerment principles of development, to fall back on technology transfer and skills-training processes and then to try and explain what went wrong.

Solutions to the problems are not obvious. Identifying and promoting the acceptance of useful criteria for evaluating community participation in media is clearly necessary. Virtually every field officer or program director has a *sense* about the level of success of their program, and their program evaluations usually describe this—projecting benefits to the community from their participation. Yet, few final reports of audiovisual projects provide comprehensive evaluations that would *validate* how the projects contribute in the long-term to broad community development goals. In the harsh reality of the competition between NGOs for limited donor funding, quantitative follow-up studies and program evaluations using *measurable* criteria regarding participation do not add much credibility to claims about the value of people's participation. Some larger NGOs in India engage staff in full-time social effects research to help identify these variables for media projects. More efforts such as these are necessary.

Community participation may extend into the process of evaluation, as well. In an unpublished paper on Video SEWA's progress, Stuart and Bery highlight some points in the potentially sensitive process of evaluating a participatory media project. All those involved in the project must have a voice, setting the criteria by which to assess their work and all those involved must benefit from the process of assessment.[12]

Many communication practitioners also stress the importance of long-term institutionalization in creating sustainable people's media programming, and the need to direct donor money in this direction. While it is possible to train local leaders to script and produce street theater performances for various purposes, local video production is still in its infancy. Financial and technical resources must be institutionalized before video by the people becomes a more established reality.

Media Choice and Ripe Circumstances

Media choice is another important topic. Finding the appropriate medium for a project is not always simple. Some situations permit a deliberate choice based on the nature of program goals and needs. For instance, when lobbying for support to projects, dramatic presentation such as street theater, songs that symbolize the project or marches in the streets, are used to draw attention to the worth of the project. Self-reflexive staff training projects typically use video. Leadership training focusing on facilitation techniques and problem-solving may require role-plays. Programming for children often incorporates drawing, painting and song. Programming designed to empower villagers in their self-expressive abilities, have used video, still-photography, and street theater. Sometimes, videos are produced in programs that focus on advocacy or rapid dissemination of critical health information, although these tend to involve considerably less direct community input. A given organization may play multiple roles in one community over time, and use different media to suit those roles.

While making media choices based on situation needs seems ideal, communication media are more often determined by the knowledge, skills and resources available to the NGO or program team, or by its own mandate in the case of *media-driven* organizations. The *golden hammer* syndrome is common: when we have control of a tool, our actions are often governed by looking for situations in which to use it, as opposed to looking for tools to match our situational needs.

This is not always a problem, if a good *match* exists. Programs such as the Fogo Island films, Video SEWA's efforts, and PRERNA's educational videotaping are such examples, having in common communities with ripe circumstances, primed for benefiting from production of audiovisual materials. All had participated in sustained community building development programs. There was a need and desire expressed in the community to reach beyond the isolation from communication media. All had felt a shared inaccessibility to centralized decision makers whose actions affected the community. Video SEWA has the benefit of a very large and well established association behind it, with all the advocacy, education, and training techniques and programs already in place. The members of the union already participate actively in the organization's initiatives, and video is a tool that allows them to extend this further. In this context, Video SEWA has been able to select uses appropriate to video and other visual media without trying to *use* them to create participation, enthusiasm, commitment, and success where it does not yet exist.

An increasingly popular trend is the incorporation of traditional media and styles in programming, as producers learn that people tend to respond with more sustained interest and confidence to their local art forms. In educational programming, this has often meant presenting messages in theatrical form, following fictional characters in dance and song. Both as an expression of local and regional cultural form, and as a tool for development communications, street theater and puppet theater have seen a revival. A benefit of such art forms is that they *force* the producer to work directly with local artisans. Where print, slide shows, radio and television broadcast, and video all have major financial and technical training considerations, street theater productions require no equipment, little or no costumes, relatively short preparation time, and the possibility for more direct involvement of spectators. Theater may often be an excellent medium for accomplishing the first necessary step in any community problem solving effort: bringing large groups of people together to collaborate and discuss issues.

Personnel

Ultimately, empowering local initiative takes place on a personal scale, and even the largest NGO does its most effective work through individuals and their personal contact with villagers. The bottom line of any project is the ability of a program coordinator to select and keep quality staff and volunteers. They are the cornerstones of participatory development efforts. Program directors often identify attitude as a key element of this quality: an attitude of collaboration, humility, and genuine good will. Such staff needs the ability to work in situations, which are not predictable, with the commitment to allow local leadership to operate. They must be able to assist the transformation of human relations in which local people are treated as full equal partners in development endeavors. "[This] may turn out to be a more important change than the many worthy development projects stultified over the years by their designer's refusal to accord local peoples (and their knowledge) the respect and seriousness that true participation involves."[13] A number of valuable skills are also regularly identified: fluency in the local dialect, beliefs, and customs; ability to translate technical jargon and complex political rhetoric into locally understandable concepts; and an interpersonal ability to facilitate discussions with a range of people.

Unfortunately, appropriately talented staff is not always available. Many smaller NGOs suffer a high turnover of trained field-workers and videographers. The current rapid expansion of the television industry has produced many jobs in advertising, news casting, and entertainment programming, with salaries, which cannot be matched in the nonprofit sector. The NGO positions are then often filled by less well trained individuals. Spaces in video production workshops are at a premium, and the need for expansion of micro-production training institutes has been stressed. Yet the intense commitment and ability of many people I met who *have* stayed with the smaller media projects is a reason for hope. It is the responsibility of program directors to continue to hire and train such people.

Conclusion

My intention in this chapter has been to highlight some of the obstacles, successes and insights that arise from attempts to bring about popular participation in the use of visual media, and video in particular. My suggestions for practitioners who wish to use participatory video are:

♦ Assess and gain clarity on the ultimate goals of a program relating to participation.
♦ Narrow the group of intended participants appropriately.
♦ Be realistic about the role and values of the program initiators.
♦ Strategize methods to address participant skepticism.
♦ Understand lessons learned from previous development efforts in this same community. (This often goes hand in hand with understanding the political implications of a project and the appropriate measures to ensure personal and emotional safety of all involved.)
♦ Be prepared to make the necessary accommodations at the organizational level in participatory programs, from adjusted time frame and financial expectations, to special care in evaluation and reporting to donors.

♦ Understand local traditional media and perspective in analyzing options with electronic media. Hire staff that is well suited for facilitating people participation.

The popularity of participatory development communication in India is due, to a large measure, to the commitment and farsighted plans of a network of individuals. In the next few years, these professionals will face some big changes: a more conservative political scene, national economic developments, a rapid increase in cable viewing of foreign television across the country, and an increased, technically aware public. They must keep sight of the goals they seek within and beyond participation because participation in and of itself is not a panacea for social problems. Understand that participation in communication is, and must be, essentially a political action. Talented, well-trained staff will be needed in NGOs and government programs to advance the development needs of all people. In the conflict which inevitably arises over the nature of the development process and the appropriate technologies for its implementation, *shared* goals of human development must be pursued: health, security, basic human rights, access to information, and participation in courses of action that determine his or her own future.

Notes

1. For a complete report of this study, see Booker, 1997.
2. Williamson, 1991, p. 272.
3. Boeren, 1994, p. 150.
4. Shinar, 1993.
5. Keenan, 1993.
6. Agrawal, 1989.
7. Stuart, 1987.
8. Roc Scott, personal communication, March 7, 1995.
9. Jayasankar and Monteiro, 1994.
10. See Protz, 1989, pp. 18–19.
11. For an excellent discussion of this topic, see Protz, 1989, pp. 18–19.
12. Stuart and Bery, 1994, p. 7.
13. Awa, 1989, p. 314.

References and Select Bibliography

Agrawal, B.C. (1989). *Communication Revolution: A Study of Video Penetration in India.* Ahmedabad: Development and Educational Communication Unit (DECU), Indian Space Research Organization.

Agrawal, S. and S. Sarkar (1994). 'Liberation through Video,' *Voices*, 2(1), 9–12. Hong Kong: CCA–URM and DAGA.

Awa, N.E. (1989). 'Participation and Indigenous Knowledge in Rural Development,' in R.F. Rich (ed.), *Knowledge: Creation, Diffusion, Utilization.* Newbury Park: Sage Publications.

Boeren, A. (1994). *In Other Words … the Cultural Dimension of Communication for Development.* The Hague: Centre for the Study of Education in Developing Countries (CESO).

Booker, D. (1997). *Profile of Participatory Programs: Visual Motion Media in Indian Development.* MS Special Project Report. Ithaca: Department of Communication, Cornell University.

Cohen, J.M. and N.T. Uphoff (1980). 'Participation's Place in Rural Development: Seeding Clarity through Specificity,' *World Development*, Vol. 8, pp. 213–35.

Jayasankar, K.P. and A. Monteiro (1994). *The Plot Thickens: A Cultural Studies Approach to Media Education in India.* Unpublished manuscript. Bombay: Tata Institute for Social Sciences.

Keenan, M. (1993). *Grassroots Video for Community Development.* Unpublished Special Project Report. Ithaca: Cornell University.

Protz, M. (1989). *Seeing and Showing Ourselves: A Guide to Using Small Format Videotape as a Participatory Tool for Development.* New Delhi: CENDIT.

Shinar, D. (1993). 'VCR Narrowcasting in the Kibbutz,' *Israel Social Science Research*, Vol. 8(1), pp. 175–96.

Stuart, S. (1987). 'Video Focuses on the Village,' *Agricultural Information Development Bulletin*, 9(4), pp. 5–7. Rome: FAO.

Stuart, S. and R. Bery (1994). *The Power of Video in the Hands of Grassroots Women: Video-SEWA, A Case Study.* Unpublished manuscript. New York: Communication for Change.

Uphoff, N.T. (1992). *Learning from Gal Oya: Possibilities for Participatory Development and Post-Newtonian Social Science.* Ithaca: Cornell University Press.

Williamson, A.H. (1991). 'The Fogo process: Development Support Communications in Canada and the Developing World,' in F.L. Casmir (ed.), *Communication in Development.* Norwood: Ablex.

16

Beyond Community Video: A Participatory Broadcast Model for Development

❋

Korula Varghese

The aim of this chapter is to discuss a participatory community broadcast (PCB) model that takes advantage of the changing mass media environment and offers the message syntax and control that communities need to channel their messages externally. The core participatory production methodology outlined here is relevant if the production illiterate and marginalized sections of society are to be able to make use of mainstream mass media space for self-expression. Both the participatory production process and the facilitatory support system of the PCB model have wider application in the use of other community level media whether it is radio, video or theater, especially where external professionals are involved in the process.

Over the past three decades, community video has given voice to numerous voiceless groups and helped bring about change in many communities. The move towards video as a community communication tool in the 1970s was partly a result of the growing disenchantment with private and state-owned mass media channels which often became tools for top-down information transfer by the state, development agencies or corporate groups. Mass media was seen as centralized, elitist, one-way, expensive and nonparticipatory. But a few central developments prompt a reassessment of the role mass media can play in participative development, especially in fostering community communication.

Status of Community Controlled Media

A critical reading of community media performance suggests that community controlled small-scale media projects have not always succeeded in providing a sustainable channel for community communication. Even after two decades, small media efforts still remain experiments. Many community media projects were short-term experiments that were terminated once the larger development projects to which these were attached ended (Mody 1991). Community media were also found to be unsustainable as it was uneconomical to operate projects which offered little scope for financial returns (Jankowski, 1989; Prehn, 1992). Also, many small media experiments were aimed only at raising critical consciousness among people rather than helping communities communicate with the wider social environment (external function).

The increasing accessibility and decentralization of mass media in developing countries offers a great opportunity for communities to extend their challenge for unmediated self-expression to media spaces offered by existing broadcasting structures and emerging cable stations. A case in point is the Indian television network which expanded from a city based phenomenon of the 1980s into a three-tier network at the national, regional and local levels (Doordarshan, 1991). Cable also rapidly mushroomed in India with more than 100,000 one-man cable operators offering connections in the country by the early '90s. Leonardo (1993) notes that the number of television households in Asia increased by 70 percent in the last five years. In many Latin American countries, like Honduras,

Brazil, Argentina, Bolivia, Colombia and Peru (Mohr, 1994a), local level television and cable stations have become increasingly available. There is growing recognition in the South of the potential role that community access to broadcasting can play in development. Community access programming like community video can serve as a forum for community self-expression on development and cultural issues, a tool for organizing, and a channel to communicate community knowledge and experience. In South Africa, the Film and Allied Workers Organisation (FAWO) is engaged in facilitating the development of the proposed Community Television Network through a community based tier of broadcasting (Mohr, 1994b). In India, limited community access is already available on radio and television for developmental purposes. In other Asian countries such as Indonesia, Papua New Guinea as well as India, the Ryerson International Development Centre of Canada and the Asia Pacific Institute for Broadcasting at Singapore are involved in testing the Kheda local television model for aiding developmental efforts (Bhatia, 1992).

And finally, there is the realization that any group interested in sending a message to the wider community cannot afford to create messages in its own language hoping that the mainstream learns it, decodes their arguments and effects change. In many ways, community video in the hands of nonprofessionals often uses video syntax that fails to effectively communicate to the mainstream audiences.

Production Illiteracy: A Barrier to the Use of Mass Media for Community Communication

Though mass media space is becoming available at local levels, a major factor limiting successful use of such space for community communication is the lack of a production methodology that is amenable to control by community members who are production illiterate and socially disadvantaged. The only model that has been widely circulated is the Kheda production model (Agrawal, 1993). which however, engaged in audience based message production and not message creation by the audience itself. At Kheda, the professional staff made all the editorial decisions though such decisions were influenced by target audience considerations.

Offering hands-on control as with Video SEWA (Stuart, 1989) appears as one way of providing complete control to community members. But on a practical level, ordinary people do not have production experience to take effective control of television production language, even though they may have some training. As one community access television producer noted:

> If you are a seasoned program maker and you are offered editorial control to make a program, you are easily able to take control as you know all the means and ways of all that is happening around you. You would understand all the language, all the grammar, all the parts of production processes, you know you can control the script, you know all the budgetary implications. (Those) who are not program makers don't know all those things. Therefore they are at a disadvantage (Varghese, 1994:188).

The following sections describe a participatory community broadcast model that takes into consideration the production illiteracy, lack of confidence and other constraints facing community members and offers communities control of their media messages. The model was designed based on insights drawn from a study of the BBC Community Programs Unit's Open Space access television production methodology (Varghese 1994).

Participatory Community Broadcasting Model (PCB)

The Participatory Community Broadcasting Model (PCB), modeled on the BBC's Community Programs Unit's Open Space program, relies on a few basic assumptions, essential for the success of any participatory model placed within a mass media structure. These include:

♦ Offer of community access for people who are interested in making use of the broadcast space.

♦ Production resources, including a production team, adequate budget and a suitable transmission slot.

♦ Offer of editorial control for accessees, including the right to make decisions on all aspects relating to the content and form of the program.

♦ A right to veto any part or the whole program from being broadcast if accessees feel it does not reflect their views.

♦ Protected program slots that are not subject to mainstream program evaluations based on audience figures. Instead, it is based on the recognition that not all programs can be of interest to the majority and attempts to select issues or make programs attractive to the majority can lead to many marginal points of view being excluded or distorted.

Shared authority or collaborative media productions involving professional producers and media nonprofessionals raise a fundamental question as to whether the nonprofessionals will be able to exercise control in such productions. The unequal relationships involved with university educated highly skilled media professionals on the one hand and production illiterate media nonprofessionals on the other, can pose a major constraint to appropriation of editorial control by the nonprofessionals.

The two core elements of the PCB model address this issue by taking into consideration the needs of accessees to be able to control program development though they lack the necessary knowledge, ability or confidence to do so. The two elements are:

1. An iterative participatory production process that is amenable to nonprofessional control.
2. A facilitatory support system that helps nonprofessionals develop confidence in the professionals and in themselves.

The Participatory Production Process

The Participatory Production Process is designed to enable nonprofessional accessees to control the development of their program ideas from idea to final tape ready for transmission. In this iterative participatory production process, the producer (professional) engages in continuous dialog with the accessees (nonprofessionals) to elicit their ideas on the content and form of the program. These ideas are redefined by the producer and translated into television production language. Each element that gets redefined by the producer is reviewed again by the accessees who suggest modifications leading to further refinement of the element. Both the content and form (structure) of the program are continually redefined by such a process. The final decision on suitability of a redefined element rests with the accessees who hold the editorial control for the program.

In the above process, the dialog provides an opportunity for the nonprofessionals to convey their expectations of the program and also control program development in the desired direction. For the professionals, the dialog provides an opportunity to learn about the subject from the nonprofessionals' point of view. This learning is necessary for the professionals to technically reproduce nonprofessionals' ideas into a finished television program that is faithful to the nonprofessionals' realities.

The Facilitatory Support System

Generating accessees' confidence in their own abilities and trust in the production crew is essential if production illiterate community members are to meaningfully exercise their editorial control in participatory production. The Facilitatory Support System provides the following strategies to achieve this: trust building, deprofessionalization, demystification, and a sensitized production approach.

Trust Building

Accessees, because of past bad experiences in their dealings with the media often find it difficult to trust professionals from a media organization. Since it is difficult to have a collaboration where there is mistrust between the two parties involved, building trust is an important component of the Facilitatory Support System. In the proposed model, professionals use the initial meetings with the accessees to engage in informal discussions. Discussing issues of interest with accessees along with their daily life experiences contributes towards lessening the initial mistrust that accessees may hold. Real trust in the professionals, however, gets generated only when accessees are offered every opportunity to make decisions on program related matters. Professionals ensure that they do not make editorial decisions unless delegated by the accessees. Once accessees accept that the professionals are not attempting to manipulate them, they are able to increase their trust in the professionals.

Deprofessionalization

The social and professional status enjoyed by the production crew is quite the opposite to that held by accessees who not only lack production knowledge but could also be illiterate, poor and socially disadvantaged (Agrawal, 1993). In this relationship, accessees can feel that their opinions are unimportant and be too willing to accept editorial suggestions offered by professionals without considering the suitability of such suggestions vis-à-vis their own needs (Ruby, 1992). To avoid this from happening, it is essential to break down the conventional image of the professional and help accessees feel that they are on equal terms and able to explore their own needs in terms of the program.

One way of relinquishing the professional image is to reject traditional notions of professional "neutrality" and identifying with the concerns of the nonprofessionals (Kronenburg, 1986). Showing that they care about the accessees opinions and concerns help the accessees to view the professional as an ally rather than an unsympathetic professional.

Demystification

For people who are entering a television production situation for the first time, the sophisticated equipment and the mystique of production is an alienating experience. Demystification is one strategy that could be used to alleviate the alienating influence of a media production situation.

Professionals can help the accessees understand the production process and help them become familiar with the technology associated with program production. Such demystification involves viewing program tapes and explaining how a program is put together; camera recording the accessee group and playing it back for viewing; and in camera editing showing how recorded material can be reduced (Dubey and Bhanja, 1993). If the studio is being used, it also includes taking the accessees to the studio and showing them around well in advance of the actual use of the studio. Professionals engage in further demystification throughout the production process by explaining the various processes involved at each production stage, if necessary.

Sensitized Production Approach

The PCB model envisions a nonintimidating production approach, sensitive to the needs of nonprofessionals. This includes:

♦ Generating a comfortable working atmosphere.
♦ Providing accessees with enough time to deal with production situations.
♦ Ensuring that accessees consider the consequences of what they are saying in the program vis-à-vis their relationship with the audience.

An informal working atmosphere where accessees do not feel stressed during production meetings, and arranging for production meetings at venues where nonprofessionals are most comfortable is one way of ensuring a less stressful production environment. Taking only minimum crew members into production situations so that accessees do not feel outnumbered by the professionals and consequently less able to express their needs is also part of this approach. Another aspect of the sensitized production approach is to give the accessees adequate time to deal with production situations. Accessees who are new to television production find it difficult to translate their ideas into the visual language of television easily. Any lack of knowledge and confidence of accessees is taken into consideration during the scripting, filming and editing stages. The accessees must seriously consider the consequences of making a particular stand or allegation in the program on their relationships with the audience. People new to the media often do not realize how views expressed in the media may affect them in their day to day life. It is essential that accessees are made aware of possible negative consequences of taking a particular stand or criticizing somebody in the program.

The PCB Model and Participatory Development

In the new notions of participative development, communities themselves determine their media needs and use media for self-development efforts (Melkote, 1991). The PCB model provides a useful tool, in this regard, as community groups and individuals determine how they use it to communicate what they wish. They determine the content of the program, the argument of the program and the visual language of the program.

Many participatory projects have remained exercises in manipulation where people have been coopted into projects whose design and goals were predefined by external agencies. In the PCB model, there are no directives on how to use the media space for a particular purpose nor how a particular issue should be treated. Community accessees themselves set the parameters on how an issue is treated. This is made possible by PCB's offer of editorial control and the model's reliance on dialog-based program development which allows accessees to constantly monitor and retain control over how the program develops from inception to final edited tape.

The PCB model adopts the central notion of the participatory development paradigm, namely, the recognition that all human beings have the ability to create knowledge and it is not the prerogative of the professionals (Chambers, 1993). By offering editorial control (a critical power which determines a program's content and form) to nonprofessionals, the model explicitly recognizes that the nonprofessionals have the ability to analyze and construct their own reality without the professionals having to spell it out for them.

Another useful question here is whether the PCB model contributes towards empowering its users. Williamson (1988), writing about the Fogo process, states that individuals seeing themselves in the Fogo films experienced an increase in self-confidence and in their power to express themselves and the value of their own lives. The facilitatory support strategies of the PCB model allow accessees to have self-confidence and the ability to make their own decisions. The process of analyzing the issue being treated during the scripting can lead to greater critical awareness among the participants vis-à-vis the wider nature of the problem and its underlying causes. Mere involvement in the production also provides participants with a greater awareness on how media is used to represent them and thus provide them more control in later dealings with the media.

The role foreseen for professionals in the PCB model reflects the role expected from professionals involved in participatory projects. PCB professionals take on the role of an enabler/facilitator to serve the nonprofessional's self-expression needs. They relinquish traditional journalistic notions of "neutrality," to empathize with the accessees and identify with the accessees' concerns rather than serving the needs of an external agency like the media organization or a developmental agency. This is similar to the role adopted by the participatory researcher where there is a "conscious commitment of the researcher to work for the cause of the community" and a rejection of "the traditional scientific principle of neutrality." (Kronenburg, 1986). The PCB professionals relinquish notions attributed to normal professionalism and take on the values of new professionals that subdue personal and professional interests in favor of the needs of their clients.

The PCB Model and Other Participatory Media Approaches

The PCB model is unique as compared to other participatory media approaches used for community communication. It not only provides for community control of the media messages, but also allows for quality productions that can reach a wider audience. A comparison with the Kheda local television approach and the Video SEWA hands-on approach makes this clear.

The major approach used at Kheda involved professionals taking up community identified issues for producing programs. However, the professionals made the decisions on content and form of the program though these decisions were shaped by formative research and pretesting conducted among audience groups. The second approach, the more participatory one, centered around scripts produced by rural community members. Available literature notes that the scripts were adapted by the professionals for recording (Bhatia, 1980; Space Applications Centre, 1981). The rural writer was invited into the process only at the time of recording the script. However, the rural writer had only a limited opportunity to control how the program was shaped as professionals made all the production decisions. Higgins (1991) notes that each person who constructs a visual sequence does it within his/her cultural perspective and there is no single true picture of reality. As such the exercise of such productions will be true to the cultural bias of the group to which the producer belongs. Similarly, Philo, et al., (1982) note that values which influence selection of material in the media are in effect a product of the person's social and political value framework. In such situations, if accessees are interested in achieving a product whose content and form should truly reflect their communicative intent, participation and exercise of editorial control is essential; aspects which are lacking in the Kheda approaches.

Another drawback of the rural writer approach is that such participation is open only to those who are able to write scripts (or outlines). This limits the involvement of the illiterate or those who are not confident enough to write scripts. In the PCB model, accessees need not be literate or able to conceptualize ideas in terms of scripts since the professionals help elicit their ideas and translate them into television language. At the same time, the dialog-based program development provides accessees with a process that can easily be monitored and controlled at all stages so that the program reflects their own aims.

While PCB thus provides the community with more control over how they represent various issues and also themselves, it does not offer the sort of control possible through hands-on production like that done by Video SEWA. In India, Nepal and elsewhere, community members, often illiterate, have used video to record their own realities and used it for horizontal and bottom-up communication.

However, while such hands-on approaches provide ultimate control, one drawback is that the product often faces the risk of being interesting only to those immediately concerned with the issue due to its poor technical quality. McLellan (1987) who studied the worldwide use of video for development notes:

> A rule of thumb is that if the image is fuzzy and wobbly and the sound bad, the person being interviewed and their relatives will still watch it. A neighbor will require a bit better quality. To show material to those in other towns even more

attention has to be paid to framing, sound, editing, style, aside from the content.

Similarly, Croll and Husband (1975) suggest that in situations where potential audiences are already familiar with certain formats, styles of presentation and camera work through exposure to other media output, it is beneficial for community media output to contain these familiar styles. In developing countries, like India, inspite of the fact that television sets are not widely available in rural areas, people have a good deal of exposure to audiovisual output through commercial films, government films shown by mobile film units and in many cases television through community sets. Thus, as audiences, they expect certain styles and techniques in audiovisual output, and if community groups are intent on using media to reach such groups, it is essential that they make use of the best possible means to do so. Similarly, if media is being used to get the attention of urban based decision makers, it will be useful if such programs possess basic production quality.

Decision makers often do not have the time or the inclination to sit and watch tapes with wobbly camera work and poor sound. Melkote (1991) notes the importance of treating messages for bottom-up communication:

> Just as top-down communication needs to focus on message design and treatment for adequate, uniform and accurate receiver comprehension, researchers and practitioners ought to examine ways of enabling the voice of recipients to be encoded in messages. Messages would need to be structured and treated for accurate and uniform comprehension by the source, ranging from change agents to high-level administrators within the project and donor agencies (p. 260).

The PCB model provides a means by which community groups can make use of media to encode their own voice in a manner that can reach the decision makers and also other community groups. Professionals provide their technical skills and experience to translate community voice into familiar television language that is acceptable to a wide range of people. At the same time, the control offered to the community groups helps them use their own local dialects and images in the media product.

Concluding Comments

The relative success of the PCB model will be dependent on a number of variables when it is adapted for use in different political environments. For example, it can be difficult to translate its ideals of public editorial control to nations that do not recognize freedom of expression for its citizens. As Wenaut (1975) observed, "If a country wants to keep its citizens in place and the, voiceless kept voiceless, then nothing is going to be accomplished" (Quoted in McLellan, 1987).

It has to be recognized, however, that where such restrictions apply, it will not only affect mass media output but also output at the small-media community level. Locating PCB within particular broadcasting structures (commercial/public broadcasting systems/state-owned enterprises) can also affect the extent of editorial autonomy that accessees enjoy. Audience influences, competitive market, media laws, professional production ideologies and staff attributes (creativity, peer pressure, career aims) can have varying degrees of influence within these different structures. Specific protective measures can be built into the model to shield the accessees' editorial autonomy in such cases.

Irrespective of where the PCB is being located, the core participatory production methodology outlined in this chapter is relevant if the production illiterate and marginalized sections of society are to be able to make use of mainstream mass media space for their self-expression purposes. Both the participatory production process and the Facilitatory Support System of the PCB model have wider application in the use of other community level media whether it is radio, video or theater, especially where external professionals are involved in the process.

References and Select Bibliography

Agrawal, B.C. (1993). 'Kheda: An Experiment in Participatory Communication,' in S.A. White, K.S. Nair and J. Ascroft (eds.), *Participatory Communication: Working for Change and Development*, pp. 387–89. New Delhi, Sage Publications.

Berrigan, F.J. (1979). *Community Communications: The Role of Community Media in Development*. New York: UNESCO.

Bhatia, B.S. (1980). 'An Experience with Rural Writers,' in B.S. Bhatia, (ed.), *Television for Education and Development*, pp. 144–45. Ahmedabad: Space Applications Centre.

——— (1992). 'Development Broadcasting,' *Media Asia*, Vol. 19(1), pp. 49–53.

Chambers, R. (1993). *Challenging the Professions: Frontiers for Rural Development*. London: Intermediate Technology Publications.

Croll, P. and C. Husband (1975). *Communication and Community: A Study of the Swindon Community Television Experiment*. London: University of Leicester.

Doordarshan (1991). *Television India 1991*. New Delhi: Audience Research Unit, Directorate General of Doordarshan.

Dubey, V.K. and S.K. Bhanja (1993). 'Using Video in Rural Development,' in K.S. Nair and S.A. White (eds.), *Perspectives on Development Communication*, pp. 195–206. New Delhi: Sage Publications.

Higgins, J.W. (1991). 'Video Pedagogy as Political Activity,' *The Journal of Film and Video*, Vol. 439(3), p. 18–29.

Jankowski, N. (1989). 'Training Dutch Citizen Groups in Video Production Techniques,' *Media Development*, Vol. 36(4), pp. 22–26.

Kronenburg, J. (1986). 'Empowerment of the Poor: A Comparative Analysis of Two Development Endeavours in Kenya,' in S.R. Melkote (ed.), *Communication for Development in the Third World: Theory and Practice*. New Delhi: Sage Publications.

Leonardo, H. (1993). 'Asian Broadcasting: The Changing Scene,' *Media Asia*, Vol. 20(3), pp. 123–26.

McLellan, I. (1987). 'Video and Narrowcasting: TV for and by Ordinary People,' *Media in Education and Development*, December, pp. 144–49.

Melkote, S.R. (1991). *Communication for Development in the Third World: Theory and Practice*. New Delhi: Sage Publications.

Mody, B. (1991). *Designing Messages for Development Communication: An Audience Participation-Based Approach*. New Delhi: Sage Publications.

Mohr, V. (1994a). 'Community TV and Local Identities,' *DEVMEDIA Digest*, No. 198. (On line) devmedia@uoguelph.ca

——— (1994b). 'Community Media in S. Africa,' *DEVMEDIA Digest*, No. 192. (On line) devmedia@uoguelph.ca

Pavelka, F. (1978). 'Community Communication Through Alternative Media,' paper presented at 'Video as Social Work,' Vienna, Austria. Also cited in H. Litwin (1984), 'Video Work in Community Organisation: Boon or Boondoggle,' *Community Development Journal*, Vol. 19(3), pp. 134–41.

Philo, G., J. Hewitt, P. Beharrell and H. Davis (1982). *Really Bad News*. Glasgow: Glasgow University Media Group.

Prehn,O. (1992). 'From Small Scale Utopianism to Large Scale Pragmatism,' in N. Jankowski, O. Prehn and J. Stappers, (eds.), 'The Peoples Voice: Local Radio and Television in Europe,' *Acamedia Research Monograph*, No. 6, pp. 247–68.

Ruby, J. (1992). 'Speaking For, Speaking About, Speaking With, or Speaking Alongside: An Anthropological and Documentary Dilemma,' *The Journal of Film and Video*, Vol. 44(1, 2), pp. 42–66.

Space Applications Centre (SAC) (1981). *Kheda Communications Project: Review.* Ahmedabad.

Stuart, S. (1989). 'Access to Media: Placing Video in the Hands of the People,' *Media Development,* Vol. 36(4), pp. 42–45.

Varghese, K. (1994). 'Exploring Media Non-Professionals' Participation in Access Television Production: Towards a Participatory Production Model for Development Broadcasting,' Ph.D. Thesis, Reading: University of Reading.

Williamson, A.H. (1988). '"The Fogo Process'": Development Support Communications in Canada and the Developing World,' unpublished Paper. Don Snowden Centre for Development Support Communication, Memorial University of Newfoundland.

17

Video Kaleidoscope: A World's Eye View of Video Power

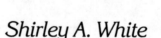

Shirley A. White

A Kaleidoscope exhibits its images in an endless variety of symmetrical forms and intense colors. In one's hand, a change of position of the scope rearranges the bits of colored glass within, creating a reflective visual that imprints on and excites one's senses. An analogy can be drawn with the images captured through video. Video's images are also of endless variety and are arranged by the hand on the camera. The resulting flow of images, as they are arranged and rearranged, imprints on one's senses and creates meaning. The kaleidoscope's images are unique and fleeting. In experiencing the flow of video images, we find that they too have their own uniqueness. Video's images can be captured by the camera—their uniqueness to be experienced over and over.

As a wrap-up for this book, it seems fitting to take a kaleidoscopic view of video—*A World's Eye View of Video Power in Context.* The endless potential of video to be tailored to meet communication needs have been lauded the world over. The realization of how technology has spread in the past two decades is amazing. It is impossible to identify the myriad uses of this powerful communication tool. The intention here is to highlight some of the interesting and useful video projects to trigger your thinking as to how you can capitalize on *video power*. The sampling of projects we present, including classic and current ones, can lead you to other accounts and contacts through the sources we identify.

For the sake of simplicity, the project write-ups are organized alphabetically, according to country. No judgment regarding the quality of either the projects or their social or political significance has been made. I would say that unless you have had personal contact with such projects, as I have in some cases, you only have limited ways to assess the project's worth. So here, we are taking these reports at face value, assuming the sources are credible. How video and its power has "survived" after the completion of projects, for the most part, is an open question because longitudinal assessments are rarely a part of follow-up. Unfortunately, computer technology has become the "technology of choice" for development focus, so video has been nudged aside a bit. It is likely that there will be a convergence of these technologies that will optimize the worth of both. The Internet, however, is a valuable source of information and therefore, I have identified a few Websites worth browsing at the end of the chapter.

Images from Africa

Zimbabwe

Julie Goodman writes in the *Daily Mail* and *Guardian*:

It is early evening and thousands of people are gathered at an old bus stop in Dzivaresekwa, a congested township in Zimbabwe's capital, Harare. Rap music pulses through large speakers, women stand with babies tied to their backs, teenagers hang off the bus-stop shelters, and the show begins.... On a large movie screen before the crown unfolds the story of

Tiyane, a young man in Harare who impregnates a woman and finds himself saddled with single parenthood when the baby is left on his doorstep. This is not a drive-in movie. Instead, the film, *Yellow Card*, is projected from a mobile truck on to a white plastic banner—a makeshift cinema easily transported from town to town. The crowd stands in clusters, some talking, some sharing drinks, but most focus on the rare spectacle of evening entertainment in their impoverished neighborhood.

This movie is just one of the several produced by the Media for Development Trust (MFD) in Harare that addresses a serious and significant social issue—the spread of AIDS. These "feature films" can be regarded as "eduentertainment"—entertainment ladened with social messages and educational information that relates to them. *Yellow Card* is MFD's most recent production, but others have been produced, using the same model, since 1987. This movie places the burden of parenthood on the male. *Consequences* tells the story of a bright young woman with lofty goals for education who becomes pregnant and is shunned by her school. The film plays out the consequences of unwanted pregnancy, encouraging youth to be cautious. Along a different theme, *Neria*, is the story of a grieving widow who has been thrown out of her husband's home by his family. *Everyone's Child*, is the story of two children, orphaned after the tragic death of both parents. This award winning film carries the strong message that people of the community often turn their backs on orphans who are truly "everyone's children." It speaks directly about love, solidarity, tolerance, hope and strength in the face of tragedy, but subtly addresses the questions of vulnerability to AIDS and other diseases.

The significant part of MFD's production practices is that not only do they produce top quality films, but also have unique strategies for distribution and use of the films strategy. Support materials are available in these languages, but also in 10 other languages. Films are released for theaters. Master copies are sold to television stations. They promote the showing of video copies for in-flight viewing on airlines, in the classroom and by community agencies. In order to have informed use of the videos they conduct workshops and provide educational materials to be used in conjunction with the videos. MFD feels a major responsibility toward the widespread distribution and use of a quality video, once it has been produced. Distribution includes a press kit, posters and a variety of promotion materials as well.

Yellow Card, for example, has been dubbed into French, Portuguese, Shona, Ndebele, Swahili and 10 other African languages, even Pidgin English (for use in West Africa). A 20-minute support video and discussion guideline manual accompanies the film. Their grass roots distribution efforts target Zimbabwe, Kenya, Uganda, Tanzania and Zambia. Premiers will be held in theaters in South Africa later this year but the goal is to have continentwide coverage. MFD is encouraging organizations across Africa to take control and intitiate their own projects which utilize the video.

MFD is supported by Media for Development International (MFDI), a not-for-profit organization based in the United States. Their guiding principle is maximizing viewership of social message videos. In conversation with Steve Smith, founder of MFDI, I learned that this group distributes videos worldwide from their headquarters in Glenwood Springs, Colorado. They have three affiliate distributors in Senegal, South Africa and Zimbabwe. They focus largely on Africa and have an impressive number of listings. Interestingly, MFDI has been addressing a crucial problem regarding utilizing video for social messages. Steve reminded me that hundreds of excellent films/videos are produced, but most are not distributed widely or packaged for action viewing contexts. They identify quality video produced by individuals or organizations and negotiate the rights to "package" them for use in social development. He noted that it is surprising that often producers of quality productions resist and are skeptical about agressive distribution efforts. Distribution is what makes this organization "tick" for the betterment of social action programs in development.

Source: Steven C. Smith, Media for Development International, 184 Crescent Lane, Glenwood Springs, Colorado 81601, USA. E-mail: ssmith@mfdi.org. Website: www.yellow-card.org; www.mg.co.za/mg/za/archive/2002mar/features/11mar-zim-cinema.html

Zimbabwe

In 2002, the Rural Libraries and Resources Development Programme (RLRDP) launched Zimbabwe's first ever, mobile donkey-drawn electro-communication library in the Nkayi district of Matabeleland North. Aside from being a donkey-drawn library cart, the innovation will serve as a center for electro-communication, providing users access to radio, television, telephone, fax, e-mail and Internet services. This will enable rural and isolated communities, heretofore deprived of communication, access to these services. The invention uses solar power supplied by a unit installed on the roof of the cart. This cart might also be provided with an aerial or satellite dish for a wider and clearer electro-communication system in the future.

The cart can travel over all sorts of terrain and serve as a networking system capable of linking several villages. In the past, the RLRDP has been successful in making information and communication accessible to disadvantaged communities. In 1995, they launched the first ever donkey-drawn mobile library. The current project builds on the experience with that effort.

Source: The Zimbabwe Mirror. Available online at http://www. africaonline.co.zw./mirror/stage/archive/990716/ national19753.html

Kenya and Tanzania

An interesting and potentially powerful project sponsored by Film Aid International started in the Fall of 2002 in two African countries. The project is using participatory video with adolescent young people to tell their 'stories' about being refugees. The two sites are the Kakuma refugee camp in Northern Kenya and in three refugee camps in western Tanzania. Project facilitators are assisting the young people in the basics of using video cameras, leaving them in the camps for the refugees to use on their own.

As is the case with groups who become enthusiastic about using participatory video (PV), they are seeking counsel from PV practitioners who have worked in that region. This is a project worthy of following since the issue of refugees is pressing, the world over. For instance, if video could take a closer look at present into the Palestinian Refugee Camps, and the images shared with the public, the world would be more than horrified and prompted to action.

Source: Creative Exchange Bulletin. Website: http://www. filmaidinternational.org. Natalia Tapies, program coordinator, Film Aid International. E-mail: nataliaT@theIRC.org

Burundi, Rwanda, Sudan

Film Aid International has established another video project in refugee camps in Burundi, Rwanda and Sudan. It is a four-pronged project:

♦ Evening feature films for entertainment to relieve the boredom and idleness in the camps.
♦ Daytime educational viewing targeting particular groups— women, children, men. Films will complement skills training and focus on problems they are experiencing in the camps. Those problems are myriad—sexual and gender-based violence, reconciliation among different ethnic groups, sexually transmitted disease, and peace education.
♦ FAI will activate participatory video (PV) with refugee youth. Working with a facilitator, young people will be given video cameras "to tell their stories and work on issues that affect and concern them." It is anticipated that this experience will make them critically aware of their situations, motivate personal development and serve as a catalyst for interaction and cooperation.
♦ The project will employ and train refugees to manage the FAI programs in the camps. Gradually these trainees will assume increased responsibility for the program.

Source: Film Aid International. Website: http://www. filmaidinternational.org/ProgramsEA.PC.Frame02.htm

Multicountry in Africa

In several African countries participatory video (PV) has been successfully introduced as a part of the "Participatory Rural Appraisal" (PRA) process. The PRA model, to refresh your understanding, involves establishing rapport; pinpointing issues; defining problems; mapping alternative solutions; establishing pilot projects; applying what has been learned from those pilot projects; and setting up new institutions.

The project facilitators found that when PV was used, project planning became quite a different process. The people chose to carefully articulate their causes and make claims about them instead of endeavoring to identify and analyze their problems. When using video they were able to present their "narratives" within the traditions of their oral culture rather than laboriously put together written reports. According to Johansson, using the PV process "led to the emergence or strengthening of new types of identity, which often supersede or replace ethnicity."

Rather than attempting to identify possible solutions, the people tended to establish "political platforms." For example, when the fisherwomen of a village shared their perspectives on their respective situations with similar identity groups, they were able to set in action mobilization efforts to unify groups with common problems. The viewing resulted in a strong tendency displayed by the groups to identify with each other and "declare their support and willingness to contribute and join in the struggle." This brought local politicians to attention and prompted organizations to join in. Through the use of PV, the initiative was shifted to local leadership. The facilitators believe that PV has made it extremely difficult for local agendas to be co-opted. It brings to attention the human factors involved shifting the emphasis to technical solutions. By enabling people to speak for themselves, progress is made toward the exertion of their democratic rights, which puts them on the pathway to empowerment. The facilitators ask: "How long can development workers continue to talk about participation and empowerment without allowing people to speak for themselves." The use of PV in the Participatory Rural Appraisal process becomes a powerful enabling force to strengthen identity and raise confidence levels.

Source: Johansson, L. (2000). 'Participatory Video and PRA: Acknowledging the politics of empowerment.' *Forestry Trees and People Newsletter,* No. 40/41, pp. 21–23. Rome: FAO. Available online at http://www.worldbank.org/afr/ik/ikvideos.htm

Images from Canada

Central Arctic

The Kaminuriak Herd Project an application of the famed "Fogo Island Process" focused on resolving an extremely complex issue. Quarry reviews this little known project centered around the conflict and hostility between the Inuit hunters of the Keewatin district in the central Arctic, and the biologists and management officials of the government over the hunting of caribou. Don Snowden of Memorial University, Newfoundland, was contacted by a federal civil servant to plan the use of video and the Fogo Process as a way for resolving the conflict.

According to Quarry, the issue, simply explained, was:

> The government biologists wanted the Inuit to stop hunting the caribou from the Kaminuriak Herd. They felt the herd was being over hunted while the Inuit believed the government had got it wrong and did not want interference in their traditional hunting rights.

It appeared that neither party was listening and hostilities were rising and blurring the vision of both. Apparently it wasn't possible to promote "face-to-face dialog" so it was thought that videotape could be used to collect and share information, document opinions and concerns. However, both the biologists and the Inuit were concerned about the disappearing Kaminuriak Herd, and had a sincere desire to resolve the conflict.

A case history of The Kaminuriak Herd documents a situation with roots "buried deep in cultural differences, in differing concepts of practice and usage, and in the interrelationship of man to other living creatures." Some Inuit perceived that natural observation and oral history were in conflict with science and mathematics.

"The project represents a serious and innovative attempt to bridge enormous gaps in perception and understanding between those whose roots are close to the natural world and those who are at home in the industrial milieu."

Snowden and his team carefully harnessed the power of video to bring about a rapprochement between the two solitudes. They began by establishing a set of principles agreed upon by both parties and under which the entire project functioned. Each group was given the opportunity to fully express their particular viewpoint that was captured on video, at leisure, in their own milieu and in their own language. The "versioned" tapes were later distributed back and forth until a gradual softening of attitudes began to take place. These tapes were "versioned" into a second language (English to Inuit and vice versa) and carefully distributed to allow each side to hear the other out via a cool medium. Gradually the management issues were clarified with the realization that each side could learn from the other. Once again the use of the Fogo Process resulted in changed attitudes on both sides. The tapes continued to do so since they were shown in schools and over native broadcasting stations long after management issues were resolved. The tapes in themselves represent a rich source of local knowledge now recorded for future generations (Quarry, p. 27).

The significance of The Kaminuriak Herd Project was that the experience broadened the conceptualization of the "Fogo Process," and brought the elements involved into sharper focus. At this point, the originators articulated more clearly the necessary components and steps in of the process that were:

♦ A trusted and respected community development worker to act as interviewer for the films so that the films truly reflect the community and to act as the crucial link for the film distribution in the community.

♦ A sensitive film crew (video cameraperson) able to work closely with the social animator.

♦ Complete trust from the community that the films would not be shown without individual editing rights.

♦ Distribution by a sensitive person knowledgeable about the community and its problems.

♦ Sensitively handled group viewing and discussion of films to help bring out community issues and knowledge, and explore ways of solving them.

♦ Judicious showing of films to power brokers, bringing views of power brokers back to community.
♦ Use of film material for peer group teaching. (Quarry, pp. 30–31)

Fogo, a filming process that transformed into a community development process, began as a communication tool. Ultimately, it became something much greater: a model for participatory development. It was evident that the tool and the process came together to achieve a greater goal than had been reached prior to its becoming a conceptual framework for participatory development.

Source: Quarry, W. (1994) 'The Fogo Process: An Experiment in Participatory Communication.' University of Guelph Thesis. Available online at http://www.devmedia.org/Papers.cfm?docid=238

Balmertown, Ontario

Remote First Nations in Northwestern Ontario, Canada are using video technologies for a variety of applications. They are making extensive use of interactive video conferencing for both point-to-point and multipoint video sessions. Uses range from public matters to family communications. For example, family members from Poplar Hill and Pikangikum First Nations video conferenced with a family member who was involved in open heart surgery at Sick Kids Hospital in Toronto. North Spirit Lake First Nation students met through video conferencing with youngsters from Lamphere High School in Caseville, Michigan and Coochland Elementary School in Virginia. Photo documentation of their activities is in the form of picture galleries that are posted on the web at http://www.photos.knet.ca.

Keewaytinook Okimakanak, a First Nations Council serving six remote First Nations, hosted a conference, First Nations Connect, in Thunder Bay in March, 2002. The conference brought together the First Nation Interactive Communication Technologies (ICT) community champions and leaders to discuss broadband connectivity issues and applications. Sessions of the conference were videotaped and clips posted at http://www.smart.knet.ca/

conference/video.html. These clips are now being used by people across Canada to show how First Nations are using ICT and video for individual and community development.

As part of the Aboriginal Smart Communities Demonstration project for Canada, Keewaytinook Okimakanak is utilizing and exploring various broadband applications (telehealth, online high school, etc.) that make use of video technologies to bring new opportunities and resources to rural and remote communities across the region. You can find more information at http://www. smartcommunities.ic.gc.ca.

Source: Brian Beaton, K-Net Services Coordinator, Keewaytinook Okimakanak. E-mail:brian.beaton@knet.ca. Website: http://www.knet.ca.

Images from Cuba

Sierra Maestra

Televisión Serrana a community video and television project in the heart of the famous Sierra Maestra in Cuba, began with a small group of videomakers in 1993. It is located in the small community of San Pablo de Yao, in Buey Arriba territory where nearly two-thirds of the population are coffee growers. The intention of the project is "to rescue the culture of peasant communities" and through alternative communication provide information and encouragement to people to "reject their daily lives and participate in the search for solutions to the problems that affect them."

Televisión Serrana has become a process of education for communication using video to reach social and education objectives— an instrument for strengthening cultural identity, and also a means of communicating with other communities in other parts of Cuba and the world. The project is intent upon developing a cultural environment within the inaccessible mountainous zones that would increase the capabilities of people to strengthen their families and their communities.

Video documentaries, news reports, and other types of programs are addressing issues of culture and identity, children's rights, gender, health, the environment and the need for education. They are encouraging self-sustaining activities for communities by offering training workshops, seminars and advisory services to individuals who desire to use video in their communities as "a tool for participatory and democratic communication." They have video production and editing facilities, a meeting room, a library, and even housing facilities for upto 10 people, and can therefore provide an optimum learning environment for those who seek assistance. They are equipped to take video into the small communities of Sierra Maestra, which they believe would help establish their presence at the community level.

One of the more interesting aspects of the project involves the children of the Sierra Maestra who produce Vídeo Cartas (video letters) that they send to other children in Cuba and other parts of the world. Through the video cartas the children share their daily life, their families and the nature that surrounds them; they talk about their school and what they do to entertain themselves; and then pose questions to the children who view their Video Carta, seeking a response.

The Video Cartas have brought recognition to the people and to the area of Sierra Maestra. The act of videotaping itself is a meaningful experience. When a videotaping team enters a community and stays with the people, their level of self-esteem is increased. When their voices are heard and the images from their daily life and culture are seen in other communities of Cuba or another part of the world, they feel recognized and respected. On occasion, documentaries have been aired on national television and people from all over Cuba have become aware of the lifestyle and conditions of the peasants from the Buey Arriba territory.

An important aspect of the communication process that Televisión Serrana has sparked is the showing of the video productions in small villages of Sierra Maestra using mules to carry TV monitors and VCRs. Each show is followed by a discussion. If a video-letter is shown, the audience may respond to it with a video-letter of their own: their need to say, "we are here" is enormous. In a true sense they experience a new sense of identity and unity. During one of the after show discussions the crew discovered an 82-year-old man who had been writing poems on Sierra Maestra for 20 years; he became the subject of a video production. Likewise, the contamination of River Yao by a coffee processing plant was first mentioned after a video show; a critical video documentary followed and pushed for the implementation of corrective measures.

Televisión Serrana faced difficulties from the beginning. Filmmakers had no experience working in a community development context. It took time for the video teams to build the confidence of the people in the local communities and for them to recognize that their presence was well intended. A plus, however, was that the training of young people in the communities in video production was enhanced by the fact that their education level was very high—upto grade 12. In the beginning, local authorities found it difficult to understand the value of a "cultural" project using video. Limited resources posed problems as well. But the project is now flourishing and has the goal of becoming a full-fledged television broadcast operation in the future.

Source: Communication Initiative Website: http://www. comminit.com/11-342-case_studies; Daniel Diez Castrillo, director and founder of Televisión Serrana.

Images from Hawaii

Maui County

An impressive community television system has been established in Maui County Hawaii with the apparent purpose of "Empowering Our Community's Voice through Access to Media." The website they have put together to support community television is equally impressive. It is a good example of how the interface of video and Internet technologies strengthens the outreach of visual media. They are using participatory approaches, which are inherent in community access efforts. Their goals are comprehensive: some of them worth noting here:

◆ Encourage the creation of programs aimed at preserving, developing and enhancing the diversity of thought, culture and heritage within Hawaii.
◆ Facilitate lifelong learning and community participation in the democratic process.

♦ Provide equipment, facilities, training and other support resources in order to meet the needs of community users.
♦ Serve as a local information exchange.

Browsing through the website is time well spent. It provides a model that illustrates how community video can be enhanced through supportive media and participatory community action.

Source: http://www.akaku.org

International Images
International Water Supply: Community Management

The International Water and Sanitation Center (IRC) is a world-wide program focused on community management of water supplies. This focus, the organization notes, is increasingly accepted as the most appropriate model for providing sustainable water supply and sanitation services to rural communities in the developing world. Currently, they are engaging in an extensive six-country training program, MANAGE, in an effort increase competencies of development facilitators to create an "enabling environment" in communities to support and sustain their own management.

The IRC project, which began in 1994, involves national partner organizations in six countries:

♦ NEWAH (Nepal Water for Health) in Nepal is an implementing organization that constructs about 200 water supply systems per year and is involved in small research projects and training.
♦ WASEP (Water and Sanitation Extension Programme of the Aga Khan Planning and Building Service) in Pakistan is an implementing organization.
♦ NETWAS (Network for Water and Sanitation) in Kenya is a training institute in the water and sanitation sector.
♦ WSMC (Water and Sanitation Management Consultants) in Cameroon is a one-person consultancy, specializing in training in the water and sanitation sector.

♦ CINARA (Instituto de Investigacion y Desarrollo en Agua Potable, Saneamiento Basico y Conservacion del Recurso Hidrico), connected to the University of Cali, does research as well as evaluations and assessments of water and sanitation projects.

♦ SER (Servicios para el Desarrollo) is a small consultancy in Guatemala, involved in research and evaluations.

These organizations have participated in research activities at the beginning of the project, and a "dissemination" phase that entails a wide range of activities and media outputs. This phase aims to improve the local management, implementation and sustainability of water supply systems.

An important part of the project was the production of seven development "video films," produced through participatory approaches: one each for the six participating organizations and one video for use in all countries. The country videos were targeted at project staff and the seventh compilation video was intended for policy makers. Ton Schouten shares the guiding principles used:

♦ The "video films" had to be directed by independent documentary filmmakers from the six countries. Directors from the countries speak the (film) language of the target groups. They know the nuances of the local film language: when people will be excited, will laugh or be "moved" by the images. They also know the rhythm of the films. We wanted independent filmmakers who would avoid the "project" type of film: selling an organization or a project. We wanted critical people who could picture the situation and opinions at the ground, independent of what the organization or the project wants to sell.

♦ The partner organizations had to produce the "video films," therefore, they needed to be in the driving seat. This was to create ownership for the videos and increase the chance that they would be used and distributed. The independent filmmakers discussed and negotiated with the partner organizations and involved them in ongoing dialog throughout the production process.

♦ The videos were made to stimulate reflection and debate: not give definite answers or some kind of golden rule or blueprint for community water management. The videos intended to show the complexities and the heterogeneity of community management, the potentials and the pitfalls.

♦ *The viewing groups should readily recognize the process communities undergo as they work to manage their water supplies.* Their response would be: "Yes, that is the reality we know. It is within our power to improve these processes."

♦ *IRC staff played the backstopping and mediation role for both the filmmakers and the partner organizations.* The latter were inexperienced in video filmmaking and the IRC helped them write drafts and synopsis for the videos. IRC also assisted in their discussions with the filmmakers so that together they could draft the process of production and decide the moments of decision-making. IRC also had regular contact with the filmmakers who were contracted by IRC.

♦ *The production was to be a learning process for the partner organizations and help them produce "video films" for their organizations.*

With the help of the Rotterdam Film Festival, the Hubert Bals Fund and the partner organizations, IRC identified independent filmmakers in the six countries. The filmmakers selected were: Sushma Joshi in Nepal, Sabiha Sumar in Pakistan, Cyrille Dieudonne Bitting in Cameroon, Albert Wandago in Kenya, Consuela Cepeda in Colombia and Alfonso Porres in Guatemala.

The productions took one year, allowing for extensive discussions and negotiations. The partner organizations were involved at every stage of the production process and had to give their final approval. The process was interesting: often there were conflicts between organizations and filmmakers. The filmmakers wanted to follow their own observations in the communities and their own judgments, the partner organizations often wanted to make a nice "project" film. In one case, IRC had to choose between a filmmaker's version and an organization's version, because the filmmaker and the organization could not agree on a final version of the film.

The videos are now widely used in the countries and most of the organizations are proud of what they produced. Ton Schouten shares some of their "lessons learned":

♦ The partner organizations should have been the contracting party, not the IRC. Some of them felt they didn't have enough power vis-à-vis the filmmaker.

♦ In one case, the partner organization was so committed, but also so stubborn, in pushing through its messages that the filmmaker pulled back. The result, in our opinion, was not good: too defensive a film, although the material allowed for a far more "nuanced" film.

♦ In one case the filmmaker was so pushy and the partner organization so inexperienced and timid, that the film became too critical. The partner organization felt more or less ashamed to show the film to other organizations and the ministry.

♦ Communication among three parties—IRC, filmmaker, and partner organization—was very time consuming and complex. It often created misunderstandings and problems.

♦ IRC at times had to mediate the conflicts between the filmmaker and the partner organization: an awkward position for all.

Ton believes that it is important to build local level capacity for the production of good video films, films that stimulate reflection and debate and help target groups take a critical look at their work, develop new insights and opinions. For such capacity building you need to have independent filmmakers who can negotiate with local people. You need to build the capacities of the organizations to make films that really matter and to work compatibly with independent filmmakers.

Ton played the role of mediator between the filmmakers and the organizations, between the interests of the organizations and the creative thinking of the filmmakers. The videos are truly the product of the three "actors"—all with their own backgrounds and experiences, who together made the videos through sharing ideas, discussions, negotiations, and creative visualization. He is convinced that this project has definitely promoted better understandings that will be reflected in future video production endeavors.

The *Seventh Video* produced by Ton Schouten was highly appreciated. It shows the nitty-gritty's of water management in rural communities, the daily realities; quite unique in the water sector. However, the video could only be made because in each country they were able to capture to these realities and the people were ready to cooperate with Ton to film with an open spirit. Ton makes his position clear:

I attach much value to the artistic freedom of the filmmaker, the personal judgements of the artist. The independence of the filmmaker guarantees critical and authentic films; critical films will stimulate reflection and discussion and therefore development and change. A film doesn't necessarily have to reflect the "way it is," because there is no "way it is." There are many different ways of looking at the same phenonema, i.e., community management of water supplies—the community's way of looking, the filmmakers way of looking, and the project's way of looking. Which one is chosen, depends on what you want to accomplish with the video.

We wanted a film that tickles the imagination of project staff, a film that does not let them get off the hook (is that English?) but makes them think and talk. A classical kind of film, with good tension, with a good story and plot, that builds up to something, an exciting film for project staff. That was the assignment for the six filmmakers (and biased by me). In the discussions and negotiations between filmmakers, the organizations and the people in the communities the films were finally made, not through structured participation, but rather through genuine negotiation.

A personal comment from Ton Schouten exhibits his enthusiasm for the power of images in development. He says:

> IRC gave me the assignment to make the seven films ... I liked the intermediate role between filmmakers and organisations: the tension between the creativity of independent people and the interests of the organisation. In the development sector we should use the dynamics of art far more, because art and artists hold the mirror and help us to walk and think a bit besides the paths we already know and tend to cherish too much.

Source: IRC International Water and Sanitation Center, Ton Schouten, program officer. http://www.irc.nl/manage; http://www.irc.nl/manage/videos/index.html

Images from Jamaica

Rural Jamaica

A pilot project experience from Jamaica offers a unique gender approach to using various participatory media at appropriate moments during a technology development and extension process—a process aimed at improving the effective use of a variety of soil nutrients. Video was used extensively in a variety of ways throughout this project. This experience points out video's power as a research tool and the versatility of its use throughout development projects. The goal of the project was to develop a participatory communication model using a variety of media to reach rural women, ones that would be supportive of indigenous knowledge, culturally relevant and empowering. Learnings from the experience are now available to extension professionals who are concerned about reaching women producers more effectively.

The first phase of the project was conducted through one-on-one farm visits followed by community screenings of videotapes that profiled Jamaican agricultural projects. Video facilities were available in each community. The level of interest in the programmes was high and the people were enthusiastic about video. Those who viewed were quite impressed with what the farmers in the videos had achieved. As was anticipated, the level of awareness of the people about the activities of other rural communities and farmer organizations in Jamaica was quite low. One person exclaimed during a screening: "A wha countri a dat dere [What country is that there]?"

A visual ethnographic approach was used for data collection in the baseline survey that was to serve a comparative purpose in evaluations. All respondents were interviewed with open-ended questions, their responses either videotaped or audio taped. According to the researcher there were several advantages of this visual and aural approach:

♦ It was easy to record women's indigenous knowledge and the tapes served as proof of their intellectual ownership.
♦ The women were able to speak for themselves instead of through someone else. The media impressed many of the

women who felt that they were being listened to and that they had something important to say.

♦ The interviewers could replay the recordings to check for instances of bias.

♦ The information could be returned to the respondents in a way that was meaningful to them.

♦ The video reports could be used for participatory evaluation when the project was completed.

♦ The exchanges were intimate and relaxed because no notes were taken.

The researchers found that transcribing or viewing the interviews was quite time consuming, but this disadvantage was outweighed by the benefits. Unexpectedly, they found that a high number of respondents had access to VCRs, so small video libraries were created.

In order to verify the baseline findings, a drama was developed. Rural women, accustomed to performing folk songs and dances for large audiences from one community were hired as indigenous actors. This experience increased the organizational skills of the involved women. The theme of the drama was extracted from the information gained in the baseline study and centered on the quality of gender relationships. Exaggeration and humor were used to minimize the threat to men. Audiences found the play realistic and it served the purpose of validating the impressions of the baseline survey. Performances were videotaped and then shown again in each community. It was possible to stop the video whenever necessary to allow particular points to be more fully discussed.

During the second phase of the project, technology introduction and testing, a "Rough Cut" instructional video was produced. The video proposed a number of techniques for conserving soil and/or increasing soil fertility. The "Rough Cut" was viewed in each community and discussed. Farmers who viewed the tape were invited to test out combinations of the techniques suggested in the video. An impressive response followed: 100 women registered, agreeing to test at least four techniques over the next year.

The positive response to video led to the formation of groups who took part in the "Participatory Video Training" conducted within each of the communities. The training resulted in a series of short, humorous and insightful programs relating to agriculture and indigenous soil fertility technologies. The video training led to the discovery of more indigenous techniques that were explored in greater depth for possible use. Wherever possible, the participants with video production skills were involved in retaping of the videos and used as narrators to continue the "farmer to farmer" communication approach.

One of the significant observations of the researchers is that women have specific information needs and are found to be responsive to visual communication technologies. In proposing appropriate agricultural technologies for rural women and their families, a participatory communication and extension methodology interfacing indigenous and scientific knowledge is found to be effective. The uniqueness of this project is that it focuses on gender issues that impact on communicating agricultural practices. This proposed methodology and the participatory communication techniques for a gender approach to agricultural projects are worthy of serious attention.

Source: Protz, M. *Developing Sustainable Agricultural Technologies with Rural Women in Jamaica: A participatory media approach.* Posted December 1998 on the FAO Sustainable Development Website: http://www.fao.org/sd/cedirect/cdan0020.htm

Images from Latin America

Rio de Janeiro, Brazil

TV Maxambomba is a project of CECIP, Centro de Criacao de Imagen Popular (Popular Image Creation Center) in Rio de Janeiro. Created in 1986 as the Popular Video Project, it became TV Maxambomba by 1990. The name carried with it powerful local significance. Slaves who once carried farm products to boats heading for the capital were referred to as *Maxambomba*. It implied that things had changed: better understanding of social events, and a movement toward community participation in the communication process. TV Maxambomba has become a strong people-driven project producing video with powerful messages for social change.

The founders of CECIP were professionals from various fields, drawn together by their common interest in helping Brazilian society. The organization focuses on enabling Brazil's disadvantaged populations to obtain access to information. The goal is to assist them in understanding their rights, identifying their problems and taking action. TV Maxambomba uses video to record the experiences of local people, different aspects of local culture and programes for children. They document and appraise action of grass roots organizations so they can better address the issues relevant to the disadvantaged.

Some of the CECIP projects are video documentaries on special issues. As many as 100 video documentaries have been produced since 1986. Various relevant social issues have been articulated visually: democracy, citizen's rights, education, gender, environment, black culture, health and sexuality. Videos are produced for specific audiences such as women and children. The videos are shown in public community based screenings in public squares and schools as well as over broadcast channels. While TV Maxambomba has grown into a production house respected for innovative techniques and high quality video productions, it keeps in regular touch with the social reality and participatory involvement of the grass roots people. Like many similar alternative video production organizations, this one faces the issues of sustainability in terms of relevance and funding resources.

Source: Claudius Ceccon, executive secretary, CECIP. Communication Initiatives Website: http://www.comminit.com/11-342-case_studies/sld-596.html

Images from Mexico
San Luis Potosí, Yucatan, Chiapas

The Programme of Integrated Rural Development in the Tropical Wetlands (PRODERITH) was operational from 1978 to 1984, and from 1986 to 1995. This project in Mexico put participatory video (PV) on record as a powerful tool to enlist people's participation in agricultural development. In light of previous failed efforts to enlist participation, project designers made a strategic decision to undergird their project with a communication process that would ensure the participation of local people. It was important that the proposals would reflect the will of the people and thereby, be appropriate to the situation.

Starting in 1977, video was used to enable peasants analyze their problems and situations, to record meeting procedures and to use as a reference document to be played back as future plans were discussed. In these initial stages of the project, video was an effective motivator for bringing peasants into the planning process. Video became the centerpiece of communication strategy as the PRODERITH project was put into full operation in 1978. Training with video as a tool was the main activity conducted at the community level. Cameras became available in the project areas, but a centralized editing facility was maintained in Cuernavaca.

The snapshot provided in the website account of the project characterizes the situation well:

The charismatic old man, with his white hair and white beard, sat cross-legged in front of a video camera for hours on end. He held forth about the past, about the Revolution, about the greatness of Mayan culture and about life today. He deplored the decline of such Mayan traditions as the family vegetable plot, explained how he cultivated his own maize, and complained that today's young people did not even know how to do that properly. He accused the young of abandoning all that had been good in Mayan culture; they would sell eggs to buy cigarettes and soft drinks, and so it was no wonder that diets today were worse than they were in his youth, and so on.

Scores of people sat in attentive silence in the villages as these tapes were played back. In the evening, under a tree, the words in Mayan flowed from the screen, and the old man's eloquent voice and emphatic gestures spread their spell. For many, it was the first time they had ever heard anyone talk about the practical values of their culture. It was also the first time they had seen a peasant like themselves on "television," and talking their own language. Frequently they asked that the tapes be repeated again and again.

The desired effect was achieved: the people began to take stock of their situation and think seriously about their values. Ultimately, community participation became the overall goal that drove the project.

Peasants often show difficulty in articulating their views of their reality, and they seldom share with outsiders their individual perceptions. PRODERITH has contributed to rural development by enabling the articulation of collective perception within the community—on the local situation, its problems and options for improving it. The video methodology prompted internal debate about the history, culture and future perspectives of the communities involved in the communication process.

During the two phases of PRODERITH more than 700 training videos and accompanying printed materials were produced, and more than 800 people participated in the training sessions. These, undoubtedly, had a great impact on the daily lives of peasants, as the topics covered farming, fishing, livestock, health, nutrition, environment, water, community organization and every other possible topic connected to the needs of the rural population. At its peak of productivity in 1981, the communication team was able to produce 100 videos in one year. In a broader perspective, PRODERITH is an example of communication becoming instrumental in moving forward a major rural development program. It shows how communication can be fully integrated if the need has been clearly identified from the inception of the programme. The Rural Communication System developed by PRODERITH was uniquely imaginative and effective, according to a FAO assessment.

Source: FAO of the UN, 1996. *Communication for Rural Development in Mexico.* Available online at the Communication Initatives Website, http://www.comminit.com/11-342-case_studies/sld-589. html

Images from South Asia

Tamil Nadu, India

Since 1966 Marupakkam translated as "the other side" in Tamil language, has been operational as a development organization. The organization now works with local groups such as NGOs, trade unions, educational institutions or just informal groups to arrange "video tours." The purpose of these tours is to expose local people to development issues pertinent to their areas. Marupakkam coordinates the "tour" with a video projector, the films the groups want and a team of facilitators to assist in organizing the event. The tour project is called "Vaanavil", meaning "rainbow" in Tamil language. The films used are feature films and documentaries produced by Marupakkam as well as low cost videos on local issues. Also screened are films made by fellow filmmakers for use in the tours. Marupakkam also organizes film festivals, translates films into Tamil from English, assists filmmakers in organizing tours with their own films, and organizing video training workshops.

Marupakkam tours started early in 2002. Some of the development issues addressed are: welfare of children, status of women, problems of aging, cultural preservation, human rights, agricultural productivity, environmental problems, access to education, political and economic development. It takes considerable organizing and mobilization of volunteers to conduct the tours that can run from one to five days. Marupakkam provides a video cassette player, a video projector, requested films, and reading materials that can be photocopied, and individuals to assist in coordinating the event.

Two to four volunteers from Marupakkam began the organization effort. They worked with local facilitators—activists, filmmakers, academicians and other locals. Up to four screenings are arranged each day: each one followed by open-ended discussion. The facilitators introduce the films and coordinate the discussions. Local people are alerted to the showings through a "write-up" sent out at least one-month prior to the tour. There is an abundance of video and film on development issues available but they are not necessarily adequately disseminated and used in Tamil Nadu. *Vaanavil* is an attempt to bridge the gap.

It will be interesting to follow this project to determine what impact it will have on development efforts in Tamil Nadu. Its success will no doubt depend upon the follow-up of local facilitators, assuming that the videos will motivate local citizens to act.

Source: Vaanavil: A Video Tour—Tamil Nadu, India
http://www.comminit.com/pds10-2001/sld-3191.html. For information contact: Amudhan rp, Marupakkam, 12-7/147, Malligai Malar Street, Mahatma Gandhi Nagar, Madurai 625014, Tamil Nadu, 98431-94528. amudhanrp@rediffmail.com

Bangladesh

ActionAid Bangladesh has embraced Participatory Video (PV) as a strong and effective communication tool for social change. Several challenging and innovative PV initiatives have been undertaken by ActionAid Bangladesh with its partners.

Our Voices, a participatory video about girls' education, was made by a group of adolescents who had developed their expertise through a program which explored PV as a tool for facilitating adolescent voices. This training was partnered by ActionAid and the Bangladesh Institute of Theater Arts (BITA) at Chittagong. These young adolescents were from the Poracolony slum area of Chittagong city in Bangladesh where the poor do not have access to any medium through which to make their voices heard. Sobhan notes:

> The video served as a tool for telling their stories, sharing their knowledge, expressing their problems, demand their rights, and suggest approaches to appropriate development initiatives and changes. The children's participatory video units identified crisis in access and relevance of primary education with particular emphasis on gender and girls' right to education as an issue to be addressed. Through this participatory video exercises, at least, the schooling system and as a whole the education system and child rights situation was scrutinized from the standpoint of the excluded children, particularly the girls. The systematic process of marginalization for the girls, both in schools or beyond the schools is portrayed by the children at the grass roots in the *Our Voices* video.
> Their work continues.

Another four-month long PV pilot project was initiated in 2000 in Tala, Sathkhira, a southwestern district of Bangladesh. This PV project intended to explore the potentials of PV as a tool: to raise awareness and solve problems at the grass roots level, to involve marginalized people in advocacy processes, and to facilitate active participation of grass roots people in education campaigns. Sobhan reports:

> Twenty-eight villagers (including women) from four villages of Tala, Satkhira received hands-on training in participatory

video production. After receiving training, they produced PV training films on various social concerns. Later, the films, produced by the "newly trained" PV personnel were screened and discussed with the fellow villagers. The process of "community viewing and receiving immediate feedback" helped create awareness about various issues in the community.

The outcome of the pilot project was the establishment of video units in each of the four villages, complete with operational resources. They began their work with a focus on the problem of accessing quality education at the grass roots level and will move on to other local problems. The videos will be viewed by community groups and discussed locally. Their goal is to influence government decision-makers and be a force for acquiring resources.

ActionAid Bangladesh is collaborating with its current partner organizations to further explore PV as a tool for amplifying the "voices of the unheard." They continue to put a priority on children's participation with a long-range goal of ensuring that the country will benefit from their knowledge and future leadership. In addition they are fostering the use of PV as an effective research tool. According to Sobhan's account there are visions for PV in ActionAid Bangladesh:

Along with constantly exploring and experimenting with the potentials of PV in Bangladesh as a tool for information and advocacy, ActionAid Bangladesh in near future plans to introduce PV as a tool for scrutinizing public services by the civil society organisations under ActionAid Bangladesh's governance support programme for strengthening civil society. Not only that, private television channels have already showed keen interest in PV and expressed willingness to telecast PV footage/programmes on TV. ActionAid Bangladesh, in the days to come, wishes to see PV as the most widespread and effective communication tool for social development. It could be made possible with the commitment of all, coupled with required funding and support.

Source: Participatory Video in ActionAid Bangladesh. Hillol Sobhan, associate coordinator, participatory video & campaign,

ActionAid Bangladesh, May 2001. Available online at http://www.elimu.org or http://www.actionaidasia.org.

Images from Southeast Asia

Korea

Video has been a forceful communicator in Korea articulating the situations and needs of laborers. Labor News Production (LNP) was established with this main goal: "to strengthen the democratic and progressive labor movement in Korea and worldwide and to play an important role in making the situation of media in the country more democratic."

During the 12 years of activity of LNP beginning 1990, the organization has undergone an important transformation evolving from changes in communication technologies and experience with participatory approaches. Video has, however, been an essential part of labor education from the beginning. It has played a critical role in facilitating information exchanges about the labor movement among working people and has enabled a visual history of working people's lives and their struggles.

At times video has represented hundreds of union members and enabled them to speak with "one voice." It has shared their perspectives with a wider audience in order to make their situations known. From its position inside the labor movement, LNP has to effectively establish the significance of democratic communication. Through the 10 years this organization has conducted participatory video training, several workers' video collectives have emerged as well as many independent documentary video-makers. LNP has trained an impressive number of people: more than 1000. Through collaboration of several labor-oriented organizations, the Human Rights Film Festival, and the International Labor Media Conference have been organized as well as other such events.

It isn't surprising that LNP now distributes its videos internationally—to Japan, USA, Australia, and other countries. Their videos are playing an important role presenting the situation of working people in Korea to workers of other nations. Some videos are broadcast by satellite by Indymedia. LNP can claim part of the credit for finally obtaining people's access to public broadcasting, cable and satellite TV in Korea. As a result of their efforts, alternative media became more attractive to users but also to government funded institutions in the film and broadcasting sector who are focusing their research on the alternative media movement. Video is at the axis of the media activities of LNP though other communication tools are used as well. LNP has established a website that has been accessible since 1998.

LNP is truly a participatory communication project. Every member contributes to the decision-making. Video production methods engage a participatory process through which LNP and workers learn from each other through on-going dialog and discussion. LNP opted for a methodology of "video production with the people not about the people." One of LNP's main intentions is to continually help rank and file workers make their own videos, which is an essential part of the participatory process encouraged within the labor movement.

Source: The Communication Initatives Website, http://www. comminit.com/11-342-case_studies/sld-621.html and the Labor News Production Website, (Korean Language) http://www. mayday.nodong.net

Images from the USA

Washington DC

The World Bank is making available videos on Indigenous Knowledge (IK) and Practices for training purposes. IK videos document success stories in applying indigenous practices. These stories demonstrate how IK can enrich the development process, through a series of best practices featuring development practitioners at work. They can be downloaded from the World Bank website.

♦ Anima's story—"IK in East Africa plays a key role in the survival strategies of border communities."
♦ Using local knowledge on medicinal plants and seeds for development.

◆ Tea growing communities in Wupperthal, South Africa secure a $15,000 export contract.
◆ Health workers in Iganga District, Uganda reduce maternal mortality by 50 percent within three years.
◆ Farmers in Pratapgarh, India increase their income within five years by 60 percent.

Videos such as these can provide a springboard for thinking in other communities, in other continents. The possibility of downloading video from websites provides an inexpensive and readily accessible source of visual materials for facilitators. Such tapes should serve, not so much as "models" to be copied, but as "trigger tapes"—the power of images—to stimulate dialog and thinking.

Source: http://www.worldbank.org/afr/ik/ikvideos.htm

Websites Worth Browsing

The Internet was a valuable tool for assembling the information I have included in this chapter. Websites were located with key word searches using various search engines and from relevant hyperlinks provided through the DevMedia List Serve. Interestingly, most of my personal contacts were also identified through the Internet.

The most informative site I used is the Communication Initiatives website originating in Victoria, British Columbia, Canada. The Communication Initiative is a partnership of development organizations "seeking to support advances in the effectiveness and scale of communication interventions for positive international development." The intent of the site is to provide information that will improve strategic thinking about the role of communication in resolving development issues—uplift the quality of "communication for change" information and advocate improved communication effectiveness for sustainable development.

The Communication Initiative is concerned about meeting the needs of individuals actively engaged in development. The site

seeks to provide a forum for your ideas, stories and actions and to connect you to information that will be of use in your work. The issues, and trends we bring forward and the work of others we profile ... are examples and samples of the many voices and actions that make the field of communication for social change dynamic and hopefully add to all of our learning and understanding.

Web Address: http://www.comminit.com/about-time.html

Another useful site is UNFAO's Sustainable Development Department's website, SD Dimensions. As stated on the site:

The Sustainable Development Department (SD) serves as a global reference centre for knowledge and advice on biophysical, biological, socio-economic and social dimensions of sustainable development. It was established by FAO in January 1995, in response to the need to take a more holistic and strategic approach to development support and poverty alleviation.

Web Address: http://www.fao.org/sd/index_en.htm. The entire FAO website is useful for development communication professionals and practioners. *Web Address*: http://www.fao.org.

The World Bank's Participation website is a focused, useful and comprehensive site. The site is put together by the bank's Participation Thematic Team. Their work "promotes methods and approaches that encourage stakeholders, especially the poor, to influence and share control over priority setting, policy-making, resource allocations and access to public goods and services." The site has extensive resource materials on every aspect of participation and development. It becomes user friendly with its site search feature than allows you to search by country or by theme, or key word. *Web Address*: http://www.worldbank.org/participation.

Another of the World Bank's sub-sites is Voices of the Poor. The content of the site is derived from extensive research on worldwide poverty. The site offers an extensive collection of materials, much of which can be downloaded from the site. I would recommend browsing the site at http://www.worldbank.org/poverty/voices/index.htm.

A smaller and perhaps one of the more user friendly sites is Reflect. The site presents an innovative approach to adult learning and social change that fuses the theories of Paulo Freire with the methodology of participatory rural appraisal. The site suggests links to other organizations and websites that focus on adult learning, social change and participatory methodologies. It can lead you into many interesting directions. It can be accessed at http://www.reflect-action.org. ActionAid is the international NGO that originally conceived Reflect. It currently uses the approach widely. The ActionAid *Web Address*: http://www. actionaid.org.

SACOD is a coalition of Southern Africa filmmakers and organizations in related services whose primary focus is the production and distribution of social responsibility films and videos. Southern Africa Communications for Development (SACOD) was founded in 1987 by independent institutions from Zimbabwe, South Africa and Mozambique, and Canada to support the growth of the independent video movement, and to support the process of democratization in Southern Africa via the audiovisual medium. SACOD now has members in eight SADC countries. South Africa (Regional Office), Zimbabwe, Swaziland, Angola, Lesotho, Zambia, Mozambique and Namibia with its regional cooperation office in Johannesburg. *Web Address*: http://www.sacod.org.za.

Comment

When I realized how much I rely on the Internet, I became curious about how much others depend on it. I learned that more than 50 percent of Internet users are in North America. If they are associated with academic institutions or other organizations, they generally utilize the Internet service provided by their institution. Others find local service providers readily available. There is sufficient use for the US Postal Services to complain that e-mail is cutting into its revenues. Another fourth of Internet users are in Europe, and the remaining scattered throughout Asia, Latin America, Africa and the rest of the world. I'm sure there are precise figures available on Internet users, figures that likely change daily.

Sources from USA tend to dominate website content. Interestingly, this pattern is similar for television and telecommunications. However, many well-designed sites are popping up all over the world in many different languages. But, as most of us discover, keeping a website updated is a huge challenge. When you browse sites you find many that haven't been updated for months or even years.

The potential benefit of the Internet in bringing about social change is virtually unexplored and unlimited. The interface of computer technologies and video technologies certainly holds promise for revolutionary changes in the way these technologies can serve the causes of development. Additionally, they can enhance the participatory aspects of the development process. But knowing what is possible, and actually accomplishing the possible, are two different issues. Great leaps forward are dependent upon access to financial support for projects and available human resources with the capacity to implement them and keep them operational.

Looking Ahead: Community Communication Centers

For a long time it has been clear to me that the only way people can make use of new communication technologies is to have access to them. For video in the USA, public access television has been a concern and a reality since the 1970s. When I established the Video Communication Laboratory at my University in the mid-70s, access was our main purpose, accompanied by training and consultation. We served the faculty and the field staff of Cooperative Extension. By 1977 we had trained nearly 200 field staff and grass roots leaders and began to establish regional access centers. We established an extensive summer school program and then a regular credit course in Video Communication. A dream that was never realized, largely because of political roadblocking, was a Walk in Learning Center on the campus where people could comfortably learn how to use a variety of instructional media at their own pace. We also began setting up mini-centers in several of the County Extension Associations.

When I became associated with the Development Communication Research Project in India at the University of Pune in the early 1980s, we conceptualized a similar resource center to be established in the village—the Community Communication Center (CCC). In cooperation with the University's affiliated colleges, we began to work toward the CCC goal. The first step in the development of such centers was to find an existing place in the village where we could simply locate a television receiver. Our focus was on video at that time: because it was possible for people who were illiterate in a traditional sense to express themselves and to learn, aurally and visually.

At that point in time most villagers had not even seen television. In a few villages the village panchayat leader had a TV in his home and did share it with villagers. The temple was often the place where people could gather so most often that was where we located the TV receivers. In cooperation with the local affiliated college we identified faculty and students who could provide outreach to the respective villages and be trained in video. These folk began their association with the Development Communication Research Project (DCRP) by assisting with data gathering for the project. The centers had great potential and the concept was well received. However, the centers were never fully developed because of lack of resources.

The Centers

The center approach is one that has been explored by many development organizations to provide rural areas access to information and communication technologies. The centers have been labeled Development Resource Centers, CyberCenters, CyberCafes, Telecenters, Village Knowledge Centers, etc. While they have originally been started to provide individuals who are unable to afford telephones and the Internet access to these technologies, these centers have expanded into a broader shared facility. Some telecenters, for example provide access to telephone, fax services, the Internet, e-mail and library services. They have the potential to link the Internet to radio and television making their services accessible to audiences for whom it is not feasible to come to the centers.

Unfortunately telecenters have come to be seen as information technology centers. Many are staffed by technicians who are focused primarily on the technical aspects of the center operations. Providing *Information and Commmunication Technologies* in isolated rural areas is not sufficient for the community. Often when a technician who operates the center is offered a better opportunity, s/he exits and it is not uncommon to find the center shutting down temporarily, or permanently. Certainly, a center must be much more than technology access in order to serve the wider purposes of the community for development. Proponents of telecenters do not seem to have the vision, the interest or the time to put the concept into broader perspective and link it to long-term goals of development. The measure of success too often is the number of telecenters established without addressing the issues of sustainability.

The Vision

My current vision of a Community Communication Center (CCC) has not been substantially altered from my original thinking about the idea. I find it quite relevant to the movement toward participatory communication and development. Such centers should be the heartbeat of communities who are moving more steadily toward participatory approaches. While my earlier thinking was to find a way to put video into the hands of local extension professionals and grass roots people, it has easily broadened to include other new communication technologies. Therefore, as a finale to this book, I would like to present my model for a CCC.

The Model

We can start by visualizing such a center located, in a small town or village. Figure 17.1 presents the components of the center. First, the CCC needs a roomy facility that can become a *communication environment* that attracts people, invites them in and gets them involved. It should be staffed by well-prepared technicians and facilitators who have an understanding of the center concept and who can effectively institute its processes. Such an environment makes it easy for people to get acquainted with one another, feel at ease, interact with others and talk about issues of concern. Dialog and interactions are ongoing in the CCC environment.

Second, the center will *provide access to information and communication technologies*. While long range plans for the center may be for a wide array of access and training offerings, these offerings should gradually be introduced as a part of the center's program. At each step of the way, it should be assured that the staff and the participants optimize the use of resources. Ongoing, *consultation,*

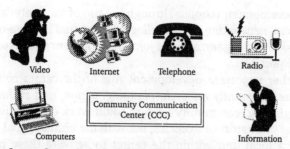

Video   Internet   Telephone   Radio

Computers   Community Communication Center (CCC)   Information

- Creates a Communication Environment that Fosters Dialog and Interaction
- Provides Access to Information and Communication Technologies
- Provides Consultation, Training and Counseling
- Serves as a Link to Community Leadership, Organizations and Services
- Facilitates Community Research, Planning, Action and Evaluation
- Initiates Resource Acquisition for Human and Economic Development

Figure 17.1
Community Communication Center Model

training, and counseling will provide the "process" base for the center's activities. Projects should focus on the needs of the local people and if feasible be linked to, and be relevant to, a specific development goal relating to health, education, or agriculture. Perhaps the recently established Village Knowledge Centers in Chennai, India, best exemplifies a substantive, process approach to establish a center that focuses on accessing and using information technologies, computers and the Internet to access a content focused area, like agriculture. This project is a partnership of the M.S. Swaminathan Research Foundation in India (MSSRF) and the International Development Research Center (IDRC) in Canada.

The mission of the center is to serve as the nerve center for community development. As such it would serve as a *link to community leadership* and draw those individuals into the life of the center. It would *also link to community organizations and services* and have information about these organizations for the use of those individuals who come to the center for assistance. Center staff could also *energize networking* among community organizations with the intent of fostering cooperation and resource planning and sharing among them. Such interaction can be a force in creating shared local development visions. Through the use of the center's Internet resources, *networking among villages* for "virtual" village-to-village discussion and organization of joint development endeavors would also be possible.

Another important development role of the center could be to *facilitate community research, planning, action, and evaluation.* In the beginning, community leaders could work cooperatively with external facilitators or agencies, but with the ultimate goal of establishing a local unit within the center to activate these processes when appropriate. Finally, a center should be in a position *to initiate resource acquisition for human and economic development.* This suggests that center leadership and community leadership would collaborate their efforts to enable the community and its citizens to move steadily toward an improved quality of life.

It is yet to be seen whether access to technology will substantially contribute to social change and development. Molding these technologies to serve social change objectives or enhancement of cultural identity through participatory processes is the challenge. Access to technologies can be empowering in itself, but unless access is linked to meaningful applications, localization of information databases, and utilization for individual development for community leadership it will lead to further disenchantment and alienation. Perhaps, centers first need to build a program around the transforming and renewing processes that catalyze interest and mobilize individuals for participatory development and then bring in the technologies that meet the people's needs.

Admittedly, this is an ambitious model. It is presented as a holistic view of an ideal center. Successful establishment of such a facility and program would depend on vision, focus, adequate resources and commitment of local leadership. The local realities would govern how far a community might be able to go in putting together such a resource facility. A regional look at the concept might find one fully developed center with several smaller, focused satellite centers in a network of villages.

Another reality looms clearly. In many depressed, poverty-stricken rural areas throughout the world, people can barely meet the necessities of daily life, much less find it possible to think about an ambitious, and unfamiliar concept such as a CCC. But hopefully this model can stimulate a more guided train of thought in those communities where such ideas are conceived. As one does on a Website: I now encourage you to link back to Chapters 2 and 3 and interrelate your understandings of involving people in the participatory process and of participatory video as a process which transforms and renews, within the CCC concept.

Kaleidoscopic Vision

Communication and information technologies are in a constant state of evolution and change. Small format video technology has changed immensely over the past three decades: from large, heavy two piece video systems to the small, lightweight digital video camera; from low grade visual quality to high quality images; from awkward camera handling to "professionalized" camera techniques, from uninformed image organizers to systematic visualizers. Each technological advancement has been accompanied with a parallel advancement of those using the technology. But one basic element remains unchanged: people must learn to manage the media to meet their own communication objective.

Video Power is also changing. As the uses of video expand, video's power increases. The technology will continue to advance. The power of images will continue to provide a frontier for exploration. But there is a constant, sustaining force of this media: its completeness, its flexibility, and its intimate visual potential that can change minds, clarify and create ideas, and alter personal behavior.

This book has shared the experiences of numerous individuals and organizations from all corners of the globe. We do hope our sharing will inspire further exploration of the uses of video and the interface of video with other technologies that can enhance *image power*. At the same time we hope our reader has gained greater understanding of the *power of participatory processes*. The potentials of both the technologies and the processes can more readily be explored if an appropriate place and space is provided for their convergence in the local context of development.

I am convinced that those who have information and communication technologies in their hand bear responsibility for the future of humanity. They can use its immense power for beneficial or

398 ❖ Shirley A. White

destructive purposes. Consequences can be good or evil. In the
final analysis there is a correlation between the technology holders
and the power holders. How technology and power is shared will
depend upon their sense of social responsibility, their understandings of human need and their respect for human life.

About the Editor and Contributors

The Editor

Shirley A. White is Professor Emeritus, Department of Communication, Cornell University. She has served as Associate Director of the Cornell Cooperative Extension and Chairman of the Department of Extension Home Economics, Kansas State University. A pioneer in the field of video and participatory communication, Shirley White's work over the last 25 years has focused on organizational renewal and change, video communication, and development communication. In India, the major thrust of her collaborative work has been as the U.S. Department of Agriculture's Chief Cooperating Scientist for the Development Communication Research Project at the University of Pune. Currently, Professor White works as a consultant in the areas of participatory communication, participatory video, interpersonal, and organizational communication.

A prolific writer, she has edited and co-edited several books, including *Perspectives on Development Communication* (1993); *Participatory Communication: Working for Change and Development* (1994); *Participatory Communication for Social Change* (1996) and *The Art of Facilitating Communication: Releasing the Power of Grassroots Communication* (1999).

Address: 485 Van Ostrand Road
Groton, New York 13073
USA
E-mail: saw4@cornell.edu

The Contributors

Wilfred Amalemba is a trainer and writer for the AIDS program at MAP International, Africa. Since 1995, he has been involved in training, facilitating and designing training programs in HIV/AIDS, pastoral counseling, youth peer education, HIV/AIDS and church policy, as well as an HIV/AIDS curriculum for theological institutions and Bible schools. Wilfred has worked extensively in Kenya, Tanzania, Uganda, Rwanda, Senegal, Zimbabwe and Namibia. He has co-authored *Growing Together—A Guide for Parents and Youth on Sexuality*, and has also edited several other MAP International Publications on AIDS.

Address: P.O. Box 21663, Nairobi, Kenya
Telephone: 254–2–729497
Fax: 254–2–714422
E-mail: wamalemba@map.org

Renuka Bery is Dissemination and Advocacy Manager, Support for Analysis and Research in Africa (SARA) Project, Academy for Educational Development. As a project director and development video trainer with Communication for Change, she has facilitated various participatory training processes to use video as a tool for communication. She has worked with grass roots women and men in Bangladesh and India, and adolescent school children in Nigeria. Renuka Bery writes and consults on health and communication issues. She has lived, traveled and worked extensively in Asia, Africa, Europe and North America.

Address: 124 Hamilton Avenue,
Silver Spring, MD 20901
Telephone: 301–589–5997(H) 202–884–8985(O)
E-mail: rbery@aed.org

David Booker, founder and director of *Nomad Digital*, has lived and worked in a dozen countries. Trained as an agriculturalist, he has set up tools and technologies to help poor farmers in Africa better survive droughts and dislocation. He has also been the manager of monitoring and evaluation for a food security program covering the Sahel countries of Africa. Currently, David Booker is the website developer for The Cochrane Collaboration, an international organization that prepares systematic reviews of the effects of health care interventions, finding ways to provide better access to the library of reviews for the doctors who subscribe to the service.

Address: 308 Eastwood Ave, Ithaca, NY 14850, USA
Telephone: (607) 279–2995 (USA), 49–(761)–696–7529 (Germany)
Fax: (707) 281–0604
E-mail: dave@nomaddigital.com
Web: www.nomaddigital.com

Stephen Crocker is Assistant Professor, Department of Sociology, Memorial University, St. Johns, Newfoundland, Canada. His areas of specialization include social theory, globalization and the sociology of the image. Prof. Crocker's articles have been published in *Cultural Values, Philosophy Today, Continental Philosophy Review, Journal of the British Society for Phenomenology*, and other publications. His book, *Between Empires: A Canadian Cultural Studies Reader* will be published in 2003 from Duke University Press.

Address: Department of Sociology, Memorial University,
St. Johns, Newfoundland, Canada, A1C557
Telephone: (709) 737–7447
Fax: (709) 737–2075
E-mail: bcrocker@mun.ca

Mary Jo Dudley is Associate Director of the Latin American Studies Program at Cornell University. She has also served as Co-director of the Cornell based Program on Gender and Global Change and as Co-director of the Cornell Participatory Action Research Network. Her research centers on using participatory and feminist methodologies with grass roots populations. An experienced videographer with production experience in both the US and Latin America, Mary Jo Dudley has produced a weekly news commentary program as part of the *More than the News* television collective, and has also collaborated on a participatory video project with domestic workers in Colombia.

Address: Latin American Studies Program, 190 Uris Hall, Cornell University, Ithaca, NY 14853, USA
Telephone: (607) 255-3345
Fax: (607) 255-8919
E-mail: mjd9@cornell.edu

Sabeena Gadihoke has been teaching Video & Television Production at the Mass Communication Research Centre, Jamia University in New Delhi for the past 12 years. A prolific writer she is also an experienced documentary filmmaker and camerawoman. Sabeena is a founder/member of Mediastorm Collective, a group of six women filmmakers. She has been a Fulbright fellow at Syracuse University in the United States during 1995–96. Her film, *Three Women and a Camera* (1998) won the second prize at Film South Asia, 1999, at Kathmandu, and a certificate of merit at the Mumbai International Film Festival, 2000. Sabeena Gadihoke has recently completed a four year project sponsored by the India Foundation for the Arts, Bangalore, that documents the work of women photographers in India.

Address: 103 Sahyog Apartments, Mayur Vihar, Phase I, New Delhi 110 091, INDIA.
Telephone: 91–011–22751580,
E-mail: sgadihok@vsnl.com

Ricardo Gómez is a development communication practitioner working with the International Development Research Centre in Ottawa, Canada. He is Executive Director of Bellanet. Ricardo obtained his Ph.D. in Communications from Cornell University in 1997, and a Masters in Communication from Université du Quebec a Montréal in 1991. He works with different communication technologies and conducts research on their potential applications for community development in Latin America and the Caribbean. He lives in Ottawa, Canada.

Address: 250 Albert St., PO Box 8500, Ottawa, ON, Canada K1G 3H9

Telephone: (613) 236–6163
Fax: (613) 567–7749
E-mail: gomez@idrc.ca
Internet: http://www.bellanet.org

Padma Guidi is a musician and world media activist. She spent several years working in the Los Angeles music business as a singer-songwriter, teacher and producer. In 1997, Padma Guidi started a rural multimedia Internet project with indigenous women in Guatemala, combining the technical, creative, and activist sides of her production skills and experience. Initiated as a social action project for her doctorate studies at the Union Institute, the project has since become a local rural movement in modern media awareness for the region of Solola. Padma still resides in the area and has no immediate plans to return to the United States.

Address: Callejon Ajachel, Bario Jucanya Panajachel,
Solola, Guatemala
Telephone: 011 (502) 293–5756
E-mail: padmaguidi@hotmail.com, mujersolola@yahoo.com

Bushra Jabre has served as Senior Communication Advisor, Johns Hopkins Center for Communication Programs, in the Near East region since 1994. Prior to that, she was the Chief of the Near East Division, 1991–1994. Bushra Jabre is an expert in strategic communication, including program design, interpersonal communication/counseling, behavior change communication (BCC) training, research and evaluation, community partnerships, and media advocacy. Ms. Jabre has worked mainly in Egypt, Morocco, Lebanon, Syria, Tunisia, Jordan, Oman and Yemen as well as in the Central Asian Republics and the South Pacific Islands.

Ms. Jabre has been actively involved in women's development programs and has overseen the development and implementation of *Arab Women Speak Out*, a self-empowerment project. She is currently working on an Emerging Leadership Initiative as well as Arab Youth Initiative.

Address: JHU/CCP, 111 Market Place, Suite 310,
Baltimore, MD 21202, USA

Telephone: 961 179–0568, 961 355–6857, 386 239–0108
E-mail: bushra@aol.com

Ndunge Kiiti is member of the Partnership Development Team in the Atlanta, Georgia office of MAP International. She has served as Director/Assistant Director for communications in MAP's East and Southern Africa office working in their HIV/AIDS, Reconciliation, Relief, and Health Development programs. She was responsible for the design, coordination and implementation of the overall communications program; training, material development, research and networking at the grass roots, national, regional and international levels.

Address: Map International, The Healey Building, 57th Forsyth St.
NW, Suite 240–G
Atlanta, Georgia 30303 USA
Telephone: 404 880–9411
Fax: 404 880–0540
E-mail: nkiiti@map.org

K. Sadanandan Nair is Professor of Anthropology and Head of the Department of Anthropology at the University of Pune, Pune, India, where he teaches and directs research in anthropology, development, and communication studies. Professor Nair has also been research director and principle investigator for the University of Pune's Development Communication Research Project, funded by the U.S. Department of Agriculture.

Address: Department of Anthropology, University of Pune,
Pune, India 411 007.
Telephone: 91–212–2383730
Fax: 91–212–2333899
E-mail: nair@unipune.ernet.in

Barbara Seidl is senior producer for a public television series specializing in documentation of development projects throughout the world. An extensive traveler, she has directed several documentaries in developing countries. Barbara Seidl also teaches at a university in Boston, Massachusetts. She holds degrees in education from the University of Wisconsin, and in communication from Cornell University.

Address: 27 Hall Av. Apt #3 Somerville, MA 02144,
Boston, Massachusetts, USA
Telephone: (781) 844–1324
E-mail: barbaras@visionaries.org

Carol Underwood is Senior Associate in the Department of Population and Family Health Sciences, Hopkins School of Public Health. She teaches a graduate seminar in Communication and Social Change. As part of the Johns Hopkins Center for Communication Programs since 1994, Dr. Underwood is involved in the development, implementation and analysis of qualitative as well as quantitative studies to inform policies and programs in the countries where she works. She is also the Senior Researcher for the innovative project *Arab Women Speaks Out* that promotes women's self-empowerment, self-(re)presentation, and active participation in social development throughout the Near East. She has an extensive background in international development and Islamic thought and has worked in Egypt, Iran, Jordan, Oman, Tunisia and Yemen as well as in the southern region of Africa. Dr. Underwood is fluent in English and Persian (*Farsi/Dari/Tajiki*).

Address: Johns Hopkins Center for Communication Programs,
Johns Hopkins School of Public Health, 111 Market Place,
Suite 310,
Baltimore, MD 20854, USA
Telephone: 410 659–6300/6142
E-mail: cunderwood@jhuccp.org

Korula Varghese holds a Ph.D in Agricultural Extension and Communication from the University of Reading, England, following which he completed a post-doctoral program at Cornell University with Shirley A. White, Department of Communication. Currently, Dr. Varghese works as a Houston based consultant for a multinational company that provides end user training and performance support for complex technology systems. His seminal research on broadcast television access and shared authority productions for community communication has helped promote a reconsideration of the once neglected mass media for community communication. Dr. Varghese has lived, traveled and worked extensively in Asia, Europe and North America.

Address: 4611 Zachary Lane,
Sugarland, Texas–77479 USA
Telephone: 281 313–1941
E-mail: kv2020@hotmail.com

Index

408 ❖ Index